LIFE WITH LABS

LIFE LESSONS FROM WOMAN'S BEST FRIENDS

TONYA WHITTLE

TONYA WHITTLE

Published by: LLH Publishing.

Cover Design © Print Shop NL 2023

Cover Photography: Sandra Woito Photography

Interior Design by: Vellum

Tonya Whittle — 1st ed.

Trade Paperback ISBN: 978-1-7388051-0-5

eBook ISBN: 978-1-7388051-1-2

First paper printing March 2023.

DEDICATION

For my beautiful girls, Tetley & Lexie Lou, you changed my life. I will love you for the rest of mine. You have become the very fabric of my being. I'm grateful you were mine.

Me, Tetley & Lexie in Gros Morne.

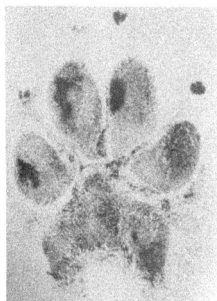

Lexie's Signature

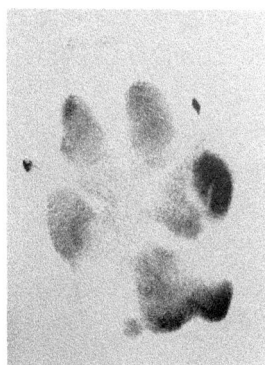

Tetley's Signature

PRAISE FOR TONYA WHITTLE

"Relatable"

Whittle's "Relentless: Life with Labs" is a heartfelt exploration of life through the eyes of beloved canine companions. With a blend of personal anecdotes and profound insights, the author reveals how dogs teach us invaluable lessons about love, loyalty, and resilience.

Whittle's engaging writing draws readers into their world, capturing the joys and sorrows of pet ownership. Each chapter resonates with anyone who has shared their life with a dog, highlighting moments that reveal the depth of these bonds.

More than a memoir, "Relentless" is a celebration of the love that dogs bring into our lives. Whittle's genuine affection shines through, making this book a must-read for animal lovers. Whether you're a dog owner or just an admirer, these reflections will deepen your appreciation for the simple joys they offer.

Joan Sullivan
Book Reviewer, Columnist
Saltwire

I finished the book a little while ago but had to let it sit with me before writing this review. It was so engaging and I loved getting the backstory of Tetley and Lexie. So many takeaways! So many life lessons! It inspired me to be an even better dog mom and friend! And it's only stuff! Tonya has such a way with words and the love and unconditional acceptance came through in spades! I laughed, I cried. It was wonderful. 🩶

Carol Ann Poole
Amazon Reviewer

"Exactly What I Needed"

As the on-scene commander for the Canadian Search and Rescue of the Titan Submersible aboard the CCGS John Cabot, I had to maintain a steady hand at the helm for my crew. Once the search ended, I retreated to my cabin, unsure of my own emotions, I began reading your book. As I settled into my chair, your storytelling resonated deeply with me, almost as if you were narrating the story in person.

Your book, especially the inclusion of your grandfather and father - fellow mariners - offered comfort and reflection during a challenging time. Yesterday, as I finished the last pages, I was moved by your words and the truth they conveyed about facing life's trials. Your story made me both laugh and cry, and it was exactly what I needed.

Sam Arnold
Commanding Officer
Canadian Coast Guard

"Relentless: Life with Labs" in true Tonya style did not disappoint. Throughout this book you not only connect as a dog lover but as a person. You feel deeply about not taking a day for granted. You see determination, perseverance and unconditional love. The lessons we learn from our animals are truly powerful. Congratulations Tonya on another inspiring book!

Tanya Barron
School Teacher
Amazon Reviewer

———

———

"It's a love story baby, just say yes!"
Simply put, dogs are amazing. Being a lab Momma I understand their quirks and the many facets of their incredible personalities. Their true loyalty and their unconditional love; author Tonya Whittle truly explores this through her words. She shares her girls; Tetley and Lexie with us, their adventures and countless relatable laughs along the way. A definite read to lab owners, dog people, animal lovers and book lovers! Dogs teach us so much!

Christine Brinson
    Dog Mom

ACKNOWLEDGMENTS

A book, like life, is a living thing. It's a community effort and it's virtually impossible to thank everyone for their support and help but I'll try. To Mark Lefebvre for your endless support in getting this book into the world. My early readers, mother-in-law Shirley, and friends: Nancy Burton and Kat Hamilton for reading the drafts and providing feedback.

A massive thank you to my friends, especially those who have been my biggest supporters and have held me through an incredibly tough year.

To my readers, clients and supporters. I wouldn't be able to do this work without you. Thank you for being here and elevating my words.

To my parents who have been there for me, always, especially this year.

To Paradise Animal Hospital, for always providing exceptional care to my girls, with particular mention to Dr.'s Meister, Slade, Mercer, Kroyer and Breynton, techs Matt & Amanda, and all admin staff. I'll be forever grateful.

And of course, my beautiful babies, my girls. I wouldn't be who I am without you. There aren't enough words to thank you for the journey.

CONTENTS

CHAPTER 1
PROLOGUE

Brigus, Newfoundland February 2022.

Tetley and I sat, she pressed into my leg, looking out over the ocean. It was bitterly cold, the tide was low but violent. We had come to let her swim but the rocky beach and low tide wasn't worth risking an injury. I told her she couldn't swim, she was in her help-me-up harness, as we made our way to the grassy picnic area. I was cold but I didn't want to leave.

Lexie stayed in the Mazda, having the sense to stay in the warmth of the vehicle on this bitterly cold day. Tetley and I sat, pressed together, on a blanket I took from the hatch of the SUV. I was wearing -40 celsius-rated running tights, a winter parka, a hat and mittens. My cheeks burned from the cold but I didn't want to risk losing this moment. I had waited for a moment like this for nearly 14 years.

Tetley would turn 14 in a month and she never sat quietly with me in public. She is a wild one, a free spirit, cuddling was a rarity with her, and it certainly wasn't something she did while outside. When she did cuddle it was early morning or post-workout. Yet, I always wanted a moment of solitude, of mutual appreciation in nature.

Lexie is the emotionally intelligent, quiet, cuddle girl but Tetley was filled with spirit, spite and wildness. So if she saw fit to give me this moment then I would stay until I couldn't handle the cold North Atlantic breeze any longer.

It wasn't windy but even the mild breeze stung exposed skin. For the first time in her life, she wasn't throwing a stick or slobbery ball in my face. This was bittersweet. I was terrified we wouldn't get more time than we had, that this surely meant the end was here.

Or maybe it was just a gift of the one thing I wanted from her that I never got. Maybe it was a goodbye, maybe it was a thank you. One thing is for sure, it was love.

Tetley had just been diagnosed with Dementia, or CCD (canine cognitive dysfunction). We had been through a tough couple of months, that escalated over the last couple of weeks, of unbearable, incessant, nonstop pacing, panting, and crying that suddenly shifted to circling and walking left. I wasn't expecting *this*.

Tetley. January 2022.

We have been doing bucket lists of our favourite places while we wait for Justin, my husband, to get home from his rotational shift at work. We were preparing for the end. The ending is on us, the journey of several thousand miles, spanning a decade and a half, the day you know is coming the moment you pick up the bouncing, wild puppy, but it still seems so far away.

I have been holding my breath since she turned 13, really, already knowing how lucky I am to have as long as I have, knowing we are outside of her "lifespan". That's the problem about it being so good, even when we know it has to end, we never believe it will, or can prepare for it.

A dog like Tetley seems endless; like she cannot possibly die and will somehow live forever because she's just too much, too big, too bold to ever be reduced to nothing.

As we sat together that day, in Brigus, she was there, with me, fully present, giving me this gift. We had hope, again, as she just started a new medication for Dementia, and she had immediate improvements.

Maybe, once again, we were skirting the inevitable. Someday we wouldn't escape it, but today was not that day. This book started to form, sitting there with her pressed against me, the story I had been trying to find the words for, beginning to take shape in my heart, a vision creating in my mind of the story I would tell about our lives together.

I had this book in my mind for years but until now, whether it was half-hearted attempts or just nothing to write, the book didn't have a scope except that I wanted to tell the story of how much my life has been impacted by my two Chocolate Labrador Retrievers, Tetley & Lexie. I've spent my life with them - Tetley was just 1 when I started my own business and Lexie was added to the pack when Tetley was 4. She was 7 months old when we rescued her. We haven't spent much time apart.

There were so many moments, good and bad, along the way. So many lessons, tidbits and a story I feel honours the bond between women and their dogs, not a man's best friend but a woman's. Those stories are less told, and I love nothing more than telling a lesser-told story.

The words are coming as I've stepped back to honour this time we have, be it short or long. If these are my last days with her, I want to have them fully with her and Lexie - going to our favourite places, road trips, charcuterie boards, games, swimming and as many of the things we've loved and enjoyed over the years as possible. Not that we haven't spent our lives that way, because we have, but also to ensure there is nothing else between us if this is the end.

With Tetley's diagnosis, I felt both guilt, shame and inconsolable grief. I had spent the last few months frustrated with her. Tetley was always a highly driven, relentless dog in getting her own way, plotting things and planning things as you'll learn throughout this book. Everyone loves her spirit but that spirit is a lot to live with day to day. As I was told of her prognosis, I found myself feeling horrible that I was losing her and didn't even know it. Some of her escalating behaviours were not related to a reduction in activity, as I had thought, but her increased pacing and nonstop activity were caused by sundowning.

As I'm writing she is sleeping at my feet after a day of raising hell. She is a fighter and she fights her sedatives until she can't; without them, she wouldn't sleep at all. We started a new medication yesterday and I have guarded positivity. I see her again, in her eyes, the way she hasn't been in over a week when she went over the ledge that led to her diagnosis.

She was lost to me, I couldn't see her anymore, I couldn't feel her anymore. She was still a tangly little beast relentless to move forward but she was lost to herself. She looked like Tetley but there was a vacancy about her. I realised how devastating this disease is, not just to animals but I felt myself hurting for everyone I know who lost family to dementia and Alzheimer's. I wish I knew more, understood more, and offered more support.

I know what it feels like to stare helplessly at your people (yes, she's my people) and not be able to help, watch her walk into walls, go in circles and have panic attacks and stay up all day and night, panting and crying. I have talked to friends and family these last few weeks and have a deeper understanding of what people go through when their human family members get this.

I am less sad today as I've seen an improvement after just

two days of being on her new medication. I can see and feel her normal presence. She's fighting and as long as she is fighting, I will help her fight.

But watching her lose herself is the hardest thing I've seen, and I've seen some hard things in this life. I promised her and myself that I won't let her suffer, no matter what! I know that when the time comes, whether it's sooner or later, it will be devastating. But I won't turn her into something or someone she isn't. I will honour the spirit of who she is, who she wants to be and how she lived before her diagnosis. I will not drag her through life less than she would want.

Tetley is a proud dog. She has a relentless spirit and a wild soul, closer to the wild than anything I've ever seen. I will honour that and I hope this book honours that. As she's laying at my bedside next to Lexie, I've realised why now is the time for the book. It's time to look back at our relationship, our journey together while they're still with me.

I've mostly talked about Tetley and that's because she's the one who's sick right now but also because she has taken up most of the space in our lives. Lexie is a domesticated dog, a perfect dog. She loves people. As long as she is with us she is happy. She is acting as a nursemaid for Tetley now, lying next to her, letting us know when she is in distress, which seems to be always with Tetley and not just because of her dementia.

Lexie spent her days running to the door to tell us that Tetley had lost her ball under the deck or running to tell us to help Tetley in some way, shape or form. Tetley was the frantic one but Lexie was the calm to her frenzy. Tetley would often be in such a panic she couldn't see a ball directly in front of her. Lexie would calmly walk to it and pick it up, setting Tetley ablaze for the ball, while Lexie would casually chew it, squeaking it then, with her head in the air as if it was the most pleasurable thing - to chew the ball while Tetley freaked out.

Lexie is a caregiver. She is a natural emotional therapy dog. I've hosted many women's retreats, and while Tetley was terrorising the guests for a game of fetch, Lexie was licking people's tears. Tetley never cared about your feelings but Lexie is up in your grill with your feelings.

They spent their days with me in the gym, when I ran a fitness studio, and Tetley used the activity to get a workout - learning to run on the treadmill, do burpees, plank hand taps and more but mostly manipulating people into throwing a ball for her. She spent much of the gym days at the top of the stairs to the gym throwing a ball down and barking until someone opened the door and threw it for her. We did nothing to deter her tyranny.

The view from the gym door. Always.

When I was training for a fitness competition I walked on the treadmill every day, twice a day, she would come into the room with me and throw her balls and toys on the belt of the treadmill. I would have to skirt the toys so as not to faceplant off the treadmill. Justin would come in and hang out while I was getting my cardio workout in and one day he decided to get her on the treadmill.

She was scared at first but he started feeding her treats while she was on the treadmill and she stayed on. Eventually, she became so addicted to the treadmill we just had to say cardio time and she would run downstairs to the treadmill, jump on and go. When I was using it I would have to give her turns! She would come to the treadmill and beg for a turn.

Lexie, on the other hand, mimicked a land seal, flopping around the floor, taking advantage of unsuspecting defenceless women suffering through pushups and planks. She'd sneak attack for an armpit lick or a neck lick - providing much-needed relief for the women working out, desperate for any reason to drop out of a plank. Lexie was happy to oblige.

My girls are yin and yang. They are as opposite as if they are completely different breeds. Tetley regularly hiked 30 plus kilometres. She would race around the car on the way to the hike and then play fetch when she got home. When Lexie hiked she stayed close to me but Tetley did the hikes, I'm sure, 3 times as she sprinted ahead and then back to us. She's the dog that makes ultramarathoners feel bad about their effort. In her younger days, Lexie came along with us and enjoyed life as an active dog. She would reach a point where she was done but Tetley never had an off button.

Eventually, due to injuries and bone and joint problems, Lexie became a house dog. When I tried to take her out for a walk or run, she dreaded every step. She came because she didn't want to stay home and miss out, but she mostly wanted to Netflix and chill. I'm sure she wondered how *this* became her life. How did she end up in a home with a personal trainer for a mom and a fitness nut, Tetley, as a sister? Her dad, Justin, is as intense and non-stop as the rest of us, but he does enjoy TV time and she would jam herself into his side while he watched sports and dodged her licking tongue.

Lexie loves the sound of people laughing and squealing. She would do anything to make it happen. Tetley loved the sound of her paws on the pavement and she would do anything to make it happen.

My life with Labs has been filled with fun, love, adventure, passion, connection, power, and heartbreak. I know my heartbreak hasn't even really started yet because as I write this, I still have them and as long as I have them I have hope. Even if my hope is marginal and feels like walking on thin ice, tiptoeing across it, feeling it breaking here and there, but somehow not.

This book is a love story.

Tetley, Tonya & Lexie on the couch.

We hear about "man's best friend" but our story is a story of woman's best friends - a life filled with adventure, wilding, finding ourselves, being ourselves, and living a life of passion, purpose and love. It was only possible because of the 2 incredible Chocolate Labs I've been blessed to call mine.

This book is about our journey together and the lessons I have learned from them along the way. I'm inviting you into our unforgettable journey together as we laugh, cry and reminisce, not about the ending that's coming but about remembering the amazing journey we had together.

The book is shared in lessons instead of in chronological order. It weaves together the past and present through the lessons and life we have lived. Join me as I walk back memory lane and remember all of the amazing gifts, and life, they gave me.

CHAPTER 2
TETLEY - THE BEGINNING

Tetley 7.5 weeks old.

t was 2008 and we were living North of 60, in Nunavut. We had been there 5 years and were preparing for our move back east to Newfoundland. We decided it was time for a dog. We knew we wanted a Lab; Justin's family were Lab people and I had fallen in love with a Chocolate Lab when I was 18. It was the first one I had ever seen, and I knew one day I would have one of my own.

Our search began in Newfoundland. We wanted a puppy to coincide with our move in the fall. We found a breeder, as we wanted a puppy that we could train ourselves for our first dog.

Oh, I was fooling myself because she trained me. But, I digress. The search in Newfoundland turned up a popular breeder, unregistered, but considered quality Labradors.

I submitted my application, carefully answering the questions, and taking my time to give details to showcase my perfection as a choice for one of their puppies. I excitedly waited for the response. I was declined. I was shocked and devastated. Would I not make a good dog owner, I wondered. They turned me down because I didn't have plans for the puppy during the day while I was working.

I told them I would make plans as needed based on what our lives looked like, that it was likely we would not have jobs immediately and would be available until she was old enough to be left alone. They said no. I told them I would bring her to daycare. They said no. I asked for suggestions on what they expected or recommended and they didn't reply.

We turned our attention elsewhere, not ready to give up. Ottawa was the hub closest to Iqaluit, Nunavut. We flew in and out of there regularly so I searched Ontario for Labrador breeders. It was an overwhelming search as there were so many to choose from. I used the popular classified search tools as most social media was in its infancy back then.

I found an ad on Kiijii titled C.K.C. REGISTERED " CHOCOLATE LAB. PUPS and I replied. They sent back information later that day that the puppies had not yet been born but would be soon.

We received pictures of both parents and were told the litter would be entirely chocolate as both parents only carried the chocolate genes. I filled out an application and we were accepted. We sent our downpayment to secure the puppy. They told us we had the pick of the litter.

Tetley was available sooner than we wanted. We wanted a fall puppy but she was born in the spring. Once born and a couple of weeks old, they sent us pictures of the females as we had decided we wanted a girl dog. Justin made the choice based on her nose and head size. Small head, short nose. That was that. We didn't visit them as we were in Iqaluit. We didn't see the puppies in person. We received a couple of pictures and I made arrangements to fly to Ottawa to pick her up.

When we gave them her name for the paperwork they laughed and said "that's an interesting name" which is a bit of a joke on how she got her name. Justin is an avid tea drinker and I mean the kind that's been cut off from hotels for drinking so much. As we were deciding on a name for her it came up among friends as a joke that Justin would call her Tetley, his preferred cup of tea. He is so obsessed with Tetley Tea that he brings it everywhere he goes, including destination vacations. I'll find baggies with tea bags in the glove compartments, luggage and even stashes in baggies in the cupboards. He's the person who buys the 1100 bag of teabags from Costco.

It might have been a joke but we liked it. It was unique, just like she turned out to be. Her tail turns orange in the summer and Justin says that she's steeped. That's how she got her name.

Tetley has many nicknames, her most popular one being toots. She's also been called toodles, wiggles, wiggies, Tetley roo, tootsie, tootsie poppers.

I flew to Ottawa and stayed with friends, Vicky and Dwayne, for the weekend to pick up Tetley, get the supplies I needed as we didn't have pet stores in Iqaluit then fly back to Nunavut with her. Once we settled into the idea of having her with us in Nunavut it made more sense, really. She would be older when we moved back east and able to stay alone a little longer. In Iqaluit, we were minutes from home at all times so checking on her during the day was easy.

If all went to plan, she would move into our new home in Newfoundland when she was 9 months old. Our home there would be a 30-45 minutes drive from the city, where we likely would be working.

On May 2, 2008, Vicky drove me to the Tim Hortons location where we were scheduled to meet the breeder. They had driven into Ottawa from Hastings, Ontario to bring the puppies to their new owners. We ended up at the wrong Tims and by the time we arrived at the right one, we were the last ones to arrive, and Tetley was the last puppy, whimpering and crying.

Microchipped, dewormed, and vet checked, #1 in black permanent marker written inside her ear, wearing a blue cat collar with a bell (which I still have), wrapped in a Winnie The Pooh blanket that smelled like her mom and siblings she was handed to me. She still has her baby blankie in her kennel. They cut pieces of the Queen size blanket to send home with each of the puppies.

They handed her to me, swaddled, and she jumped up and bit my nose and grabbed a mouthful of hair, yanking on it. She was tangly.

The breeder said "She is the smallest puppy in the litter but she is the boss of them all, including her mom" - all signs of what was to come. Not the smallest but the boss for sure. She was born wild, with the spirit of a wolf and the determination of a honey badger, declared to be the most determined animal on the planet - only because they haven't met Tetley.

I handed her to Vicky so we could complete the paperwork because she would *not* stop moving. She was wild. As we drove back to Vicky's house she was biting my face and eating my hair so I tucked her into the crook of my arm with her little white puppy belly sticking out. I had borrowed a small fabric pet carry-on from a friend to transport her back to Iqaluit but I kept her in my arms for that drive.

Vicky and I went to Pet Smart to get the supplies I needed. We left Tetley with Dwayne and I gave strict instructions for her to be kept in her kennel as I had a plan for her training. I read a book and I had a plan. That's who I was back then, a woman with a plan, always. Tetley taught me plans are just suggestions. When we got back from shopping, she was tucked into his arm laying on the couch, both of them asleep. He said she wouldn't stop crying so he picked her up and she settled down. Oh, Tetley.

The first night with her, at Vicky and Dwayne's, she did not stop crying. I promised myself I wouldn't let her sleep in my bed, that she would be a dog, a loved dog, a house dog but she wouldn't be sleeping in my bed. I'm not sure why I thought that. Maybe some ideation of adulthood?

I didn't want her to keep them awake. So, I took her to bed with me, "just for tonight" I whispered to myself as she settled into the crook of my arm. It would be the first of many sleepless nights with her. She bit my face, ate my hair, chewed my toes, and peed on me. I loved her. She was mine, and I was hers, then and there.

We travelled back to Iqaluit the next day, where she met hundreds of people, who couldn't help doting on her. It was the perfect hundreds of people socialisation recommended for a puppy, at least that's what my book said. I was scared she would bark on the plane ride, or get sick, but she didn't make a sound and just made a lot of friends. She even did her business on paper towels in the bathroom. She was smart. I praised her and she loved that.

Walking a 7.5-week-old Chocolate Lab puppy through a busy airport felt like walking a celebrity through the place, everyone just had to meet her.

The first night in her new home, a shady apartment in Iqaluit's West 40, where we shared a 3-apartment unit with other families, felt like we were sleeping in a sauna. One of the neighbours controlled our heat and it was either too hot or too cold, always. That night it was blistering hot. We were in transition in this apartment, saving money for the move back east and the new home build.

By living there, we saved about a thousand dollars a month on rent and other expenses, money we wanted to put into our new home. Trust me, you get what you pay for. The dishwasher was in the living room, the laundry was in the kitchen and our table was smaller than a two seater at a restaurant. It was small and had a rocking chair and a reclining loveseat with a small folding table next to it. It was all we had room for. The stackable washer and dryer were in the kitchen behind the tiny table without even a folding door or curtain to cover it up.

I stared at the stackable unit over Justin's shoulder during every meal, while he stared at the TV over my shoulder. My chair touched the love seat and the loveseat was 5 feet from the TV.

When Tetley moved in, she moved in with an attitude. She would run under the folding table, hide in the laundry - clean and dirty, jump into the shower when you least expected it, rip apart the shower curtain, soak the floor and cover herself in shampoo and claw her way into the tub. Her early love of the shower and baths would not last.

We had a very long hallway for such a small apartment. The cold porch, standard in Nunavut, entered the hallway where looking right you saw the kitchen and living room, directly ahead was the bathroom and to the left was a very large bedroom. I'm not sure who designed the place but it was a terrible layout. The bedroom was huge and the living space was too small. Tetley learned to play fetch using small pieces of sausages in that hallway. It was love at first fetch. It took one, maybe two fetches. Get it. Rewarded. She was trained. A pure retriever. Her parents were hunters, after all.

Justin used bits of sausage to train her to fetch and give paw. It took virtually no time to get her to do it. She was house-trained in a few days. She was smart, typical of her breed. It would turn out that she was a little too smart for our good and very dramatic.

The first night with us in Iqaluit, she threw up in her kennel. We were committed to crate training as I had read the Training Puppies for Dummies books, and I was ready. I knew we wanted to crate train because it was safer for her and easier to train her.

Then she threw up. She was inconsolable. I picked her up, cuddled her, cleaned her up and took her to bed. "Just this one time," I said to Justin. I mean, she was far from home, it is a new setting, a new place, there was a strange man here now, and she doesn't have her mommy or daddy or siblings. Imagine sleeping with 13 other siblings and your mother for 7 weeks then suddenly sleeping in a crate alone. That's all the things I said to Justin as she snuggled into the crook of my arm, belly up.

She eventually settled down and went to sleep. The next night, not long after closing her kennel door and turning the lights out, we heard her urging again. "Oh no!" I said "We are thousands of miles from a vet! What do we do now? What if she has something wrong with her?" I said to Justin. She came with her vaccination papers, so we knew she was vet checked, vaccinated and dewormed, but it could be anything and we were North of 60 with no vet close by.

When we opened the kennel door a sick puppy didn't have to be pulled out like the night before. No, a bouncing puppy barrelled her way to the bed, paws up, as if to say, "Hello you forgot me". At 7.5 weeks old this foreshadowed the coming years. It was Daddy's night, and it was clear he had no intentions of staying up with her. He sat on the edge of the bed with his shirt in his hand, asleep. This also foreshadowed the coming years of who would always be on night duty, and well, dog duty. She bit his toes, and his ears, ripped on his hair and eventually fell asleep wrapped around his head on his pillow.

"Just for tonight", Justin said.

By night 3 we realised she had no intentions of staying in a cage. She faked sick, again. Faking sick became a regular occurrence for her. She still fakes sick to get her own way. She stares at me while fake urging. In a baby voice, I say "Oh is my baby sicky icky" and she keeps doing it. She gets her way, then she stops. This is why we call her a skeet. A skeet is a Newfoundland saying that no one really knows the definition of. They say you know a skeet when you see one.

Skeets are not necessarily criminals, maybe some low-key stuff but mostly it's the skeety behaviour like Tetley's faking sickness that we mean. Skeets are, well, skeets. And Tetley is a skeet. The urban dictionary says it's an "unruly" person involved in petty crime. But other definitions are "poorly educated, drinking, smoking weed in the trees, wearing tight clothing"… it's an odd conglomerate of prejudices thrown together. In Newfoundland, most of us would agree with "unruly" as a good word for a skeet. They aren't necessarily involved in petty crime but you're not sure they're not either. And I'd have to agree with the term "unruly" for Tetley's behaviour. It fits.

She raised hell in her kennel when we left for work and had to be chased to go in it. She ran through that tiny apartment, slid under the bed, piled herself into the laundry baskets and escaped every way she could. She always settled in and it helped house train her quickly. She only had 1 accident in her kennel and then learned to hold it. She was never left for more than 2 or 3 hours when we first brought her home.

I would sit in my vehicle outside and wait to see how long she cried after leaving her and it wasn't long. We never asked if we could have a dog and we didn't want her causing a ruckus among the neighbours. Within a few moments, she settled down. Eventually, she came to love her kennel and was allowed to free-roam the house by the time she was 6 months old. She still uses it with the door open, of course. It's her room.

She became a drama Queen of the finest kind. We would open the apartment door, in hindsight a terrible idea in Canada's Great White North with so many predators, and find her in the back of the building terrorising the kids who lived there, while we were putting on boots, hats and mittens. She was on someone's head, every time. No one seemed to care. We could hear the kids screaming "my hair my hair" and we knew she had gone in for the tangle of hair she could ram into her mouth and tear on to illicit screams from the kids. She loved tearing hair.

She would run behind that apartment building onto the rocks and we gave chase. Despite being a small puppy, she was fast and even more determined not to go indoors than she is now. She never wanted outdoor time to end, even as a baby.

We walked daily to Sylvia Grinnell Park, as the entrance was across the street from us, and we would carry her back, asleep. She always went on full speed until there was nothing left, even at that age. There was no off button for her. There still isn't. While she has slowed down, she doesn't stop much, changing rooms, in and outside, swimming, up and down, she just has one speed and it's bust, even if that bust level has changed over the years.

As a baby, she was afraid of water and wouldn't go near it. We tried to get her in by walking through puddles or throwing balls in the water but she would not go in. My friend Catherine, who also had a Chocolate Lab named Bruiser, tossed her in the water one day. Not exactly an approved way of teaching a dog to swim because it can work or it can go wrong. She didn't swim that day. She scrambled back out of the water looking like a drowned rat.

She didn't see water for a few months after that and tried to drag Justin's mother, Shirley, into the pond when she took her to Bowering Park for a walk one day, not long after our move to

Newfoundland. "I think Tetley wanted to go swimming," she told us. We took her that night, not to Bowering Park, mind you.

And swim, she did. We went to Octagon Pond in Paradise and she nearly dragged Justin into the water. She's still swimming every day and I have my doubts that her fur has ever really dried out. She has a very thick, woolly undercoat that water cannot penetrate.

She has swum in every kind of puddle, ditch, swamp, bog, mud, pond, river and ocean that one can conjure up, even in the winter. I've seen her come from what looks like the depths of hell, green slim, rank bog, black dirt and even Quidi Vidi when I had no choice but to drop the leash or be dragged in with her. The bystanders were as horrified as I was. It took days to get the stink off her.

She never cared. She was always happiest when she was running and dirty. She taught me that - running and dirt can fix almost everything in life. She never slept past 5 a.m. until she was about 11 years old. She woke me up by jumping into the bed and hauling the sheets off me. If I tried to roll over and go back to sleep, she would jump and hit me with her front paws directly on the chest, sometimes slamming into my throat and choking me out a little bit. If that didn't work or I was taking too long to catch my breath she would bite my toes, lick me and eventually resort to full-on barking by 5:20 a.m.

She started to do what Justin calls the Polar Bear jump, standing in the doorway, she lifted off her front paws onto her back ones, rising up in the air, slamming her paws onto the floor, with a single "WOOF" over and over to get me up. She would go into downward dog and pounce onto the bed. She wanted what she wanted when she wanted it and she did not mind being dramatic to get it, with her lips pursed, ears pinned back and a low growl to get her own way.

It didn't matter if it was sleet, rain, hail, snow, hurricanes, or blizzards, we put on our flashers, glow-in-the-dark collars, and headlamps. It just didn't matter, we had to go. There is one season for Tetley and it is go season. There is no bad weather, she taught me, just bad attitudes, and gear.

I learned that trees protect you from the wind and even sideways rain. Ocean water is good for the skin as it gives you a salt scrub from being flung in your face and can heal a lot of wounds, more than physical. Insulated rubber boots, to the knees, are a lifesaver in the winter and insulated gear is a necessity, not an option.

The North Atlantic Ocean is about the coldest thing you can experience in the winter *and* summer, and gale-force winds just make the waves more fun to ride. If you slam into them face first and get the stick right away, you can ride the wave back to shore for another go. It's like a free circus ride.

It is a fact that there is only so wet you can get and once you're wet nothing else matters so you might as well stay out longer. The right socks will prevent blisters and even gators for your hikers won't matter when the water is waist deep. While there is only so wet you can get, dirt is endless. I have found mud in places I didn't know it could get. She ruined 3 vehicles from her escapades.

Sometimes our hikes didn't end near a water source and the trails had no shortage of mud that towels alone couldn't fix, no matter how hard I scrubbed. She made sure to haul the blankets off the seats and grind herself, dirt and all, into them in her effort to completely dry off. We started packing buckets of water but by then the damage was done and the vehicles were totalled.

She ripped the side panel off my SUV door, twice, from standing on the door armrest, hanging out the window, larger than life, catching the wind in her mouth, ears and eyeballs. The faster we drove the more she wanted her head out. She didn't hang out the window with just her head, she stood on the armrest and was up to her waist out the window.

Tetley didn't love the vehicle when we first got her. I drove a 1994 Suzuki Tracker, in 2008. In her defence, the roads in Iqaluit were craters of potholes and if you drove over 20 it was a violent safari ride. She grew to love the vehicle because it meant adventures.

It was in the car that I started singing to her. I used the words to the old song "Daddy's girl" but I changed it to "Mommy's girl, mommy's girl, you're the centre of mommy's world, I love you like you are my teabag, mommy's girl". I always thought the song was horrible saying "I love you like you are my son" what a message to send girls. I took the song and made it about my little teabag.

I was always terrified she would fall out and kept the window up a certain distance so she couldn't. She never did fall out but she did jump a couple of times when she couldn't control her excitement. When we arrived at her favourite destination, the car stopped and she could not control herself. She jumped out the window and into the river, while we scrambled to get out of the car and catch up. I regularly heard from friends and family that they saw us driving with Tetley half out of the vehicle. They knew it was us by the Chocolate Lab hanging out the window everywhere we went.

She somehow always knew when it was the last fetch and time to go, she would go into the pond or river and lay down, refusing to come out. I swear she is telepathic. Every adventure ended with us getting in the car and driving back and forth on the road, near the pond where we could still see her, saying goodbye out the window. The first few times it worked but she caught on that we weren't going to leave her behind... Eventually, her games would end, and she would reluctantly come to us. It was *always* a fight.

Country Path became her domain. She was the only dog on the street that I know of when we first moved to the area. She made sure everyone knew her. I didn't see another dog on our street until a few years later. She stole the neighbour's balls, gloves, and window scraper as they chased her back to our place. The good thing is she forced us to meet Janice and Mike and we liked them, and they loved her. Janice would take her for walks and drives when I was working in the city before I left my corporate job.

They moved to Labrador not long after and got a yellow Lab named Daisy. They brought her to meet Tetley once. Daisy has long since passed, at just 8, from cancer.

She tore up another neighbour's cabbage beds and chased the garbage truck every week. A man from the next street was a runner and she chased him home all the time, going for a run because she wanted to. She never went inside with them and they would call to tell us she was there. Justin wasn't working the first year we moved back to Newfoundland, and it led to many fights between us - how she wasn't tied on or fenced in when I was at work. He was working on the house or in the yard and he didn't want a dog tied on; he didn't think it was a good life for them.

I was getting calls every other day because my number was on her tag. She was everywhere except home. We were one of the first new builds in our area and as construction progressed to other homes, you could be sure of where to find Tetley, running around the sites trying to get someone to throw a ball for her, leading to many cut pads as a construction zone was no place for a dog.

It led to an epic blow-up one morning but eventually, Justin got the message that it was not safe for her to be off-lead because she wasn't yet trained and didn't have the recall necessary. She was just too young. I came home that day to a tie-out set up for her on a clothesline so she could run 40 feet in every direction. She hated it. A chain is still a chain, but I was happy that she was safe when we turned our backs.

When the satellite company showed up to install our TV service, the installer threw a golf ball for her, it took him hours to get the installation completed because he couldn't get up the ladder before she returned with the ball. Justin told him not to engage her. People never listened and they paid for it with their time. She stood with her head cocked to the side, side-eyeing you and the ball, her ears perked up with the fuzz standing up, with a line of drool flowing out of her mouth. Not many people resisted her. She was relentless and pretty cute about it.

On our flight to Newfoundland, we checked in at the Westin Hotel because we had an overnight stay in Ottawa. I wanted to do some shopping at stores we didn't have in Newfoundland and we needed the break in between flights. She had to travel cargo this time so I felt better about splitting the travel.

At the hotel, she had a heavenly dog bed and bowls. The bell-hops would come to my room and take her out for walks when I was shopping. They even took her to the park! Of course, as I was walking her out one day, she decided that the Westin Hotel lobby was the perfect place for a poop. I was mortified. She couldn't care less. It would become her motto for her poop, whenever wherever.

Lexie, on the other hand, gets up in the morning and reminds me of an old man, getting his glasses and paper and heading to the toilet. Lexie goes, spends an insane amount of time searching for the perfect place and does all the things like circling and sniffing and changing her mind a few times until she could go. It was always off the grass in the bushes. Even if we were walking, she did the same process on the side of the road, in the bushes or woods, not to be seen as Tetley and I waited, sometimes for up to ten minutes, while she was finding the perfect place to go.

Tetley was always too excited to take time for that. Every-thing was big and intense and powerful, and she didn't have time to stop for a decent poop. She would hold it until she started her workout, walk, run or hike then she'd just stop where she was and go. There was nothing perfect or deliberate about it. She stopped mid-trail and went where she was. She sure wasn't wasting any time over where to go. There was life to be lived and where to poop was the least of her worries.

When we left for adventures in the morning, she held it until we got where we were going. I always encouraged her to go "Do your poop!" But she was always afraid of missing something and never went. By the time we got to the trail heads, sometimes 90 minute drives, she jumped out of the vehicle and squatted immediately for a poop.

Meanwhile, she hated poop. If Lexie dared to poop next to her, or wherever she herself just pooped, she dramatically ran away from it as if it was somehow horrid that she would have to do such a thing. As she always carried a ball or stick, she often pooped with it in her mouth, which she then dropped as she ran away, and I had to rescue it if it was in a 3-foot vicinity of said poop. For someone who couldn't care less about where she pooped, she was particular about if it was near her.

Life with Tetley became a whirlwind. Life blurred together between working and running her, finding adventures, finishing our house, planning a wedding and running a business. Tetley was relentless in her pursuit of activity so her workout became a priority in order to get anything else done. There were no days off, ever.

My appendix ruptured in 2010 and I had emergency surgery in the middle of the night. I was kept in the hospital for 5 days on IV. Justin was taking care of Tetley, working and visiting me. When I got home from the hospital, she flew through the door, over the patio and raced around the yard. Exuberant is a mild word to describe how she met me.

I knew something was wrong but I didn't think something burst inside of me. I was working out regularly, hiking and running, thinking I had indigestion. When I finally went to see my doctor they sent me to the emergency room. I wasn't going to go because I had started to feel better that day. It was weird, coming and going. I was sure I was going to waste my time.

But I decided to go and get it checked, just in case, as I had taken the day off. They kept me. Justin showed up at the hospital to check on me but I hadn't been seen yet. I was waiting on an ultrasound so I sent him home to check on Tetley and get her settled, always my priority. He just arrived home, from a 45 minute drive, when the doctors called him to say I needed surgery and for him to come back to the hospital. I didn't even know yet.

They did a CT scan instead of an ultrasound and told me my appendix was "angry" and I needed surgery right away, which happened in the middle of the night. The next morning they told me how serious it was and read me the riot act for overlooking it. I told them I didn't think it was that serious, I just didn't think something burst inside of me. I had atypical appendicitis, where I had back pain instead of side or front pain.

When I was finally released 5 days later, I was given strict instructions on exercise and movement. I was a full-time personal trainer by then so this wasn't an easy feat.

But aside from that, those doctors didn't live with Tetley. She didn't care that I could hardly walk, she got up with the same gusto she did every day. She either didn't have the empathy genes most dogs have when their people are sick, or she simply didn't care.

I drove to the railroad tracks as I couldn't have her on leash because that was a recipe for a hernia. I took baby steps, doubled over, sweating and barely moving, and she was beyond frustrated with the pace of our walk, she ran ahead and back, ahead and back as if to say "Hurry up!" She was fed up.

Over the next year, I came down with the Norwalk Virus and H1N1. They were not reasons to stay in bed. Justin would leave for work and I had to negotiate my rest by taking Tetley for swims, walks and runs. Once she was settled, I got in bed until she ripped the sheets off me again. Tetley did cuddle but after her workout. Cuddles are for recovery not a way of life. Justin always told me to wait and he would walk her when he got home. There was no waiting.

It doesn't matter what is happening, Tetley gets her activity, still at almost 15! She has an appointment twice a day in my calendar. I loved our adventures. It was our thing. The activity was great for both of us. But sometimes I wanted a day off and that just wasn't an option. It still isn't. Sleeping in and days off are for dead people. If we are breathing, we are moving.

A tired dog is a happy dog became my motto. She didn't destroy many things in her life because we kept her active, however, there were exceptions such as Justin's seal skin mittens from Nunavut and 12 pairs of my most expensive shoes that time we left her all day for our bachelor parties. I always said she had great taste. There was also the steering wheel in the car when Justin put her back in the vehicle at the ballpark because she ran into the field chasing the ball. We can't really confirm if it was Tetley or Lexie.

We initially blamed Lex because she was newly with us and was a holy terror for destroying everything. Later we thought it might just have been Tetley because she could get very spiteful when she didn't get her own way. Someone also chewed the corners off the railing in the house but we couldn't determine the culprit.

She dramatically flopped when she lay down, the sound of her elbows smacking against the floor was cringeworthy and we're pretty sure she chewed the edges off those to make the smacking less painful. I mean, I often hit the elbow-height ones and wanted to rip them off, so I understood.

Tetley wanted one thing and that was her own way. She still does. There is no compromise unless it ends up with whatever she wants. She is relentless in her determination and it is impossible to not give in. It would be a good thing and a bad thing in her life, her determination.

One thing about Tetley is while she is wild, and still is, she also has a very sweet side that few get to see. Outside was all bets off adventure and nonstop antics but inside, when she was tired, she was always the sweetest girl.

For all of her wildness, she loved to be comfortable and cozy. She loved hot towels and blankets from the dryer and snuggling in the blankets with her head on my pillow after her adventures.

I dressed her up in my blue bathrobe and pretended she was

Tetley Crawley, heavyweight champion of Holyrood, as she wrestled me on the bed, chewing and vocalising as we ramped around.

Tetley - heavyweight champion

Tetley's intelligence was my biggest downfall, she played me, played Lexie, played Justin and her and I went toe to paw on many occasions. I knew she was playing me most of the time. When I said no she barked back. When I said no more she defied me, slamming her paws against the pantry cabinet for treats, or slamming a stick against me for another go. She stared with defiance that dared me to say no.

I snuck around the house when I didn't want to wake her, I still sneak around the house when I don't want to wake her. When I'm up, she's up and when we're up it means let's do stuff. I sneak around, tiptoeing, creeping in and out of rooms, sometimes even hiding behind doors, holding my breath, hoping she will go back to sleep. Just at the moment I think I've won, she finds me. I sigh. And we do whatever she wants.

Her intelligence knows no bounds. When we leave a place of play, I take her stick and hide in a bush or somewhere we can get it and I say "For next time". She leaves the stick but the next time we go there, she heads for the bush where her stick is left behind, whether it is the next day or even weeks later.

As we approach the places she loves she loses it. I always say she has an inner map, tracing the twists and turns in the road, she knows the streets and where we are, and even now, in her very old age, she perks up when we take a familiar road. Adventure and where they happen are embedded in her cells.

I tried, sometimes, to get the upper hand but it quickly resorted back to being Tetley's way or the highway. In a battle of wills, she will always win. We were a match made in heaven.

CHAPTER 3
LEXIE - THE BEGINNING

The first picture I took of Lexie.

Lexie became part of the family, sort of by accident when Tetley was 4 and she was 7 months old. I didn't want another dog. I was already a busy entrepreneur. I was struggling with some things in my personal life, working 18-hour days and I just didn't need the extra work or responsibility. We had never talked about being a 2 dog home.

A woman Justin worked with, Cindy, knew someone

rehoming a Chocolate Lab due to allergies. It was a male and they wanted a great home for him. I believe he was 4, around the same age as Tetley. She told Justin about the dog, knowing we would give him an amazing home. We had sort of already gleaned a reputation as amazing dog owners by then. We talked about it over the weekend, a second dog is a big commitment. The cost of food, insurance, vet care, plus the work and time of 2 dogs.

What if it was like Tetley? Could we really handle that? Could I take 2 dogs to work with me? How would it impact Tetley's life? Would she get along with another dog in her home? Could I walk 2 dogs? I had so many questions. But ultimately decided we were already doing so much for 1 dog, would it really be that much more for a second one? And they could be good company for each other. The lie all multiple-dog households tell themselves before they get a second dog.

We decided to meet the dog. When he told Cindy on Monday, she said the dog had already been rehomed. That was that. It wasn't meant to be and I was a little bit relieved, honestly. But it left an opening where one had not been. We were not looking or considering until then. Someone sent me a link for a dog being rehomed. It was a Chocolate Lab.

I replied to the ad.

A woman responded telling me they were rehoming her because they just had a baby. I can't remember the details exactly. We exchanged a few emails but eventually, I didn't reply. I just let it be. We had a big snowstorm over the next few days followed by a bitter cold front. Newfoundland's weather is sketchy at best, with no norms, we fluctuate between warm and cold fronts as we are pummelled by various systems. We had more than 4 feet of snow, followed by a -20 Celsius windchill. We don't usually get that cold so it was a bitterly cold day that reminded me of living in the North.

I didn't tell Justin and I never followed up. My vehicle had gone into the garage for servicing before the storm and while most workplaces had closed due to the weather, cleanup was underway, and things were reopening. I got a call from Hickman Motors that my vehicle was ready for pickup. Justin was off due to the storm so we headed to the garage. My Blackberry dinged constantly and it was the woman about the dog. It was March 12, 2012.

I replied and said we weren't sure. She kept sending me emails. "Ding Ding Ding". Justin asked "Who is messaging you like that?" I told him about the dog. He said, "Well, let's go take a look, we might not want her, *what's the harm*?" We went to the garage, paid for my vehicle and picked up the keys. I emailed her back and said we would come to see Lexie. She replied, "I'll get her things ready". I wrote her back reminding her that we were just looking, not making a decision.

We then headed toward downtown, where she was located. I gave Justin the address, mispronouncing the name as I wasn't from St. John's. He groaned, saying we were headed to a rough area.

The snowbanks were piled high as everyone was out shovelling snow, clearing out their vehicles and driveways. They all turned to stare. We were clearly outsiders. We pulled up to the house, beat our way through the knee-deep snow, up the steps and knocked on the door. A woman opened the door and there was Lexie, in the porch, looking exactly like Tetley, with her stuff packed, sitting next to her. She wasn't wanted. It was clear.

The porch was a disaster and the house smelled like smoke and something I can't quite name. I asked to come in because it was so cold out but Justin pulled me back by the elbow and said no. She said no anyway. How could we see if Tetley and her liked each other? How could we see what she was like? Lexie threw herself at me.

I asked if we could take her for a walk and she said yes. She handed me a leash that wasn't very sturdy, nothing that could hold back a crazy Lab. She was small but also nearly adult sized.

We went for a walk down the street, with everyone in the neighbourhood watching us. She was wild on a leash. She kept grabbing the leash and tearing on it, sending my arm flailing as she did. She ran backwards grabbing the leash and yanking. Tetley was walking along next to her, on leash, with Justin. They seemed interested in each other and played a little. She was 7 months old and it was clear she had never been on a leash, or possibly ever walked in her life.

I wasn't sure. It was a lot and I had no real idea of what she was like. She looked just like Tetley. There was *something* about her. I asked for a night with her. If I could put a down payment on her and take her home with us to see how she is at our house and if they get along? She went into the house to talk to someone else and came back to tell me "My man says someone from Whitbourne is coming to get her to breed puppies". I walked away. I said no way am I getting involved with this. There were just too many red flags. I felt they were trying to manipulate me.

Justin drove me back to the garage to get my vehicle and I called him immediately and asked him to go back for her. I couldn't leave her there. Something in my gut told me to go back and get her. I did worry she might be used for breeding. The flags were red and I didn't care. I knew if she wasn't ok with us, if she and Tetley didn't get along or if it was too much, I would find her a great home. I was involved in the rescue community and I knew I had support. Plus, I knew thousands of people through fitness. Finding her a home would be easy.

Justin took out the $400 they were asking for, I didn't negotiate with them, I said, "Just pay for her". She came with a water bowl, collar and leash. She didn't have a toy or blanket, food, or anything else with her. Just herself.

Justin called me and told me he had her and was en route home. She was in the backseat of the car and when he hit the brakes she fell over, that was something Tetley had mastered at a few weeks old. I knew she had not spent much time in a vehicle.

When she arrived home, I emailed asking for her vet records

as they told me they had them and was supposed to give them to Justin. She told me she was fully vetted but not spayed. I wanted to know what food she was eating so we could transition her properly, what kind of schedule she had been on, etc. The trail went cold. No vet records. No food records. No return phone calls or emails. What appeared to be burn marks on her nose, which they said happened from a scrap with their other dog. True or not? Who knows. But here I was with an untrained, quickly discovered not house-broken, fully-sized Lab. What had I gotten myself into this time?

She was adorable, though. When she got home with Justin, I was cooking dinner for them. I cooked most of their meals. She lay in front of me with her beautiful face looking at me that night. That would be the first night of a lifetime of cooking dinner stepping over her as she planted herself between the fridge and stove. I gave her a treat and almost lost my fingers. "It's a good thing she's cute," I told Justin.

I can't imagine what she must have felt when she got here. We have a huge property, backing onto the forest, with a large yard. She lived on a downtown city street and I'm not sure of her backyard or outdoor access situation. They were townhouse-style properties, attached 4 together in row housing. I'm sure they had backyards as most properties like that do. But I really didn't know as I couldn't see it from the road.

We lived in the woods, on several acres backing onto forest. We have hectares of forest behind us. She had come from the busy downtown core, close to the police station, fire station and St. Clare's hospital. It was loud where she lived and our home was so quiet we could hear the highway traffic several kilometres away.

I was teaching fitness classes that evening, in spite of the storm, we were cleaned up and most of the town was back operating. I taught fitness classes, semi-private and personal training, in the city in my fitness studio, located on Forbes Street, which then moved to Crosbie Road, from 10 a.m. to 2:00 p.m. most days. Early on I taught from 6 a.m. to 2:00 p.m. but I hired Trish, another personal trainer, to take over those early morning shifts. She also taught evening classes in the studio.

Eventually, I hired more staff and we operated every day with classes and private training happening most of the day, evenings and weekends. I had rented space from another trainer when I first started training in St. John's. His studio was located on Golf Avenue at that time, not far from Lexie's first home.

As my reputation and demand for my services grew, I decided to rent a very small space on Forbes Street. There was a rub-and-tug massage parlour underneath my studio. I was so green behind the ears when the landlord told me that a massage parlour was located in the building I said "Oh that fits right in with us, probably a lot of my clients will use their services".

She didn't say anything and it didn't take long to find out that it wasn't a clinic. Language is key to understanding a lie. She didn't lie. I just didn't know the difference between massage parlours and clinics.

We kept the music loud to drown out the spanking and yelling. I looked for a new location as the running joke was "Yes, above the rub and tug". It was a joke but we wanted out of the area. Thankfully, we did leave, as the violence increased in the area with prostitution, drugs, and gun-related violence becoming prevalent. I found a larger and more centrally located studio that allowed for growth, on Crosbie Road. We made that home.

I also taught fitness classes in my home studio from 5:30 p.m. to 9 p.m. Before I built a studio in my house I had rented spaces in school gyms and community centres.

After I rented community centres and school gyms in Holyrood, I did rent a studio space locally. Unfortunately, the cost of the space plus maintenance in a small town was far more than I could afford to pay. Prime locations in St. John's were less than half the price I was paying in a small town and I was getting taken for a ride on the snow clearing that wasn't included in my contract.

When I had that space, Tetley came to the studio but had to be kennelled during the workouts. Otherwise, she was in the way. While she was crazy in the home studio, Justin was home and she was outside with him. She had settled enough to hang out in the studio without terrorising people.

That first night with Lexie, she bounced downstairs into the fitness studio to meet everyone. Mary Ann was a Lab lover, as she had a black Lab, Sammy, who died several years earlier. Sammy was her baby, much like my girls are mine. While M-A or Auntie Mary Ann (what she became known as) and Tetley were great friends, Lexie quickly became her best friend. She had that effect on people. You couldn't help but love Lexie.

We did have to put up a baby gate, much Like when Tetley had to have a kennel when she first came to the studio until she learned to interact with people.

What a new world for Lexie. I often wonder what that was like for her. There were so many people and she loved people. While she was greeting everyone and making friends, a baby gate gave us the space to still have workouts without her on top of people. She came in at the beginning and end of classes and, eventually when she stopped jumping on people, she was allowed in all the time.

It quickly became clear that Lexie needed more attention than we initially thought she would. At her age we certainly expected her to be housetrained. She was not. She frequently peed in the house. The first time she did it I reacted with a slight yell "Oh my God, what are you doing?" and "No stop!" All my dog training out the window as I rushed to get her outside, but as I got close to her, she cowered and shook.

My heart sank. I knew then how she was trained and how she had lived. If we raised our voice or hand to pet her, she cowered and peed on herself. If we tried to walk her on a leash, she wrestled us. She was starving and didn't appear to know what kibble was. She sought out junk food or table food but soon learned to eat kibble. I cooked most of their food so they had some kibble with cooked meats added to the top.

She tried to get on the table while we were eating. She constantly got into the garbages and we had to keep all the garbage covered until she was 4 or 5 years old. She ate pens and pencils, tore up books and magazines, toilet paper, bust all the balls in the gym, tore up mats, and chewed off leashes. Life with Tetley was a whirlwind, this was chaos.

I couldn't give her up though. This wasn't her fault. We tried to change her name but she didn't seem to adapt to anything. We settled on lou lou but friends of ours got a new dog that week and said they named her lou lou! What are the chances? We kept Lexie but over the years she became known mostly as Lex, lolly and lollypoppers, and baby chomps. Justin calls her flipper because of the way she lies on her side with her arm in the air for a rub down, like a seal.

She is also called lobster jo and lolly jo and I have no idea how many other nicknames over the years they both had. Justin went through a phase of calling them Cory and Trevor from the Trailer Park Boys and he mostly called Lexie Junior, after Tetley.

Her first vet check showed she was over 6 months old and not yet fully grown, which did align with the information her original owners gave us. We had her checked for tattoos and microchips as we wanted to make sure she wasn't stolen. They told us she was born in August but we didn't know for sure so we made up a birthday for her that was August 15, 2011. Babette Miester, our vet, took her by the face and said "you just hit the doggy lottery".

I never understood why people thought we were the unicorn of dog owners. I just took care of my girls and made them important. I didn't think we did anything special so I was always surprised to hear these types of comments. They are family, not disposable when they require extra work.

In spite of the challenges, I was happy that Lexie was with us. She was silly, fun and goofy. She joined the pack 2 days before Tetley's 4th Birthday. On her first night with us, she got to meet dozens of people coming and going for fitness classes and the next night she had a birthday party, complete with party hats, cake and treats. I like to think she felt the love right away. We celebrated her gotcha day and Tetley's birthday.

She was with us a few months before I opened my Forbes Street studio. By June, they didn't have to stay home anymore while I went to St. John's to work. I bought a kennel for the studio for Lexie and took them both with me.

Our mornings, and days, changed then. When I was renting space, Justin walked Tetley, then both of them, in the mornings while I headed to St. John's. Now I had more time in the mornings, with Trish handling my early morning sessions, we headed out for adventures, did our morning workout, and had breakfast before heading to the St. John's studio for client sessions.

We often went early and stopped at a pet store near the studio by the village mall and grabbed pizzles to keep them chewing and content during the workouts. They kept meeting more and more people with the circle around them growing.

It wasn't easy and a couple of times in those first few months I wondered if we should find her a new home. It was a lot but she had already won me over. I didn't know if someone else would give her what she needed. I also didn't want to put her through another rehoming, given the issues we were seeing with her being scared. We didn't want to break her trust and we felt she was ours now.

She was the best rash decision I ever made. Not only because of taking her from that place, where we believe she was abused, but we became the sole focus of her love after she felt safe with us. She was wild and crazy but she also balanced out the intensity of Tetley. Our family felt complete. Crazy, but complete.

In the first couple of years with her she exhibited some behaviours that we know could have ended her life with other people. If we put our feet near her, she growled. Justin has a habit of pointing at Tetley when telling her to do something or not do something.

He did the same with Lexie but she didn't like his finger-pointing. She growled at him when he did it. She snarled, with her lip pulled back and her teeth barred. It was off-putting as we weren't sure if she was serious or if she might bite. I would remind him to stop putting his finger in her face as she clearly didn't like it. It was a habit neither of them would break. He pointed and she growled.

It didn't take us long to figure out if she would bite. She bit my nephew, Kyle, on the face. Thankfully it was a surface bite and he wasn't hurt. My family was helping build our garage and my mother was in the house with Kyle while everyone else was outside. Mom was washing the dishes and had her back turned for a moment. She said Kyle was watching TV. We don't know exactly what happened but the bite happened.

Without the full picture, it was hard to know what to do next. We told my family we would call our dog trainer in the morning and have her assessed. We knew that our trust in Lexie had been broken and we needed to find out what was going on with her.

That night I put her in her kennel for bed and leaned in to kiss her, as I did every night, and she bit me on the face. A quick hit but I was bleeding. Blood ran down my chin and onto my shirt. It wasn't serious in terms of wounding but it was the second bite in a matter of hours and we knew this needed to be dealt with. We spent a lot of time with family, kids and clients. We had to ensure this didn't escalate but also give Lexie a chance.

The next morning we called our dog trainer who put her through a battery of assessments. Thankfully, my family was understanding of our desire to work with her.

Glenn, our trainer, told us that Lexie was most likely experiencing PTSD in those moments. She wasn't safe and didn't know if she would be safe. We had to make her safe.

We really didn't know what she had been through and we didn't decompress her. We didn't even know about decompressing at that time. Glenn determined she wasn't at risk for aggression. She never did it again.

He was a behaviour specialist for animals and said she did not have a mean bone in her body. He didn't feel she was a risk and he told us that if a dog wants to harm you, it will. They communicated with their mouths and she was sending a message. We followed his recommendations and Lexie's snarling, growling and snapping stopped.

Lexie desperately loved Tetley and wanted to be friends. Tetley was never happy about sharing me, she loved Lexie but mostly wanted things her way. Another dog meant compromise and she didn't like not getting her own way. They adjusted well to each other and played a lot. They became great friends but Tetley, still, lets her know who's the first dog in the house.

Lexie turned out to be the dog we didn't know we needed. She was nothing like the rest of us. She didn't want to work out or get up early. She ended up with a host of bone and joint problems, having multiple surgeries for dysplasia and a cruciate ligament repair. She was the chill dog. She was fine to go or stay as long as she was with us. She was a front-seat, console-seat dog who needed to be always touching someone. She desperately wanted attention all the time. Working out? She was on the mat. In bed? She was there. Treadmill? She was next to it.

If someone was in bed, that's where she was, too.

Lexie is a domesticated dog and a very good dog. She's the kindest soul and most loving girl. She really grew into herself as she settled down, learned to trust us, and made her home with us. She has the gentlest disposition. Every day I put my hand under her chin, lift it up, look into her eyes and ask her "how did mommy get so lucky to have you?"

Lexie always looked like this.

Training Lexie, though, was an ordeal. None of the things we used to train Tetley worked. She just became afraid of us. I couldn't live with that. To get her out of her fear state and make her safe, I stopped all training and focused on making her trust us and feel safe with us. I started singing to her. I don't sing and you can be thankful for that but somehow my singing helped Lexie.

She was afraid of everything; towels, hairdryers, if you moved a chair suddenly, or banged a cupboard door, she ran downstairs and peed on the floor or cowered under the table. As I sang, she came closer and closer to me. I made up a song about getting her hair done and she would come in and get blow-dried. She still loves to be blow-dried.

"You've gotta get your hair all diddy diddy do do do" and over and over I sang that while I was blow drying my hair. I still sing it to her after she comes from the groomer or she comes in to get blow-dried while I'm doing my hair.

In spite of the rough start, Lexie became the comic relief, silly girl, and love bug to our family. She blended in soon enough. She loved the classes and clients that came and went, the car rides and adventures, and she picked up some of Tetley's habits and learned to do the wiggles and bring toys to the door to greet us. Lexie became so obsessed with bringing something to whoever came to the door, she would rummage through their toy basket as quickly as she could to find something.

Because she often took their toys outside there wasn't anything left in the toy basket so she would run to the laundry basket of socks and grab one. It was always my socks, never Justin's, that she took. I wear odd socks every day because Lexie has robbed most of my socks. I find them in the woods, driveway and yard regularly.

Once I even found a client's socks in her kennel. I had taught yoga one night and when I put her to bed, a pair of socks were in there. I sent a text to the group asking if someone has lost their socks and sure enough, someone said they couldn't find them when it was time to go!

"Why didn't you say something?" I asked. She said she didn't think the dog had stolen them, she had no idea what happened and left with her bare feet in her shoes. Oh, Lexie.

Lexie loves to be a helper. While she's less so these days, she loved to let me know when something was wrong or help Tetley. One of her favourite things to do was "help" Tetley up the base-ment stairs, or any stairs. Tetley was always hesitant on stairs while Lexie went up, unafraid. Lexie would stand at the top of the stairs and dance, her toenails clicking on the hardwood floor.

Lexie would rush down the carpeted stairs and squeal and nudge Tetley, which just made Tetley more afraid and cautious, beelining it back to the bottom. "Lexie, I know you're trying to help, but you're not right now," I said every single time. And the girls hit those stairs several times a day and Tetley was cautious and Lexie was frantically trying to show her the way up and how easy it was.

When we hiked the East Coast Trail or came across any stairs on our adventures, Lexie rushed to the top and edged back down for Tetley, crying, dancing, clicking her toenails, and ramming her snout into Tetley's neck. Lexie would need to be managed and held onto at the top, otherwise, Tetley would lean into the wall or head back to the bottom.

One particular spot in Mad Rock, Bay Roberts has long open grated stairs to a beach. We always went down to the beach. The girls had a swim and we enjoyed it until we had to come back up. Lexie would race up the stairs, uninhibited while I would have to crawl up the rocks, under the stairs with Tetley, while Lexie raced around the stairs trying to "help".

I always came home telling Justin that Lexie is trying to be helpful and it was the only thing she was *not* afraid of. It made no sense. She loved the risks outside, getting way too close to ledges, climbing rock walls, racing up and down stairs and yet if we slammed a door too loudly she scuttled under something, terrified.

I suppose inside houses, loud noises hurt her when she was a baby, but outside nothing hurt. She was free. She was wild. She wasn't scared out there. She loved it as much as the rest of us, but for her, it hurt her physically to do it.

We had a deacon's bench near the back door when she first arrived and eventually moved to the front porch, but their collars, leashes, boots, hankies, and clothing are kept in the bench. When Lexie came home she had a collar, leash and a water bowl that was an upside-down water bottle style. She hated the water bowl and we found it cumbersome so we gave it away to an animal rescue.

Tetley lay down to drink so we used a large bowl for them and Lexie drank from that too. Plus, Lexie liked to blow bubbles in the water bowl so she needed a big bowl to contain the mess. She has droopy lips and leaves a trail of water wherever she goes. When she was younger she would put her face in the water bowl and blow out, making bubbles. She always seemed surprised by it and kept doing it. Almost as if she was thinking "Woah!"I kept yelling, sounding like my mother "Lexie, will you drink your water, not play with it".

The leash and collar she came with made her nervous. I didn't wash them when we got her, I just replaced them and put the old ones in the deacons' bench and put a pink collar on her with her fuschia tag that labelled her mine.

Each time I opened the deacon's bench she backed away. I finally figured out it was the collar and leash she hated. I held it up to her one day to see if it was the problem and she backed away, snarling. I threw them away that day. I cleaned out the bench, and put some bounce sheets in it and she never again was sketchy around the bench.

We took these as signs, beyond what we already knew, about her past. People's behaviour will tell you everything you need to know. Her first owner vanished once Lexie was out of her sight. She didn't deliver on anything she said she would and she never followed up on her. I can imagine if I had to rehome a dog I would want to know how she was doing, especially in those first weeks.

But they never asked.

Sometimes, I thought of taking a drive to the street we got her to see how she would react but I never did. I always knew it was better not to trigger anything in her memory or create any additional fear. We have never gone back to that street. There was no point. She was all we needed from there and there was no reason to look back.

She loved everyone and she had access to thousands of people and all sorts of adventures. The things that were not good about her were minor compared to what was amazing about her.

I had to share the hair dryer with Lexie and the treadmill with Tetley. There is no space where I exist without them. They consume all parts of my life from work to home, fitness, errands and shopping. It is rare to see me without them.

They wreaked havoc in many stores and businesses, including CBDC when I had a business meeting but was asked to "bring the dogs', where they ramped around on the office floor, running through the halls and creating utter chaos in their wake. Such was my life from the moment they arrived. It was me and them.

Life with both was wild.

As my constant 24/7 companions, their individual personalities and gifts taught me more about life, love and adventure than anything else in my life.

The girls, as they became known to everyone in our lives, are the ones who opened me to truly living life. As our adventure is winding down, naturally, there is so much to share in the life we lived, the lessons we learned and the incredible journey we had. Dogs have been long hailed as man's best friend but I found myself, my passion, and a life worth living because of the girls.

They gave me everything and I gave them everything. Tetley and Lexie taught me more about being a better human than anything else. Maybe that's why we have dogs, they teach us and allow us to become better people.

Those who are fortunate enough to journey with a dog, not just to live with them or coexist, but those who truly get to experience the soul of a dog, develop a bond that is beyond mere words.

While this book is an attempt to put that journey into words, I know words alone cannot really do it justice, because words are just too small for the expansiveness of the journey for those who are blessed to know the depth of a dog's love.

For the most part, I think I gave them an incredible life, the care they needed, an amazing adventure, raised off leash in the woods with days, weeks and years filled with people, adventure, and love. They gave me more than I can describe. It's a feeling, an energy that is indescribable. They came to work with me almost every day, went on boat rides, camping trips, retreats, and weekends away, and our family vacations were booked only in places they could go.

As I walk back on our journey, I reflect on how it started with Tetley. A friend of mine told me to read *Marley and Me*. So, on day 1 when we returned to Nunavut, she a 7.5-week-old puppy and me a 28-year-old independent woman, lay on the couch as I had booked a couple of days off to stay home with her, with her moving between asleep in the crook of my arm to biting me and eating my hair, while I was reading *Marley & Me*. That book set me up for the life I would have with the girls.

It set up our relationship in a way where I started out thinking of the end and kept that end at the forefront of my mind. It made me too soft on them at times but it started my life with Labs with the realisation that this is all temporary. A short journey together compared to the journey of a human life.

Sometimes Justin would say that I bring trouble on myself because I have no rules or boundaries with them, and I would exclaim but they're going to be dead someday! And he would say, but she's 2, or 3 or 8 or whatever year it was until Tetley hit 11 and then he stopped saying it because he knew too, someday they'll be dead and it will be sooner than we can handle, even if they're 20.

Because there will never be enough time, but I hope, with this book, that there will be fewer regrets, for you, too. That's what *Marley and Me* gave me and what I hope to pass on to other dog lovers - this is all temporary and the more we live the less we regret.

CHAPTER 4
UNCONDITIONAL LOVE

Princess. My first dog.

Unconditional love and dogs just go together. If you want to feel loved, get a dog. Growing up, my father always said "dogs need love and kindness too" as he got on the floor in the kitchen or living room and played with the dogs. Love, respect and care for animals is learned.

People learn to be afraid, hate, neglect or feel superior to animals. It's not human behaviour and it's not biblical in having dominion over all things, it's human conditioning. I'll never understand the people who have animals as lawn ornaments or are kept in cages their entire lives, who insist on an archaic belief that animals will behave or hunt better if kept separate from affection so they can only focus on work.

How cold is a person to chain a dog to a house and leave it there? I worked with several animal rescues over the years, picking up neglected, abused, no longer wanted animals and it tore my heart to pieces how many of these dogs were once house dogs, then put outside and left there for years, laying on concrete, ignored, only to be given away in their senior years. But for every person who neglected them, there was always a willing family to step in and take care of them and provide love and care in their final days.

Like B (name altered for rescue purposes), a dog who lived as a house dog who slept in bed with his humans until he was 7. They had kids and B was moved to the garage where he slept on a concrete floor for another 7 years. I facilitated his rescue, loaded him up in my SUV as the owner told me his story. I try my best to be understanding and compassionate at all times. I try to be grateful that people are *finally* doing the right thing and I try hard not to shame people, especially at the moment they are doing the right thing.

It took everything in me that day to be polite. I wanted to scream at her "Why didn't you give him away 7 years ago?" B was taken into fospice by Joy and her 5 children. We knew they wouldn't have long with him so we wanted to be sure it was ok for the children. She said, "I want my children to learn that this is how we help. We don't abandon people or dogs in their final days but we lean in to help them". Because of this attitude, B's final days were surrounded by love and dignity.

One of our family dogs, Sailor, was a Black Lab mix known in Newfoundland as a Cape Shore Waterdog. When he was adopted, Mom insisted that he would live outdoors if he was going to be a hunting dog. It *was* recommended as the best way to keep hunting dogs at that time. He lasted 3 days, if that, outside while his crying reverberated through the house and a bunch of animal lovers couldn't take it anymore. We could not have Teddy in the house and Sailor outside. We just couldn't.

Sailor went on to be one of the best hunting dogs in the area and also wore t-shirts and lipstick and had his ears pinned back in scrunchies, while tucked in on the couch with a pillow under his head and a blanket covering him up, getting his nose wiped when it dripped.

When anyone touched the gun case or even crept around the house early in the morning, Sailor was at the ready. He was born to hunt. He would stay in the blind in the morning covered in ice (his coat and fur are made for this) not move a muscle until he was told and then come home to a loaf of homemade bread dipped in something or other, to sleep on his bed, *in the house.*

Other men constantly remarked to my father that he would be "ruined" for hunting if he lived in the house, only to be proven wrong. Perhaps love is the common denominator to making someone great, animals or people. Mutual respect, love, care, and attention seem to be the ingredients to a great recipe. Sailor never disappointed in the hunt, one time even swimming for hours after a duck in the frigid winter ocean. They were sure he was lost because he was gone so long. A friend of Dad's borrowed him to hunt and Sailor went after a duck that was too far out. He came back with the duck, and stood on the beach, ready to go again. He was a machine.

When my father was building a cabin in Red Island he took

Sailor with him. Red Island is a small island off Placentia that was part of the resettlement program in the 1960s and it's where my mother is from. One day, as he was working on the roof, he noticed something out of the corner of his eye and realised Sailor had climbed the ladder and was peeking over the eave!

Sailor climbing a ladder.

This became his thing, a ladder-climbing dog, of which we have many videos and pictures. He became so good at it that ladders had to be put away all the time because if there was a ladder there was going to be a very large dog on the roof. Dad would have to go up and get him down, which wasn't an easy feat by any means. My father is a strong man but carrying a large dog down a ladder was dangerous, so he figured if he could learn to go up, he could learn to come down it.

Sailor going back down the ladder.

And learn it he did. Sailor started going up and down ladders on his own. It was a sight to see, a dog so committed to excellence that he was willing to do whatever his person asked him to do. He was a gift for my brother Tommy, at 16, who wanted a hunting dog. He became my other brother Kevin's dog, really, for hunting but a family dog for everyone and a companion to my father.

He was the kind of dog that set the bar for other dogs in your life, his intelligence, fearlessness, bravery and his passion for the hunt, at least. He was insane though. His parents were not domesticated by any means. These dogs are bred for hunting in the frigid cold North Atlantic, and since domestication is a trait that's passed down from generation to generation, Sailor did not have it.

He ate his way through a French door, chewed off every phone cord that came into the house and destroyed much of everything in his path. He ate shoes and slippers like it was his job. He was wild but he was a good dog and he still lived in the house. He walked to the end of the driveway with mom and carried the newspaper for her in the mornings and brought in bags of groceries from the car. He took pride in doing a great job.

He just couldn't help destroying things. He loved massages and would back in between my legs while I massaged his back muscles. He really loved this as he got older.

I believe that unconditional love is the main ingredient for a great dog. And not just for dogs. I believe a dog or anyone, who feels loved will step into their greatest potential. Sailor was living proof of that. Growing up in the 80s, 90s, and early 2000s, in rural Newfoundland, with a lot of people who have a lot of opinions on how things should be done because that's how things have always been done is one of the ways we lose access to change. People back then thought that a dog should be chained on with little socialisation or it would make them not want to hunt.

Sadly, many people still think this way. Sailor proved them

wrong. And it changed the way I viewed people who kept dogs in cages and chained outside because I knew that those dogs were like all other dogs, despite the social messages that they aren't.

I have a neighbour who keeps dogs outside in cages while he walks a small indoor dog. The compartmentalisation of the difference in these dogs makes me wonder if it's the same mentality of racism and sexism - that they can only see the untruths in their thinking - that somehow people of different colours are different from white people or that women don't make great leaders or belong in the workforce.

I muse to myself sometimes why would one see a hunting dog differently than a house dog? Maybe a Yorkie isn't going to kill rabbits with you or dive into the frigid North Atlantic Ocean but surely the hunting dog desires companionship, love, affection, and attention just as much? Perhaps even more, as a reward for their hard work.

That dog will work harder for you when you share your life with him. Like all of us, we do a better job when we feel cared for, loved, and appreciated.

Dogs are pack animals so separating them from other dogs or people is cruel… to be taken out for a momentary hunt and then caged again, with no regard for how it helps them eat, while they lay their head on a soft pillow, in a warm bed while their dog curls up in below-freezing temperatures nearby. I've often wondered how they can sleep because I surely can't knowing they're out there and there's nothing I can do about it. Legally, they're taken care of and have adequate shelter.

I'm preaching to the choir here as I know those people don't read these books but in writing this piece, I hope to teach the lesson so we can all tolerate less of it from the people in our lives. I've heard people say "He's a good man" or "a good provider" as if we can overlook the stark contradiction in behaviour.

My friend, Jeanette and I, on a trip to Germany a few years

ago, stayed in a suite owned by Peter, Tina Turner's guitarist. He was an amazing chef as well and in the private eatery he had a sign that said "If your friends aren't nice to the server, they're not nice people". I have never forgotten that.

In our society, we like to change stories and narratives and make people better than they are. Is a person a good person who cages and chains animals but because he is good to his neighbours, he is good? Is a person a good person when they are racist, but they are good to the white people they know? Is a person a good person who is a misogynist who dislikes women in positions of authority or power, but because he is a good friend to the boys, he is good?

I don't believe as humans we are as cut and dry as good and bad. We all have traits that make us more of some things and less of others. When we examine ourselves under a microscope we all have challenges and characteristics that make us less than perfect. But can we overlook moral codes such as animal neglect or abuse, though many would disagree that it's abusive? Times change and we must upgrade and change with them. I will always be a voice for those who have no voice.

Love, then, is the thing that makes our animals great, not control. Control makes an animal afraid and submissive. Nothing can be great when it's shrinking into itself. But a dog, like a person, can unfold into their greatest potential when they have love. And a dog can help a person unfold into their greatest potential when they have love.

Dogs are easy to love. They are easy to open our hearts to. When we've been broken or damaged, or they have, we can open our hearts in a way that nothing else does. Dogs were revered in ancient Egypt, buried in the graves of the Pharaohs and those who owned them.

While I had several dogs growing up, Lexie was the dog that helped me understand, and be open to, deep unconditional love. She came to me at the time in my life when I needed it most. But the dogs before her, including Tetley, set the stage to open to the love she offered. She adored me. She loved me so deeply that I started to love myself. I saw myself through her eyes and felt what real love felt like. I knew I deserved better in all my relationships, most importantly, the one with myself.

The love Tetley and I have for each other is deep, soul-level love, it's the kind of love where she will never give me what I want but what I need. She is the dog who pushes and drives me. That's her way of loving me. She knows that I'm stubborn and it's her relentlessness that is frustrating but usually exactly what I need.

But Lexie is the dog who just loves me. She doesn't care if I get up, if I take her places, if we do anything except be together. She is the dog that makes you know love because you exist. And we need that kind of love too. I think Tetley would disagree and she would say we get love when doing good, existing isn't doing good! Tetley is the epitome of a working dog, she loves to do a great job and then get love, attention, and affection. She gives it the same way. She side eyes, judges, and stares when things aren't going the way she thinks they should.

When Lexie stays in bed and won't get up for breakfast, I yell "come on Lex, it's brekkie time" and she doesn't come, Tetley pins her ears back, walks in the hallway, bounces and barks a big "woof" and Lexie will come dragging herself out of bed. Tetley is incredulous that she would sleep in and I think a little disgusted.

We always joke that Tetley thinks "of all the dogs you could have gotten, this is what you brought me?" Yes, Tetley, because if we had 2 of you, we would end up institutionalised!

Princess was the first dog I loved. I'll never forget when she came to our house in Point Verde, stray, abandoned, having just had puppies. She was some sort of collie mix with her long black fur with white and brown markings. I fed her my banana, at 5 years old, and ran into the house to tell mom a wolf was outside!

We kept her. It was thought she was dumped but no one really knows where she came from. I don't remember anyone looking for her, but she became a constant in my life until I was in grade 9, when she just left one day, as quickly as she had shown up. We searched for her for what seemed like forever, but she vanished without a trace. She had to have been old at that point. We had her for 11 years and she wasn't a puppy when she arrived. I don't remember her being sick or struggling to walk around. She was always a part of things, came on camping trips, in the woods, and walked to Placentia with my brother, Craig, when he went to dances on Friday nights. She followed us everywhere. She was just there, always.

We often walked a couple of kilometres to Green's Store in Point Verde for a chocolate chunk and she would follow us out there. She ate the Christmas turkey once, we think, on behalf of the cat who threw it on the floor. There were cat teeth and claw marks and Princess had never touched anything in her life. She was the type of dog where we could eat our breakfast or mini pizzas at the coffee table while watching cartoons on Saturday and she wouldn't touch it. She had pride and stealing food wasn't on the list of things she would do, unless the cat started it!

Years later my grandfather found her body, she had died under a tree, they knew her fur and she had a cracked tooth that was visible in her jawbone. It was nice to know where she was and get closure. She was our first family dog and taught us a lot about love and loyalty. They say dogs do that - leave to die - but I've never researched it to know if there's truth to it, but I know it happened to us.

That's how we were as a family. If something or someone showed up and needed something we just did it, we helped, and we gave where we could. So, we kept her. She added so much to our childhood. She was a constant companion. We were never alone. I hung off her neck with her long black fur rubbing in my face. My youngest brother, Kevin, was a baby and would grab her nose saying it was a rubber ball, like the old Pepsi balls we would get at the store.

I remember standing on the back bridge yelling to her every

day. We all did. Thinking she would come back. Hoping she would come back. Mom drove us around in her white station wagon searching for her. We searched the woods around the house. We never knew what actually happened until Pop found her body. Her loss left an opening for a dog.

On a trip to the scrap yard for something Dad and Kevin found a puppy in a tin can, so they came home with him. We called him Teddy and he was the dumbest dog that ever lived. He was a part Sheppard and part who knows what. One ear crooked to the side and the other went straight up. He was a doofus, and he became my dog. He was the family dog but by this time I was a teenager, and he slept in bed with me every night and joined me on my daily walks, he never had a collar or a leash and didn't need one. He wouldn't leave my side during our walks.

Teddy. My first real love.

Except for one day, a dog rushed into the street with its teeth bared and full intentions to attack me, but Teddy intervened and in one swoop flipped him on his back with his teeth on his throat. He didn't hurt him but he gave him a message. Every time we walked past that house afterwards the dog sat on the lawn and watched us go by. He wouldn't even make a sound. Teddy was a goofy, not overly intellectually smart dog but he was instinctually smart and loyal. He knew his people and he protected them.

I watched him do the same when a neighbourhood dog came into our yard, he didn't hesitate, or hurt the dog, but gave a warning message that he didn't belong. He was at dad's fish flake that was drying on the lawn. A fish flake is a net that lets you salt and dry fish, a long Newfoundland tradition dating back to colonisation and the merchant fishing trade of the "new world". The dog was a neighbour's dog, but Teddy didn't care, he wasn't welcome to steal drying fish.

Teddy died when I was 22. He was 10. I was at university studying for exams when they called to tell me he was gone. Even though I hadn't lived home in 4 years I felt Teddy was my dog and the loss was hard. I'm not sure if I ever really grieved all those dogs because I'm crying as I write the story. I missed him. I still do. Back then I didn't know how to feel my feelings, so I pushed them down.

Teddy had some strange behaviours like backing out of the house instead of just walking out. He was afraid of the forced air grates for the furnace. He also had to sit in the front seat of the car and we would have to sit in the back of moms car. He loved the homemade bread and milk loaf mom made him. She would tear up the bun of fresh bread and dip it in tin milk and water mixture that he loved. Probably not the healthiest but he loved it and it was the 90s in rural Newfoundland.

He ate 4 tubs of ice cream and smelled like vanilla ice cream for days during blackout 1994, a 5-day power outage caused by a storm when we used the snowbanks for a deep freeze while the power was out. As we were eating dinner, he came into the house sticky and smelling like ice cream. Mom rushed out to find the four tubs of ice cream that she had gotten on sale at the grocery store were gone. We don't know if he ate all 16 litres of ice cream or if he had help from some other neighbourhood dogs who were kicking around. Sailor came when Teddy was about four or five years old. He arrived in December and I moved to St. John's for university the following September and I would see them both on my weekend and holidays trips home.

The dogs brought so much joy to my life and I have a deep love for dogs so as an adult when it came time to settle down and I knew I was putting down roots and could properly take care of a dog, it was time. Little did I know what was going to happen in my life and how much we would need each other and just how much living we would do together.

Unconditional love from dogs is easy and perhaps the only place we'll truly get it. All other love, even our parents, is conditional. People say they love you no matter what but it's not true. There are always conditions on that love. As children, we learn how to get love and what a lack of love feels like. We know that when we are good love flows easily to us from people but when we are bad that love is easily revoked.

Love often requires us to be something that someone else wants us to be. It also means we must understand, without really being told, what will get us love and remove love. We try our best to be good and get love but from person to person good is a relative term and we spend most of our lives twisting ourselves into the version of what we think is most lovable. Or we eventually give up on that ever happening and we just isolate ourselves in the cages inside of ourselves, desperately seeking love that feels too painful and confusing to reach out for.

But with dogs, who we are, what we have and even the mistakes we make do not matter to the love we receive. Even when we are angry, frustrated and disconnected, our dogs bring us back to ourselves. They forgive us easily for our mistakes and are the most excited to see us, ever. When we leave, they chase us to the door and when we return they meet us at the door. They seek us out when we're sad, laying their head on whatever part of us they can reach, sometimes full body, as if they could absorb the feelings we have.

I wonder if that's why dogs exist at all - to teach us unconditional love.

Tetley pushes me to get outside. Sometimes I get frustrated with that because I am often in the middle of something, but she relentlessly pushes until I go out with her. Sometimes it is pouring rain or frigid temperatures and I vent to myself (and friends sometimes!) that I wish she would just stop and let me have a day off occasionally.

Not only is that never happening but the truth is I need those moments outside, in the woods, or by the pond with the wind blowing on me. I can get really in my head and hyper-vigilant and focused on what I'm doing - sometimes to the point where I forget to eat. Her pushing me to take a break, and go outside is less about her and more about me. She is unconditionally loving me in those moments to help me loosen up, be in the moment, and just live fully. Nothing is ever so urgent that a run in the forest can't fix or bring clarity to the situation.

I never regret going but I always regret my frustration.

Lexie is unconditional love personified. Whenever I get frustrated, especially with Tetley, she sits directly in front of me, ears back, eyes wide, the tip of her tail wagging, and pawing at me, bringing me back to myself. Tetley is the push every button you have dog and Lexie is the put the buttons back in place dog.

Lexie would absorb my pain if she could and I'm not convinced she can't. A shaman I once worked with told me that dogs take on the energy of the house and their people, it's why they often get so sick, whereas cats eat the energy, and dogs try to take it away and end up taking it on themselves. Whether there's any truth to it I don't know but I know myself, and many dog owners, will tell you that when we're stressed our dogs are stressed. Lexie had all sorts of maladies from skin conditions and allergic reactions. The calmer I became in life the less stressed she was, and she went from taking all sorts of medications to taking none.

Lexie is the dog that gives me constant unconditional love. It pours out of her, not just to me, but to so many other people. I am her person though. She sticks close to me but she will fling herself at anyone for a little love. She exudes love. She is impossible not to fall in love with.

She has a knack for knowing how to get people on the floor in a cuddle fest with her. She offers her belly as if it is a gift to you. And it is. There is something about her calm demeanour that allows you to destress by rubbing her gut.

She never asks anything of me, except to be myself. She wants to be with me constantly but she never asks for anything other than love in return. She never demands anything and never judges me. She is faithful. No matter where I am, she is there too. It's that simple. She is present and she loves me. She looks at me with pure adoration.

Tetley is demanding. I know how deeply Tetley and I love each other but there are demands, constantly, from Tetley, and judgment. Oh, can Tetley exude judgment. No one can do a side eye like her. While Tetley is the wild one, she was also the disciplined one and took pride in following the rules, well the ones she wanted to, and obeying her commands.

She liked to pretend to do some of them. When Justin said "down" she went half down in a squat position, with her elbows not quite touching the ground under her. On repeat, she would go all the way down but she hated it. She gave her passwords (kisses) for treats and took pride in returning the ball, putting it in my hand when asked and going to her bed for her snacks. Lexie has never done a command in her life. When my parents watched them for us, my mother always said "that Lexie doesn't listen". And she really doesn't.

Lexie lives by her nose. She shuts down, emotionally, when I ask her for anything and we didn't care. Tetley cared though. She knew Lexie wasn't doing commands and stared at her, then back to me as if to say "is this for real?". Lexie was happy while Tetley was driven. Lexie got a snack every time Tetley worked for one, for the sake of "fairness". And in all fairness, Lexie never asked for snacks, and Tetley was in constant demand.

She has to be tended to 24/7. It's like living in constant negotiation. Working from home requires a level of peace and quiet to get work done. Life with Tetley has been chronically filled with negotiation of workout time to buy quiet time.

With Lex, there are no demands, no judgment, just love.

Lexie is the only person in my life that I don't have to do or perform or be something for. She exists to love. You can feel the love emanating from her. And me toward her. While I felt a lot of frustration and stress early on in our relationship, that was quickly replaced with love. She was too silly and lovable to stay frustrated with and her quirks just made her more love-able. I just had to remember she was still a baby. Because she was fully grown when I got her it was easy to forget she was still a baby.

I felt guilt early on for needing to split my attention between both of them. But I also felt the need to protect her, make her better, heal her and help her be a dog. Somewhere in those first months with her, we fell in love.

She helped me be a better person. She didn't ask for anything but she gave relentlessly of herself, for love, for attention, for cuddles. In spite of being let down by humans in her early life, she didn't write us off, instead, she loved us harder.

Lexie gave me permission and really demanded that I slow down. She taught me that rest doesn't have to be earned, the value of an afternoon nap with her pressed into me, and that morning cuddles and all-day snuggles are truly the best medi-cine for this chronic, over-exhausted life we are struggling to live.

Lexie and I have something different. I believe she came to me at the time I needed that kind of love most but it wasn't available anywhere else. Many of my relationships were like the one with Tetley. Still a lot of love but based on demands, doing and the tough love kind of love. I needed that too. But with Lexie, it was the first time I had the soft kind, the kind where being who you were, where you were, was just fine. It was that non-demanding love that helped me open up. Lexie demands being. You can lose hours in her fur, snout to mouth, scratching her chest and holding her paw while doing it, her slight snoring feels like a lullaby to your soul.

Lexie was a front-seat girl before she couldn't get up there anymore. I used to think it was partly because Tetley never stopped moving and often jumped on her but it was really to be as close to a person as possible. When there was a human passenger and she lost her seat, she started using the console. It started as her putting her chin on the console but quickly became her sitting on the seat with her bum, her back feet on the floor with her chest leaning on the console and her head leaning on my shoulder with one paw on my leg.

She is love. Justin often stayed in bed with her while Tetley hauled me out of the house in any and all weather. He got up brushing fur off his face and out of his scruff and said it was Lexie's fault he stayed in bed so late. She doesn't get in bed much anymore with her mobility and he isn't here much as he travels for work so now we get on the floor and her bed with her and the same thing happens. You can lose hours of your life in a cuddle fest with her.

She taught me that downtime is not optional but necessary in life. We live to do and in chronic doing we are burned out, exhausted, frustrated and unhappy with our lives. There's real value in just laying on the floor snuggling with a dog. I call it recharging. Somehow they can tell our batteries are low and are like a charging port for us. Dogs are a soft place to land in a world that's neither soft nor lets us land anywhere.

Most dog owners will say we don't need studies or science to tell us things we know from sharing our lives with dogs. We just know. We know when they are sick, when they aren't themselves when they are happy, excited or whatever else they have going on. We just know.

They just know, too. It's why they are called (wo)man's best friends. It comes without conditions. They forgive, love and grieve with us. They are constant in our lives and, whatever else we have in our lives, they have just us. They are part of our world, but we are their entire world and they are unapologetic about it. They own that role as if their lives depend on giving us as much love as they can, filling us up from the tips of our toes to the ends of our hair. They know no limits in what they give.

Humans aren't always the same and often the only love we can feel is the safe love of an animal that won't let us down. We have them with us for such a short time. How can we not return that wholly?

I know many people in my life have judged me for giving so much to my dogs. But they have given me more than I ever could give back to them. For some people, it's just a dog but for me, they're my family. They're not *like* family, they *are* my family. In many cases, they are better than a lot of people I know. I'm not sure how many times people have shown me that they were excited to see me, but the dogs sure did, every single day.

I don't recall anyone else in my life just accepting me as I am, trauma, warts, mistakes and imperfections. I always feel the need to perform the way people want me to perform in order to get love, even with Tetley. She demands it. But Lexie gives it, freely, easily and powerfully, she is pure unconditional love. A love that I never knew existed in this way. Lexie came to me at the time I needed this softness most. It's unexplainable in many ways, how she came to me, at the time she came to me, and how soft I had to be with her in order for her to heal. I had to find softness within myself to help her and I got it back in return, tenfold.

That softness came in the very essence of who she is, she made me more of me. I believe if we see people with their dogs without our performance face that we put on for the outside world we can see who people really are. I think that's why we find the loss of dogs so incredibly difficult, they might be the only ones who know the real us.

Lexie loves being sung to and touched. I do the itsy bitsy spider rhyme on her body, I crawl my fingers up her body starting on her hip and I sing the words and my fingers make their way to her head between her eyes, tapping a few times before I run my hands down her body as I say the "washed the spider out" and she does her hair toss. I call it her hair toss because she flips her head to look back at me, which is where she throws her head to look over at me with her big mouth smiling and wheezing the way she does when she's excited. Justin asks her if she has asthma when she breathes that way but it's just an overexcited noise she makes. Then I'd do it all over again. Justin says he is getting worried about me but he made up rap songs about them so he can't really talk.

Lexie. Always with me.

Dogs help us get out of our shells, they let us play, and have fun and love is the core ingredient. When we feel safe and loved we can open up. They make us more of who we really are. Dogs open up when loved too. What I gave to Lexie came back to me tenfold. Love, not control, is what makes us great.

Isn't it the least we can do for their unconditional love? To return it?

CHAPTER 5
PRESENCE

Photo by Lori Browne Photography. The girls. As they looked in the woods!

I saw a photo several years ago of a man and his dog sitting in a park with thought bubbles over their heads. The man was thinking of vacations, bills, work, women, etc. and the dog was thinking of just him. That's the difference between animals and humans, their presence. They are in the moment, always.

I know firsthand that they can plot and plan things so I don't believe they only operate that way and can't think about things. Tetley and Lexie vie for attention constantly. They love each other and over the years had some serious play fests but they didn't cuddle much, and jealousy was the name of the game when it came to getting their people's attention.

They sleep on beds next to each other and there have been the occasional times they ended up on the same bed. They also slept in bed with us most of their lives but not next to each other. Tetley was behind my legs while Lexie was between us or in front of one of us, spooning.

They slept on top of each other in the car, until someone inevitably got pissed off and sat up staring out the window, usually Lexie. When Tetley lay down in the car she was exhausted so there was no way she was getting up. Lexie, rotted, would get in the console or sulk, staring out the window.

While Lexie was mostly happy she could get a mood on her, sitting staring at the wall, or sulking, with her back turned when she wasn't getting attention.

While they didn't cuddle they did beat the devil most days in their romping fests. They stopped this as their senior years set in but they frequently romped to the point we worried it might turn serious. They were vocal, bowing and bouncing, locked in an embrace kicking each other in the guts with their back legs. One would pin the other down and chew and snort on each other, then they would change positions and the other would be the ring leader.

They could do this for hours some days. They were friends but they were also jealous of the attention the other one got.

They ran between us getting their butt scratched and wiggle bums in. Tetley always wiggled her butt when she was spoken to. She couldn't control her booty shake so we called it the wiggles. She even wiggled to the word. If you said "wiggle", her butt moved uncontrollably. We used to say she was going to put her back out from wiggling. She didn't exactly wag her tail with it, just her whole back end moved side to side. We even made up a song and she would come running, jam herself between our legs and get her bum scratched. She lifted her feet up and down and her whole body was into it, tail, back end, and paws as she raised her head into the air, ears flapping.

We sang "Do the wiggity wiggity wiggity wigs" and she would lose it. Lexie learned to do this too and still does it but Tetley's tail doesn't wag much anymore. It's one of the saddest things to see, how little her tail moves now when it was in constant movement.

Her tail wagged relentlessly. When she was swimming it acted like a rudder as she swished it through the water, and she wagged it in an almost circular motion as we walked. It still acts as a rudder as she swims daily but it doesn't wag much these days. Almost every day we walked to the river on Country Path, she ran ahead with her tail going round and round in a circle while she carried a ball, stick or the occasional teddy bear if she couldn't find anything else. She *had* to carry something.

She ran ahead to the river, doing 360 spins in a circle as she got closer to the water, dropped her ball and bounced into the water, no matter the time of year, or the force of the water. She smiled big smiles and wasn't at all patient in the pursuit of the ultimate game of fetch. She just loved being outside and heading for adventure.

We called her running in circles 360 spins. When I got out of bed or finished getting dressed and she knew we were leaving for an adventure she raced out the hallway and through the kitchen to the back door, spinning around constantly as she did it. I had several black eyes from her slamming into my face as she bounced under me while putting my boots on. Several times I was sure I had a broken nose as I slid to the floor, gripping my face and saying "you hurt mommy" and she would rush to me, nuzzling my face with her tail between her legs. As soon as I would say "it's ok, come on" off she went again, over it.

She was keeping an eye that we were still coming and amping herself up for the adventure that was ahead. Whether it was in the house, car or on the trails, she started spinning when she was excited. Tetley didn't run away from you, she spun away from you. When it was time to go on an adventure I couldn't get past "Do you..." and she was off her bed and running to the door. Our phrase became "Let's roll" and she jumped up and started spinning.

She has a special place where she sits outside, off the patio on the lawn. It's an elevated section where she can see into the kitchen, the back patio doors, the driveway and even the road in the front yard. Justin calls it her security station. She won't miss anything from there.

She doesn't spin anymore but she still jumps up with the "Do you..." and "Let's roll" or as her hearing declines, the hand wave. She's always ready to go.

And she planned things. I would tell her it was bedtime and that tomorrow we would go on an adventure. Or she would get super excited and start running around, frantically, and I would say "tomorrow", and she would run to her kennel and go to bed so it could be tomorrow already. I know scientific research says that dogs that are treated like family learn as much as 5-year-olds in their lifetime and think about how much a 5-year-old knows!

When Lexie was getting attention or in bed with us and Tetley wanted to get rid of her or wanted the attention for herself she would go to the door and start barking. We knew what she was doing but poor Lexie fell for it every single time. She would bark and Lexie would do her little poof poof poof bark, eventually giving up her spot or space and go chase after what Tetley was telling her. There was never anything there and as soon as Lexie gave up her spot Tetley would either take it or go rest in her kennel, her job done.

Lexie is no better, especially as Tetley has aged and gotten sicker this year. When I lay on the floor with Tetley, Lexie always pushes her way in, backs in and gets spooned. She will often start pawing Tetley's face and head, pissing her off until she leaves. Lexie exhales a sigh of relief and pushes deeper into your body. She is unapologetic about it.

I know they can plan and think ahead and of course, I know dogs, like all animals, have more basal instincts and less to worry about than people do. I mean, we make their lives pretty easy so they don't even have to worry about their food but presence is something they can teach us about, in spite of their plotting.

I drive past dog parks and see dogs running around the park or sitting, staring at their owners, who are on their phones. I know I'm making assumptions because they could be taking an important call or something, but we know how easily our responsibility to them can turn into an obligation and it's easy to check out of the day-to-day living with them. But they never check out.

If they are chasing a squirrel, they are chasing it full out. If they are getting petted, they are fully in whole-body rub-down mode. If they are chasing a stick or ball or diving into the ocean, they are fully present, but can we say the same? I'm constantly doing ten things at once. I am working and cooking dinner, feeding the dogs and making my dinner, I'm working out and checking my email, I am writing a blog and watching tv, I am watching tv and texting a friend, I am laying on the dog bed and petting them while scrolling through mindless social media. I check myself often, laying my phone down, to be fully present in their moment, feel their fur under my hands, count their toes, sing their favourite songs, play games and be with them, tell them stories of our lives together and I often tell them the stories of how we got them. It's less about the words and more about the feelings and quality time.

My parents always told us the stories of when we were born,

how much we weighed, where we were born and all the details that are part of our origin stories. I think myth and story have always been how we know where we are from and who we are a part of. I like to think they understand, maybe not the words, but how much they matter to me, how much they are a part of me becoming who I am. I believe that the moments of talking to them, sharing with them, and laying on the floor with them make a difference to them. We are a part of each other, woven into the fabric of each other. I am as much a part of them as they are of me.

I wasn't present most of my life. I had my head in a book or headphones in my ears. I didn't really choose my experience but sort of blocked out most of the experiences.

I can't say exactly what changed for me or when but I know it had to do with hiking, woods and Tetley. I hated the corporate accounting jobs I was working but I hadn't exactly found my place. I did enjoy the work at times and I worked for great companies with great pay and benefits.

By the time we made Holyrood our permanent home, Tetley was 9 months old and completely insane. The days of walking her on the road leashed or on a trail in St. John's were over. Justin had returned to work by then and I was working full-time, teaching fitness classes in the evenings, taking care of a new home and planning a wedding.

By the time Tetley was 1.5, Justin was in school and only came home on weekends. She was difficult to walk because of her energy level, even at a full-paced run I could not keep up with her. She pulled and towed me relentlessly. It was frustrating and exhausting. We enrolled in private lessons with Glenn, the dog trainer who taught me that I was the problem, and how to properly correct Tetley and use nonverbal communication.

I was scared of yanking on her leash and hurting her so Glenn put the collar around my arm so I could feel the yank that a dog would feel. It didn't hurt so I felt better about doing it to

Tetley. After a few lessons, we learned how to communicate better, how to correct her and why I needed to be firm with her.

I tried. At least, I think I tried. Or I lie to myself that I tried. She was just so filled with energy and intensity that I could hardly hold onto her in order to do the leash correction. I felt frustrated during and after every walk, so I changed gears. I headed to the old railroad tracks to run her off leash and she brought a stick or ball and we walked and fetched the entire time. She always walked home with a slack leash.

At the time I didn't see the problem with this, creating a fixation on fetch but also on letting her walk and fetch instead of learning to just walk.

Fetching and walking let me burn the crazy out of her. She had so much energy that a walk alone was not enough. I now realise I should have separated the two things but here we are, 15 years later with both of us a little crazier.

The railroad tracks were often littered with broken bottles and sharp rocks, leading to several pad cuts, plus the really windy days were horrible with dust and debris blowing into our eyes and mouths. Justin had found an old woods path behind our house and he took us on it a few times. He constantly encouraged me to use it with her. He cleared out the branches so it was easy to navigate. He covered over mud holes and tagged the trees for us to easily find our way.

But I was scared of the woods alone. I didn't know my way and I wasn't sure of what else was in there. We had a lot of moose around when we first moved to Holyrood. The area is far more populated than it was back then and while we still see them, it's less than it was. We often encountered them on our morning road walks so I was apprehensive about the woods. That was their domain.

Justin said the moose would avoid me with Tetley and take off into the trees if they heard us. But Tetley abandoned me once already when we encountered a massive moose on one of our morning walks. There was an old woods road next door to us before it was turned into a road, and one morning a moose was heading up the path. Tetley barked at it and it turned and came toward us. It was massive and started swaying its antlers back and forth. I knew that wasn't a good sign.

Tetley bolted, leaving me standing facing the moose. I quickly followed suit and bolted home, finding her on the back patio waiting to go inside. She was young then and it was the only time in her life that she ran from a moose. But at this point, I wasn't sure about the woods, Tetley, moose and me.

The old railroad tracks felt like an extension of the road, safer, somehow. But one day I decided to give the woods a try. I promptly got lost. In about 5 minutes I was tangled up. The path veered off but it was overgrown. If you didn't know it well it was easy to lose. I called Justin at work, and he guided me through the initial part of the trail. I almost turned around and went home but we continued on and something changed that day. I was proud of myself for going into the woods alone, with Tetley, and nothing bad happened. It opened up experiences to us in a new way. Tetley seemed more confident, even protective, in a way.

We saw squirrels and birds, some bunnies, she hauled trees out of the ground, ripped branches off trees, and we walked about 4 kilometres until we came to a marsh before turning back. It had a bit of everything, including a freshwater stream that let Tetley get in and get her belly wet, even enough to do a couple of fetches and get a drink of fresh stream water.

We crossed over bog holes and makeshift bridges, made out of logs, much of which was rotting away. We followed offshoot trails that led to people's backyards, even ending up in what felt like scenes out of movies with their magical fairy forest look.

Not only did nothing scary happen but we both returned feeling more content than on any other walk we had done. Tetley didn't relentlessly drop a stick at my feet but she raced ahead of me, back and forth, revelling in the forest.

Somehow I felt more content, peaceful and alive after that

walk in the woods. We kept going back. Most days during the late fall, winter and early spring we spent our mornings heading to the woods and the afternoons walking to the river or heading out on adventures. In summer it became too overgrown with spider webs, mosquitos and thick brush so we stuck to more open trails during those months. On weekends we would meet up with friends and do some of our favourite St. John's trails.

I continued to teach fitness classes and find solace in the woods with Tetley. The more time I spent hiking the less time I could tolerate being in an office doing work that I didn't love. I loved fitness and helping people and I loved being outdoors with Tetley. I often packed my fitness gear and hit a trail or park somewhere I could work out using what was available, park benches, swing sets, trees, stumps, and rocks. I became more and more creative with it the more I did it.

I started inviting my clients to do outdoor workouts. At first, I was a bit scared, I didn't know if other people would like it. But they quickly said yes. Many people, like me, were tired of the gym and needed a fresh new experience. We hiked to the top of George Cove Mountain and Murray's Peak in Holyrood and did workouts on the top. We hit up parks and playgrounds for workouts, using the swings, monkey bars, and benches to get amazing workouts that felt fun instead of another chore we had to do. There was a difference between people who trained that way versus the more routine workouts in the gym.

I became despondent heading to work every day. I knew I was supposed to be happy with my career. I had growth opportunities, great pay, benefits, and a pension. Isn't that the dream we're supposed to have? How could I throw that away?

But the feeling wouldn't go away, it kept growing bigger inside of me. What if I could make a difference and create a different life for myself? What if I could make my fitness business work, have more time for things I loved, and spend more time outside?

Me & Tetley looking at an ice burg. Lexie had stopped hiking with us by this time.

The more I thought about it the more I wanted it. The more I wanted it the more I hated my morning and evening commute. I started feeling exhausted, frustrated and struggling with the desire to suppress what I wanted, to keep doing what I was supposed to do. But it wouldn't go away.

I had a conversation with my doctor and we discussed if I might be suffering from depression. She suggested I take a few days to think about it. She could prescribe medication to help me so I could stay in my job. Justin and I chatted about it and he asked me straight out: "Are you depressed with anything other than your job?" To which I replied, "No. I am happy in my life, with my fitness work, Tetley, our new home". I didn't even hate the company I was working for, I just wanted something different.

We decided that I should give it a try. Worst-case scenario I could get a job if I changed my mind or it didn't work out. What's the harm in trying? I had to know if I could do it. I knew I would regret not taking the chance on myself.

3 days later I gave notice at my job. I finished out the year with a fresh start in January 2010 as an entrepreneur. I had no idea what I was doing but I was happy to give it a try. I had been working part-time in this business as a side hustle for 3 years so I had clients, a reputation, and a brand. I wasn't starting from scratch.

That became life. I took Tetley with me to work, on the trails, to the studios where she could go, the fields, and parks and we started hiking the East Coast Trail. She spent her days with people exercising and we spent our free time in nature.

It wasn't always easy but it felt worth it. Nature gave me the courage to decide what I wanted. I believe it was in the presence that nature offers us, solace for our overburdened and overworked souls, that allowed me to find a way that felt good to me.

I don't think if we had stayed on those roads with leashes and corrections or if we had used martingale collars or choke chains to teach Tetley to be manageable that I would have found the courage to live the life I wanted to live.

I don't think I would have found the courage to do what I wanted instead of what I was told. My parents always told me that I could do whatever I wanted. My mother pushed education. Women with education and their own money have more choices. Education was valued and I made sure to get it. It's a bonus that I loved learning. My father left a secure job on the Argentia Naval Base and became a fisherman the year I was born.

My family didn't tell me to follow the line or do what I should! Dad always said that we should find something we loved or life would be hard. He talked often about how fishing gave him opportunities to have time off, go camping, go ice fishing, walk in the woods, and hunt. It wasn't squeezed into weekends here and there but it was a way of life.

Not always an option in our urbanised world. We are often at odds with what we want and what we have to do. The world, not my parents, told me who to be. At university, I was taking an English degree but was told by the career counsellor that writing wasn't a viable career choice. He told me that I could be a researcher or continue on to get an Education degree. I didn't want to do either of those so he recommended I change my degree. So I did. I took Criminology and Sociology as more suitable career choices for me.

I listened to their limitations. I listened to the world tell me that the ideal job was something with a 25 or 30-year career with a pension to retire. No one out there told me to choose. They told me to conform. The world taught me pension over passion. But the woods and Tetley taught me that passion is everything.

Hemingway said, "to write about life you must have first lived it". I now understand that this was all part of something to write about. But back then I didn't know that. Back then I was just ticking boxes of what would help me be successful so I could do more than survive, find success and be happy.

After university, I moved to Iqaluit and got a job in a prison, where I lasted 3 days. Then I found myself working in a women's shelter, which I truly adored. I loved my work in that field, helping vulnerable women and children, and tackling the homeless crisis for Indigenous women leaving abusive homes. I also worked another full-time job at an electrical company. I found myself immersed in busyness and money, as I strove to pay off my student loans. Which I did, in record time of 18 months. Being a workaholic proved successful.

Conformity and workaholism ultimately led me to kick and scream for life. I know that Tetley was the biggest catalyst for that. Her personality, her wildness, and her untamed soul was not easily managed and in that unmanageable space, I didn't try to contain her but found ways to let her burn off that energy. The woods did it. She slept so well after our adventures in the woods.

While the woods placated her, it awakened me. With each step I took in the woods I felt myself become less of who I was supposed to be and more of who I could be, who I was born to be, and who I was meant to be. Tetley unchained me from life's conditioning, her wildness helped me find mine. The presence that came to me was life-altering.

I didn't go seeking it, I didn't find it on a meditation mat, and I didn't find it in doing exercises to breathe. While I tried those experiences later, I always found I had to work really hard at them to get clarity, focus and peace and be able to stop over-thinking. My mind doesn't stop. But on those walks in the woods, I didn't actively try to be present, I just was. I didn't have to remind myself to pay attention or be there. I just was.

I found with every step I took the chaos, noise, and over-thinking melted away. I didn't think about my problems or challenges but somehow the solutions were available when I returned from the woods.

There was something about the trees, roots, air, rotten stumps, squirrels, birds and eventually moose that felt more like life than anything I'd ever experienced. One morning as we walked in the woods, my friend Vanessa joined us with her dogs, Harley and Archie, we were sure we heard cracking in the trees. This wasn't unusual at this point in my hiking journey so we continued on, unfazed, the dogs running ahead. As I rounded a turn in the path a giant moose stepped in front of me, separating me and the dogs, with Vanessa behind me.

I could taste the musky odour from it and its gut stood taller than my head. I'm not tall but that's still over 5 feet! The dogs started barking and the moose bolted into the trees. Justin was right! Tetley was fierce at that point and loved giving chase to moose. She came back when I called her. Adrenaline was pumping through everyone after such a close encounter but we continued on our way with the dogs leading the way and us laughing about the moose. There was magic in the forest. We were no longer afraid.

There was beauty in the way the sun shone through the trees, glistening on the webs, shining on the morning dew or snow crystals in winter.

There was something about the sounds of the forest that kept me acutely aware of the life all around me that I take for granted as if it's not a part of me. In the woods, I started breathing deeply and in that breathing, I grounded and in that grounding, I no longer felt lost.

When I didn't feel lost I could finally find my way. And it

wasn't in the ways I thought would bring me happiness. It wasn't in the way we are told to chase happiness, through other people, money, and social climbing.

I felt no need to be anywhere other than where I was. When I could combine my work with fitness, and eventually retreats and women's empowerment work, and the dogs, I was in bliss. We don't have to follow the way people tell us to go. In fact, it's usually off the beaten path that we find our greatest happiness.

It was in the woods I learned what presence was. I didn't feel it as much on my yoga mat. It wasn't as prevalent in the reading, meditating, studying and searching for meaning when I started that journey. I couldn't always find it where I was seeking it but I could always find it with a walk in the woods, where life lives.

When Lexie joined us, she joined us in the woods too and that became our place. They chewed sticks, hauled branches off trees, sought out puddles and mud, they chased each other and the squirrels, searching for the elusive moose they could always smell but not always see. And sometimes we lay on the ground in the forest, in a sun spot, where they would chill out, chewing sticks and me enjoying the peace.

Photo by Sandra Woito Photography. In their prime.

Presence isn't always about sitting and staring at each other in the way we're taught it is. It's about being in the moment that we are in. The girls loved the sunbeams coming into the house from the windows. After our morning runs in the woods or on the trails, they gobbled breakfast and either got in my bed where

I covered them up in blankets, tucking them in or I might find them sprawled in a sunbeam on the floor or on one of the couches.

Lexie loves baking by the wood stove. Lexie loves to be comfortable. In the winter she often heads to the wood stove, lays in front of it and bakes until she can't take anymore, then she heads outside and lays in the snowbanks to cool off. She does that on repeat some days.

She always did hot yoga with the groups I led. Tetley usually came for a quick visit and sometimes stayed but Lexie would plant herself in front of the stove and stay there until she had to be physically removed. Justin often had to drag her upstairs because she was wheezing from the heat. If we were there she was there, not enough sense to leave. She does the same thing in the sun. I have to sit under the umbrella or she will stay in the sun, baking, panting and wheezing.

She loves the heated seats in the vehicle and presses her back against the seats. Or she did while she was still able to get in the front passenger seat. After her knee surgery, she stopped scaling the console to the front. She would put her chin on the dash and I was always afraid she would break her neck if we got into an accident. I would open the glove compartment and she lay her head on it, a little more comfortable of an angle for her, but no safer.

Presence gave me choice and choice gave me more presence. The more choices I made that aligned with the life I wanted to build instead of the one I thought I needed to build, the better my life became. Creating a life that gave me freedom, community and dogs while being able to help people with their health was my dream life, which I didn't even know was my dream life until I was in it. I just kept following what felt good.

In spite of the girls getting older, my dedication to our adventures remains constant. While Lexie stayed home more and Tetley and I continued to walk in the mornings, I made our afternoon adventures a place where Lexie could go too. As Tetley's mobility declined we switched our adventures to the ocean, ponds and wherever we could get into a body of water with close vehicle access.

While the experience is different it is still our adventure time and most importantly, our time together. I am taking the time away from obligation, duty, and work to be in nature with them. Lexie isn't the type of dog who would have forced that. Lexie has always been content to stay or go, even when she was young. She wasn't the dog who would force you to change your entire way of life and pull your soul back to you, like Tetley.

Lexie is chill, and it's not a bad thing. We could not handle 2 dogs like Tetley. Who could? Lexie's ability to go with the flow to the storms Tetley created, and to be the best supporting actress to Tetley's leading lady is what made it work. Lexie, too, got the benefits of the adventure she would have never experienced if she didn't end up with Tetley as her sister.

With a dog like Lexie on her own, we would have had an easy life, an enjoyable life, a special life but not a wild or adventurous life. Lexie got the family she needed and it helped her be a better, calmer, freer dog because of the adventure she lived. Tetley is a whole lot. A lot. I could write a lot 400 more times and it would not account for the amount of a lot's that she is.

But it's that which brought us all peace, interestingly enough. Tetley's inability to conform to the domesticated, good girl dog, brought us all adventure and in those adventures we all found freedom.

Lexie learned to trust people and find her place in the world, she got to experience life in a way that she would never have had she not come to us. She became the amazing, soul-filled, loving dog that she did because of the life we lived. I wholeheartedly believe in the wrong hands Lexie would have turned nasty. Those early days required dedication and patience.

While she doesn't do much anymore, she still comes to the gym with me, does outdoor workouts in the garage, and flops around for belly rubs. She doesn't look or act old but she is a little old lady. Her demeanour is a result of her wilding. Her wilding is a result of the insanity of Tetley that only the woods could calm.

In the freedom we found, Lexie got to be herself and I got to find myself, choosing an unconventional but deeply fulfilling life. Even on the hardest of days, the challenge of balancing it all, not enough money or clients some days, I never once regretted my decision to forge my own path. Sometimes I thought of going back to work for someone else where it could be easier but I no longer saw that path as easy.

I knew it would pay my bills but what would it really cost me that couldn't be measured in dollars or cents? I didn't want to give up the trails and the days with the girls or the life I had found a way to build. Instead, I found ways to keep going. I found more contracts and more clients. I realised that when the motivation is high enough we'll find a way. I found my way and I never wanted to give it up.

That was presence to me. To the life we had chosen, not always easy, but always worth it. Seeing the sunrise while hiking, walking or running every morning, being outside for sunsets most days, doing bear crawls out the driveway with one dog throwing a ball on the back of my head and the other crawling with me trying to sneak armpit licks, was the life I wanted to live.

I found that presence wasn't a meditative experience but it was about being in the moments and the experiences we were having. When I started writing again, I found even more presence. Lexie would lay next to me while I wrote, on the couch or bed pressed next to me. These days she is on the floor by the bed or the couch, table or patio furniture when it's nice enough to start my days outside.

While I do miss our morning hikes on the trails I have to admit I don't mind this phase of slow mornings with coffee, nowhere to go, and walking them to the end.

I don't stop writing these days and they have been a catalyst behind my words. They have guided me back to me, to the life I really want to live, giving me something to write about. Hemingway was right.

Presence is less about being inside of ourselves as we're often taught it is. Present to our breath, to our thoughts, to ourselves? I find presence is more about where we are. The people, the places, the sunbeams, the woods, the words, the books, the baths, the food we're eating and less about meditation.

Can we fully experience life without needing to be elsewhere? Can we be here, with them, your people, pets, parents, work and whatever else brings you joy? I have that presence through the girls and it was never what I thought it was. It was never about silencing the thinking but more about the experience of living.

CHAPTER 6
FEARLESS

Tetley at the fireworks show.

I am not fearless. I work on feeling the fear and doing it anyway. I work on the courage, to love, feel, heal and be here in this world. As a trauma survivor, fading away was normal and facing the fear of loving and living to the fullest was hard. Learning to embrace fear as my friend was hard. People think I'm fearless because of how I live in choosing my business, running women's retreats, doing international hikes, facing my trauma, writing books and claiming my life. The truth is I did it all afraid. I did it all because the passion and drive to create my life were stronger than the fear of what could go wrong.

But Tetley, she's fearless, naturally. She was born wild and free. She has no fear of things that even normal dogs fear. The only thing she has ever been afraid of is open back stairs. She was just a baby and we had her for 2 days when she chased Justin out of the house as he was leaving for work. She bounced down 2 stairs and backed up only to fall out behind the stairs, landing under the steps.

They were high so she had a good startle when she hit the ground. She wasn't hurt but she developed a fear of open back stairs and heights. She would bark and bark to get off the bed. She jumped on with no problem but she freaked out trying to get off it. When she was tiny it was cute but as she grew and it was still a problem we worked with our trainer on it. Glenn taught us that talking to her in a puppy voice while trying to get her to jump off the bed was counterproductive. He asked me to speak how I rewarded her in the tone of voice and of course, I did the baby voice. Then he asked me to do the voice I use to get her off the stairs and the bed and I did the same voice.

It made perfect sense that I was reinforcing her fear, as dogs do not speak our language, as much as we want them to. While they do understand words, they mostly understand vibration and energy. Glenn taught us nonverbal communication. Leash her and take her with us, with no hesitation, and no fear. "She will respond", he told us. She did. The bed became a joy of jumping on and off and running around on and running away from medication, over and under, so it worked. Do not reinforce them in their fear, do not feed the fears and just keep going through it. Sound advice for so much more than dog training.

She maintained a healthy fear of open back stairs but only high ones. She could manage a few but she always needed a little support to navigate the steep ones, which was a good thing on some of the trails we took. Had she approached those stairs the way she approached everything else in life it would have been dangerous!

She wasn't afraid of much whereas Lexie was afraid of everything. She was terrified of the vacuum where Tetley faced the vacuum like she was in the Roman Coliseum facing down the enemy. Justin does our vacuuming and she chased him around the house until he took off the hose and vacuumed her with it. She attacked it with her mouth, fighting with it and making loud growling noises. She attacked everything with gusto. Justin kept his hand over the hose so it wouldn't suck her fur or skin into it or hurt her mouth or face but she constantly chased the vacuum. She even chased our cleaners to do it for her!

Normal dogs are afraid of vacuums. Lexie would run and hide. She struggled with loud noises and sudden movements, while she got over the hair dryer and other household things she has remained fearful of a lot of things, especially loud noises like thunder and lightning, wind storms and fireworks or a chair scraping across the floor or doors banging.

For Tetley, the louder life is the better. She loved guns being fired, fireworks and storms. She sat on the patio when the neighbours had fireworks and stared at the lights. We took her to the fireworks shows. After we adopted Lexie, fireworks and storms became very stressful events. We assumed Lexie was like Tetley so the first time we took her to the fireworks and she tried to crawl under the boardwalk in Holyrood we were in shock. We realised we had 2 very different dogs.

Several years later we went to Brigus for a walk, not knowing the fireworks were happening for their Blueberry Festival that night. We just went for a stroll around the town as we did occasionally. We stopped at the fireworks viewing location and I kept saying this isn't a good thing, we were far from our vehicle now and Lexie wasn't going to be ok. Justin thought she might be ok and wanted us to give it a try, but she wasn't. We had taken her to a friend's house for the most recent New Year's' celebrations and while she wasn't great she wasn't panicked either. He felt it was worth a try. Maybe she would be ok now.

That night she panicked and ran until she collapsed in a ditch about 7 kilometres from where we started. She dragged Justin the entire way. We ended up going the longest way back to our vehicle because she was panicking and running. Justin kept her tightly on leash as she dragged him. Tetley and I jogged behind, struggling to keep up.

Kind people staying in a yellow cottage on the main road came out and offered her water and stayed with us. She was in full panic mode and was trying to crawl into a culvert in the ditch. Justin ran for the car and came back to get us, while I sat in the ditch with Lexie, Tetley and some strangers. Justin is diabetic and his blood sugars started going low, Lexie was in a panic and exhausted, so we headed home. After that, her fear escalated to an out-of-control level, and we now have to medicate her with Xanax when storms or fireworks come through.

She has pulled a large flat-screen TV down on top of herself, trapped herself behind the wall unit, jammed herself in the under-the-stairs closet and had hours-long panic attacks. We give her medication now when we know in advance, like Canada Day or New Year's Eve, or as soon as something happens. She deserves that. She has developed a fear of storms and high winds now so we have started to give her medication for those as well. We seem to have never-ending storm systems rolling through these days.

We hightail it out of an area when something happens, prepare as much as we can advance for things, and keep medication on hand for unexpected situations.

Tetley, on the other hand, lives for storms, bad weather, hurricanes and blizzards. The more violent the storm the more she thrives. She always loved the snow over her head and woke up in the winter mornings to ram her face into the snowbanks. She never let me break the snow after a snowfall when we hiked.

Tetley had to be in the lead and break the snow. I would fight with her to go first so I could break the path with my snowshoes but it was to no avail as she just flew around me through woods and chest-deep snow. She took pride in that. Being in the lead and a strong girl. Lexie stayed behind me and let us break the snow for her. We always say Lex has common sense.

She would lay down on one shoulder and with her two back legs push herself on her side through the snow, rolling over eventually on her back with her four paws in the air. Tetley picked this up from her and far too many of our winter hikes were me walking with the two of them on their sides pushing their way through it. I laughed so hard at them as I told them they were hiking wrong. In hindsight, maybe I should have been doing what they were.

Hurricanes, for Tetley, just meant it felt like driving with her head out the window, all the time. Justin sometimes takes her to fireworks or goes outside to sit on the patio with her while the neighbours do their light show. I stay in the bathroom, closet or bedroom with Lexie, with music and fans on to ride it out.

Tetley's true fearlessness and strength came through when she was hit by a car. I will never forget the moment of impact or the slow motion-like events of that morning - the sound of the impact and the vision of her being tossed in the air or her yelp. It was a slow-motion nightmare. Tetley was traffic smart, traffic trained, always careful of traffic and always looked both ways before she crossed the street. People who witnessed her street smarts couldn't believe it. There were times we would cross the road; she would wait on the other side and watch me for her signal to cross. She was always a brilliant dog.

It was a random series of events that led to her being hit. I slept in, having just returned from a retreat in Florida and we were out for our morning walk later than normal. I hadn't even brushed my teeth and wasn't wearing a bra. I just got up and left as we normally did but 6:00 a.m. dishevelled is different from

8:00 a.m. dishevelled. We often walked down the street to the river, but sometimes, for a change, we walked towards Salmonier Line. She would stop in the small stream with the culvert that went under the road and splash around a bit chasing a ball up and down and all around, crossing under the street in the culvert and coming back around.

That morning I turned back early, feeling a bit tired and rushed, but Tetley did her normal don't want to go home vibe and she was so happy I let her have her way, again. I was just back from a 2-week retreat so why not spend a little extra time that morning? I had Lexie on a leash because that was life with Lexie, she could not be off-leash. Tetley would stick close without a leash, but Lexie would still be in the driveway sniffing bushes if she wasn't on a leash or end up wherever her nose took her. I kept going and was laughing at her antics.

Less than 5 minutes later the accident happened. We had just arrived at the mini river and Tetley ran under the road through the culvert, Lexie was sniffing a bush and I heard a vehicle accelerate very quickly, I turned my head to look but didn't see anything, thinking it went the other way. Before I was able to turn fully back around Tetley had been hit. I heard the impact and her yelp. It was very quick with virtually no reaction time.

I never let them be on the opposite side of the road from me or I would step into the street or put my hand up or something. I've gone over it a million times in my mind about how I could have prevented it. I'm not sure I could have. If she had been leashed or I had gone back or not slept in or gone a different way that morning, maybe. We live in a rural area on a quiet road. We're not talking about a city street, we're talking about a road that doesn't even have a yellow line in the middle of it. The reality is Tetley wasn't even on the road, she was on the side of the road, but the driver left the road. I believe she saw me and Lexie and overcorrected, went too far to the other side and slammed into Tetley.

I have no idea really and she later said Tetley ran in front of her but that's just not true, even her tire marks were on the gravel and Tetley was on the grass on the side of the road, close to 2 feet off the pavement. As the car passed, I saw Tetley jump to her feet, with her yellow tennis ball in her mouth, it was clear that her back leg was hurt. There was no blood or anything gruesome, it was clean, she was clean, but there was a kind of out-of-socket look to her back leg. She stood there making eye contact with me, the full intensity of her yellow eyes coming into that stare.

Tetley has yellow eyes, which is rare in the Chocolate Labrador. They said she would grow into brown eyes but she kept her yellow eyes. She has the wild intensity of something that seems almost feral when she trains those eyes on you in the way she does as if she can see through you. Lexie also has yellow eyes.

I'll be forever grateful that the driver stopped that day, just on the cusp of the hill. She exited her vehicle screaming "Is she dead". I had to calm her down and tell her to get in her vehicle and back up to where we were standing.

"Get in your car and back up to me, I need you to drive me to my house". She did. I picked Tetley up, who was twenty pounds heavier than she is now, and I was twenty-five pounds lighter than I am now but strength is amazing when we need it. I put Lexie in the hatch of the SUV and Tetley in the backseat and I got in with her. She kept her ball in her mouth and stood up the entire drive back to our place.

She brought me to my house, exactly 1 kilometre away. I transferred the dogs to my SUV, jumped in and put my hazard lights on and drove as I've never driven before. I called my vet clinic and told them Tetley was hit by a car and we were en route. A client, Amanda, worked at our vet clinic and later told me she told them to be ready faster than they thought possible. I pulled in exactly 22 minutes later in what would normally be a 35 minute drive.

They mobilised their team rapidly. They had a backboard and several staff removed her from the vehicle, where she was still standing with her ball in her mouth. In hindsight, she may have been in shock, or it may have been just Tetley being herself. She stood up, leaning against the back seat, the entire drive, with Lexie safely in the passenger seat. I was as careful as I could be driving as fast as I was.

I called my friend Carolyn because I needed to be strong. I couldn't freak out and I needed someone to talk to me while I drove there. I knew we most likely needed the specialty centre but my vet was closer to the highway so I stopped there, knowing we would start the process.

While I was waiting for her results at Paradise Animal Hospital, I took Lexie into the exam room with me. I was in shock and reality was hitting me, the adrenaline was leaving my body and I started shaking. I wasn't wearing a bra and was thankful I was wearing a puffy winter jacket. My entire body was covered in goosebumps and my legs and hands started to tremble. The staff came to see if I needed anything, I asked for coffee and gum, and they brought them to me.

It's funny how during such a tragedy we remember small gestures of kindness and feel like someone cares about us for something so simple. What can anyone do at that moment? I remember the feel of that room that day as if it happened just a moment ago. The surrealness of it and as if I were in a pillow of clouds, with the purple walls, Lexie trying to make me feel better with kisses on my face and laying next to me licking the palm of my hand, and the feel of her fur under my fingers, the awareness of my unbrushed teeth, unwashed face and bralessness under my jacket.

They took her in immediately, sedated her and ran x-rays, which showed that her greater trochanter was broken. They said they often break that bone for ortho surgeries but where hers was broken was in the worst possible place because it's so small. They couldn't fix it and needed to either amputate her leg or send her to the VSC (Speciality Center), which could repair it as they have a full team of specialists. We were transferred to the VSC as we wanted to save her leg.

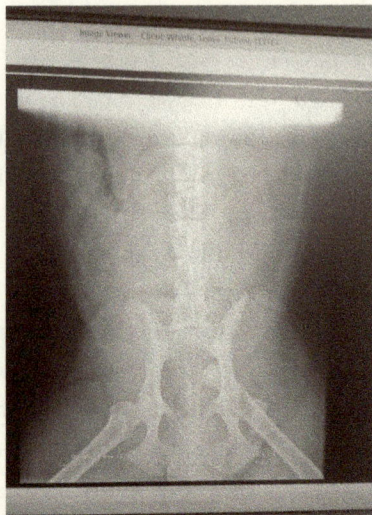

Tetley's hip fracture.

When it was time to take Tetley to the VSC I used my vehicle to transport her but two staff were sent with me. I drove and they transferred her to the vehicle on a board with tubes and the bagging device she was connected to. Her tongue was hanging out of her mouth as she was half removed from sedation for the transport but was still semi-sedated. She couldn't move but the staff from Paradise Animal Hospital were incredible and in the backseat with her for the short drive to the VSC.

Once at the VSC she was she was fully sedated again and assessed, had x-rays again and we confirmed that we would do the surgery. I put the deposit down for her surgery and got into my car and went to pay Paradise Animal Hospital and pick Lexie up, as they kept her in the back while we got Tetley taken care of.

It's such a surreal experience to just walk around as if things are normal while everything has just changed in an instant. It's like being in an alternate state. The world is churning but yours has been interrupted.

Somewhere in the mix of things I managed to talk to Justin. I had sent a text that said, "call me". I couldn't reach him because he wasn't allowed to have his phone on at work so when he called, I relayed the information to him about Tetley, the technical information from the vet, that we just had to wait for her surgery. He told me that he knew it was about Tetley when he saw my text message. I assured him it was ok; she would be ok and that there was nothing we could do for now.

When he got off work later that day we drove to the vet clinic so he could see her. She hadn't had her surgery yet and if I remember correctly, it would be the next day before she did. He sat in her kennel with her, crying, as she was completely sedated and it was hard to see her that way.

The next day at the scheduled time of her surgery, I sat outside the clinic praying the entire time that she would have a successful surgery. She did. My longtime mentor and spiritual Shaman, Regina Wright, was at St. Francis of Assisi at the time this happened and she would go to the daily prayers and pray for Tetley. She inserted prayers into the wall and did journeys and spiritual healings on her behalf. She had a lot of support while she was in the hospital.

She spent 5 days in the hospital. She had some swelling from her lymph glands and we opted to keep her there to be taken care of instead of me being extra stressed at home. The cost was high for the extra time but we felt it was better for her to be there until we knew she was fully safe to come home. I would visit with her every day.

They let me in the back to see her because she wasn't able to be taken out of her kennel until day 4. I played meditation music in the back and all the dogs would calm down and settle.

They told me after her surgery they usually pee in their kennel so they put pee pads in there for them, but Tetley refused and had to be taken out to do her business. She always had an insane drive but also a lot of pride. If she could force her way through it, she would. I knew my little fighter was in there doing her thing so she could come home.

She was released with a 12-week recovery and I slept on a dog bed next to her on the floor. I set my office up in the kitchen so I could be with her. We kept her in the kitchen as they have beds there, with our open-concept living and kitchen. Honestly, they have beds everywhere, even in the garage. The ones in the kitchen kept us close to the door for outside access, food and water.

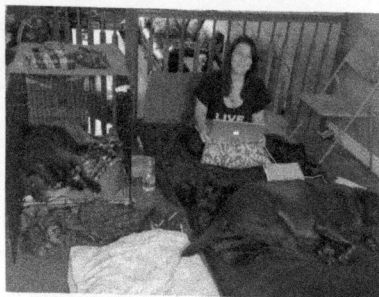

My life for the first 6 weeks after Tetley's accident.

Those first few days and weeks were tough. She was fierce and had no intentions of slowing down. She was walking assisted with her post-op help me up harness, hobbling around the yard and trying to go for a run. We took her out to pee, do her business then give her a minute or so each time to add it to her use of the leg.

Justin carried her around in her harness and helped her around when he was home. She never wanted to come in and sometimes he would lay outside on a blanket with her. Her determination was palatable during that time. She showed no signs of weakness and was fierce in pushing herself forward every day. She tried to walk further each time and it was only us preventing it, with confinement and medications.

Lexie loved this time. She loved easy days and an easy life. She took advantage of Tetley's inability to do much. She got extra love and belly rubs, slept on the makeshift bed with me, stole Tetley's snacks and provided comic relief and emotional support when necessary.

The vet said Tetley needed to use it or she would lose it. She must have thought they meant to go full tilt because we had a hard time controlling her. She had to be mostly sedated to be managed as they were nervous that the hardware installed in her would fail before it could heal if she wouldn't settle. During her recovery, she took 240 medications and the day she decided she was done with medication she stared into my eyes with those yellow eyes of hers, filled with intensity and determination that said "enough".

She bit down on my hand, slower and slower while staring at me. I kept trying to pry her jaw open, and I had gotten pretty good at that, but she clamped down harder until I gave up. She won. As always.

Tetley and her antics around medication could fill an entire book. All medications that can be liquid are liquid. We have to get them from the people's pharmacy sometimes because they don't carry them at the vet's. She won't eat Tim Bits anymore unless we take a bite because we used to put pills in there. She won't eat melted cheese because we used that trick. Pill pockets, ice cream, yogurt, chocolate, peanut butter, you name it, we did it.

Sometimes we can get her pills in with freshly cooked sausages but mostly it's a battle of wills and she mostly wins. Sometimes I can get it at the back of her throat, prying her jaw open, holding her snout closed and rubbing her neck to swallow. And I can't count how many times she cheeked her pills, only to find them under her bed later.

Just tonight I tried to give her melatonin and had to give up and I said to Justin "I'm so exhausted from fighting with her about medication". She's almost 15, clamps down, stares at me and will hold her breath and fight until she gets it out of her mouth. She cheeks it out and she even flicks the liquid stuff off her tongue, as much as she can.

After her clearance from her surgery, she graduated quickly to full, *leashed* walks. I wondered when it was time to leave our yard and take her on the street if she would be fearful of traffic or cars or the road, but she wasn't. She was excited, trying to run and tow me as I held her back with the leash. When she was allowed full walks, the first place we walked was the scene of the accident and she grabbed her ball and ran into the little river and underneath the road through the culvert and up the other side. I thought how amazing she was that she didn't hold that fear inside of her. What had happened had happened and it was over.

She was not living in the past, nor living in fear, and she was not storing anything in her system. She had a lot to make up for. She lost 12 weeks of adventure. I became so afraid to take her off leash or take her anywhere for adventures for several months. We stuck close to home, walking the road and groomed trails, leashed.

During her recovery, she had to be sedated and x-rayed several times for checkups on her hip to ensure it was healing properly. On her final x-ray, 12 weeks after the accident, we were told they found a slight tear in her ACL and wanted to operate on both of her knees.

I refused the surgery. We talked to our regular vet, who discussed the probable age of her injury - it appeared old. We also talked about the financial impact for us as well as the recovery impact of another massive surgery for Tetley. We just didn't feel it was necessary. We needed time to get our lives back, recover financially from the surgery as well as let Tetley live again.

I knew the risks of off-leash and as my vet said "you take the risk you want, this will likely never be a problem. It's clearly an old injury and may never worsen. It could also still be rehabbed because it's not a complete tear".

We went to our holistic vet who gave us various herbs for ligaments and tendons to help promote healing. We added collagen to her diet. It wasn't a full tear, just an old partial. We couldn't and certainly, Tetley couldn't face another 12 - 16 week recovery unless it was critical.

She was kept leashed. She became depressed. She would get in her kennel and stay there. She gained a lot of weight and seemed to stop caring about everything. She walked every day, twice a day, but on a leash. She felt no joy or release from it.

One morning I woke up and thought "it's time" so off we went to Mad Rock Trail in Bay Roberts, a place we had spent a lot of time hiking together. With several beaches, forests, trails, and ocean front it's a beautiful hike and the perfect one for our first big adventure instead of the safe leashed road walks we had been doing. She was even leashed in the woods behind our house!

I wasn't sure how she would do on the hike so I planned just for a short 2 or 3-kilometre hike and that Sunday morning we left the house, with snacks, coffee and water packed. She came back to herself, fully alive with the wildness in her eyes. She rode the armrest with her head out the window, running from one side of the vehicle to the other and jumping front to back like before the accident. Lexie was safely planted in the front seat to avoid her chaos.

Her car antics were of a dog that anticipated the best adventure every time she was in the vehicle, and this was no different. I can't count how many times my head was smashed against the driver's side window as she jumped into the passenger seat and back again or how many times Lexie yelped because she jumped on her. Or how we always had to say "errands" for the times we weren't doing adventures so she would calm down in the car. Lexie would put her head on the console and Tetley's feet would be planted on either side of her head.

This particular day, she was alive again, not just existing, not just a dog on a leash walking on pavement, this day she was permitted to run free again, to feel the earth under her paws, not slow down or stop or wait or be careful. She felt the rocks, gravel and grass under her feet and the cold ocean water under her belly when she slammed into the waves.

That day is etched in my memories forever, when I knew I would let her live fully, no matter how short or long, and that whatever time she had left as she was now 9, I wouldn't hold her back. She wasn't afraid so why should I be? It wasn't her fault that she was hit by a car, she did what she was trained to do. The driver made the mistake of speeding and then going off the road.

Yes, I should have had her on a leash, but she isn't a leash dog. We should have walked in the woods that day, but we didn't. We could have walked the other way but we didn't. We could go on about what else we could have done differently, and I know the judgment that the hardcore leashers will take, who will say "this is what happens" and maybe it is and maybe we took the risk and maybe for dogs like Tetley the risk is worth the reward. But in the end, she was on the side of the road, leashed or not and the driver left the road.

She wasn't afraid and I wasn't going to be either. I wouldn't collar and leash her wild nature or her spirit to hang onto her safely because I was afraid of losing her. What was harder was watching what I was losing as I was keeping her safe and holding her too close.

Tetley wasn't born for that. She was born wild and free, and I had to give it back to her. That started our adventures again. Those adventures haven't ended and neither has my promise to her. As long as she can, as long as wants to, as long as there is drive and relentlessness in her personality, I will take her. If she wants to swim, I will drive 30 minutes to the place where we can get in safely, as her mobility has declined this year. We will visit new and old destinations alike.

I did the same for Lexie. Because her mobility suffered we

often drove to locations we could have both the fetch and swimming for Tetley and the lollygagging and sniffing for Lexie. She got in the water and she could be included and not left home. We adjusted our lives to their needs and abilities.

Tetley's fearlessness taught me to face life differently. She has what my grandfather Whittle had. She faces life and death the same way, with courage, faith and belief. When he was diagnosed with cancer he told me he was offered treatment and he asked the doctor what that would mean for his life. The doctors told him he would be sick, but he would get an extra few years, maybe. He asked if he would be able to still fish and hunt and go into the woods; would he have a quality of life? They said no. He asked why he would want extra years if he was just going to be sick and couldn't live his life the way he wanted to. He wanted to die with dignity.

Pop told me that there is a time to live and a time to die and that he was 84 years old, and he could honestly say he had 83 good years. What more could he want? He said that when a man can't fish anymore, to haul up his boat, and go home and die. He told me he lived his life, and his only wish was not to have the pain he was having. He died in January. I was 22 years old and had lived next door to him my entire life. I was away at university those last few years of his life, but he would call me sometimes and he bought me a door plaque, with my name on it, for my bedroom door at university. He was so proud of it and I was so proud to have it. I still have it.

The story is a bit hazy for me as I was hearing it second hand so I confirmed with my father the details. I thought he was crab fishing and came home and went into the woods for a load of wood, but Dad told me he was actually buying wood his last year alive. He did cut up his own wood still and he was out in the boat fishing... Dad had to start his chainsaw for him because he could no longer do it. He kept saying "I don't know what's wrong with me". He had multiple mylema but didn't know it.

He had some heart issues that year, with fluid building on his heart because he strained it earlier that year, in the woods. He was of an era when they made men like steel. He got a hospital card that year, which was a shock to our family as he had many accidents and injuries in his lifetime. Something was always bleeding.

He went into the woods on his Honda three-wheeler ATV once and nearly ripped his ear off, he used turpentine to put it back together. More than once he flipped that bike on himself and my father would hear him yelling for help. No one could count how many accidents, cuts or contusions he had. When he first got that bike I was 5. He took me for a ride on it and flipped it on us. He told me not to tell or that I wouldn't be allowed to go again. I told. We were all still allowed to go with him. It was the 80s in rural Newfoundland where the beds of pickup trucks were for kids and dogs and we always defied the odds, somehow, with him.

He didn't want to fight death. He had lived his life and accepted death as a part of that. He told me he wasn't afraid because he knew where he was going. That experience changed my life. Watching how he faced death and watching the world as we're so addicted to living, even when it's a miserable, long-outlived existence, people cling to life as if there aren't worse things than dying but I think it's worse to never live at all.

Tetley reminds me of my grandfather, and I lean into their courage, their fearlessness as well as their absolute reckless abandon for life and living. When you've lived well and you have no regrets, facing death isn't as scary.

It reminds me of a quote from the movie Snow White & The Huntsmen when the awakened Snow White exclaimed "And I'd rather die today than live another day of this death! Who will ride with me? Who will be my brother?" They all knelt to her. Because we all love a story of someone willing to die in the pursuit of living.

I feel the same. If we aren't living at all, aren't choosing life over existence what is the point of it? So, I promised her I would let her live and live, we have. We didn't slow down our adventures after her accident, we picked them up. I made more time for them. I had a healthy fear of her dying before but now I had a reality of how fast it can happen and how fast it could be over. I didn't want to live with regret. In so many ways.

CHAPTER 7
ALWAYS GET UP

Lexie after her CCL surgery. Always happy. She took her teddy to surgery.

Tetley and Lexie have always been the get-up type and keep-going type. They never stayed down, even after surgeries. While Tetley might seem to be the relentless one, Lexie struggles with chronic pain, and poor mobility and while she is slow, she still shows up every day. Dogs amaze me with their ability to push through pain. Sometimes I wonder how much pain they have that we just do not know. There are times, of course, that we know they have to be in pain, after surgeries and such. But what other things do they have that we never know about?

When my appendix was removed, I was in horrific pain. I couldn't take pain medication because I would not be allowed to drive. I wasn't supposed to drive anyway because if I had to brake or got in an accident, the impact could hurt me. But I had to drive - to the trailheads for Tetley. Plus, I was newly self-employed. I couldn't take 6 weeks off. I took advil to help and that was that. I took the stronger stuff when Justin was home in the evenings and could care for the banshee we were living with.

After Lexie's spay surgery, I was keeping a very close eye on her when she wasn't kennelled. She was wearing her cone and I hooked her onto a very short tie out while I took care of a couple of things inside. I was gone indoors for maybe a couple of minutes. She slipped the tie out and was nowhere to be seen. Neither was Tetley. They went on an escapade. I called out to them and they came back from the woods, they were covered in mud.

Lexie's cone was destroyed and she was up to her elbows in mud. Neither was remorseful and Tetley actually looked proud of herself for having hitched Lexie out of her cage. Her incision was checked at the vet's and determined to be ok but she ended up kennelled for the rest of the week to ensure recovery and no more escapades. Her sister was not a good influence!

Since then she's had elbow dysplasia, knee surgeries and dental surgeries. She was quick to *try* to return to normal. It amazed me every time they had something major, how they just kept going, acting normal. It took years for the chronic pain to catch up to and lead her to a house dog life but in those younger, earlier days she bounced back as wild as Tetley.

We tried every pain medication we could get our hands on. She was allergic to everything, developing scabs and skin infections with each one. We then had to do rounds of steroids to help her recover, then start all over again with other medications. Eventually, we settled on Gabapentin as the only medication she could take. We even tried CBD and natural therapies but all led to allergies and skin issues.

She gave in eventually to being a house dog and thrived in that. We did the best we could to help her, from acupuncture to injections and laser treatments, but nothing really worked until she just slowed down. She suffered less and I realised that maybe she should have been a house dog long before she was. We don't let her do much anymore and in spite of it all, she is happy. She was always happy, even when in pain. She taught me that - our circumstances don't have to determine our attitude.

She sees a holistic vet in addition to her regular vet, and a naturopath, who put her on a strict raw diet, with various herbs to help with skin issues, inflammation and pain. Her natural vet said her pain was weight-bearing so as long as she was chilling out she wasn't in pain. That gave us some comfort and helped us make the decision to keep her home more or bring blankets pond side so she could mosey and chill while Tetley turned the water into a jacuzzi.

While Lexie lives with pain she gets up every day and shows up for life. She finds the stairs difficult these days but she will still manage them if I'm at the bottom or top of them, helping her. I moved my workouts into the garage this year so they could still be with me working out as Tetley can't do the stairs at all and they are really difficult on Lexie. She comes to the garage, outside for workouts, downstairs for yoga and fitness classes, and lying by the wood stove, she doesn't miss out on much because of her pain and she shows us every day how to keep going, with a great attitude, in spite of it. I ordered a double foam, extra large yoga mat so Lexie could be on it with me.

Lexie was diagnosed with elbow dysplasia just before she turned 2. We had started hiking the East Coast Trail that year so she was doing some long hikes, upwards of 15 kilometres. Her normal up to then was anywhere from 5 to 7, sometimes 10. She was very active, running, hiking, and swimming so we didn't think anything of it. We started with short ones around 7 and 8 kilometres. After a few months of long hikes, Lexie developed a limp. I booked a vet appointment to get her checked, believing it was a pulled muscle or strain.

Elbow dysplasia. I hadn't yet signed her up for the insurance program that Tetley was on. I cringed, knowing this was now a preexisting condition. She would require surgery. We met with our vet, who recommended the specialty orthopedic vet who was coming to town in a couple of weeks, to discuss surgical options.

The day the vet arrived we had a conflict of information. Our vet, whom we knew and trusted suggested that Lexie's x-rays might indicate it wasn't as bad as they thought but the specialist recommended surgery saying that she was in significant pain and that the x-rays wouldn't always show that. I didn't know what to do and the specialist vet wasn't in town for long, so I opted to do the surgery. I didn't want her to suffer, so I said yes.

Lexie and I bonded deeply during her recovery. We were already in love but I think her trust in me deepened during that time. She woke up from her surgery crying. She always struggled waking up from anesthesia, crying and whining as if she were scared or in pain. The vets assured me this was normal for most dogs but of course, Tetley wasn't most dogs, she woke up from anesthesia trying to run!

The night of Lexie's surgery I slept in the spare bedroom on the floor with her. She was in her kennel to prevent movement and I kept the door open with my pillow next to her head. She cried all night and I lay with her. Her eyes glistened with pain, knowing there was nothing I could do except stay with her so she wasn't alone.

By morning she was back to herself. She was on very restrictive movement to let her elbows heal from surgery so we slept on the mattress on the floor for a few weeks. She was hand fed and coddled. She had physio, exercises and icing a couple of times a day.

She was babied and she loved being babied. Something changed in our relationship then. She was still a handful with her training and into the garbage but the depth of our relationship changed. I think it was then she knew I would do anything for her. Not necessarily the surgery but caring for her when she was sick.

It was that recovery that finally made her know she was safe, that she belonged with us, to me. We were family and she was just as important as Tetley. She became my shadow after that. She was always with me but now she was addicted to me.

Her elbow surgery was a major surgery. She did see an immediate change but it didn't take long before we felt the surgery wasn't as successful as we had hoped it would be. I do recognise that we allowed Lexie to return to normal activities when the vets warned me that she would never be able to be a normal dog for activity purposes. We never let her do long hikes but she did several kilometres a day and sometimes up to 8 when we went on longer adventures.

When we came home from those hikes, Lexie was iced, then had her physiotherapy exercises and stretches, to reduce any pain and inflammation. We managed what she was allowed to do by monitoring her pain level post-hike.

It took years before the effects of those elbows would really present themselves. With added weight and challenges, Lexie walked with us to the end of the driveway where she would sit and stay. She refused to come. She knew better than I did that exercise wasn't her friend anymore. She remained moderately active until she was 8 or so.

She still came in the woods but to my deepest shame, I allowed her to do far more than I should have. I found it difficult to leave her home, even when it was in her best interest. If she wanted to stay home I let her but if she wanted to come I also let her. It's one of my only regrets, that I let her do too much.

Lexie was also suspected to have hip dysplasia but we never got the official diagnosis. We did take her to a different vet clinic because she was having trouble getting around and we couldn't get in with our regular clinic. They sedated her and x-rayed her hips and knees. They said she had a luxating patella and possibly hip dysplasia.

Lexie was on pain medication and really there was nothing more that could be done except pain management, nothing was immediately critical, just chronic. The clinic discharged her and asked me to come pick her up. They helped me put her in the vehicle. It was usual for them not to be fully functioning, especially Lexie, after sedation but this was extreme. I got her home and she couldn't stand up and was drooling excessively. I had to bring her back where they did a sedation reversal.

I was so scared at the time. My regular vet requested the records and they determined the other clinic gave Lexie the max dose of sedation. She was sensitive to sedation so it was a lot for her. We never again went to a different vet for anything major, especially sedation.

We knew she really couldn't have any more surgery and was already being managed as best she could for pain. But one of her back knees buckled one day and she started favouring it. We took her for a check up and she had torn her CCL and had to have a surgical repair. While we didn't want to do it, it was a full tear and she needed it. We opted for the smaller surgery because we knew her elbows couldn't handle a larger recovery. The surgery was not successful.

That is how she finally became a house dog. She ventured into the woods behind the house sometimes and still comes swimming but otherwise, she became a house dog. She had a knee brace for a time that helped stabilise her.

I found that her continuing on, even slowly, likely hid the extent of her pain. Dogs have an incredible pain tolerance and it took a long time for me to really understand that. If I had my time back I would do so many things differently, like wait on that first elbow surgery. I wish I had asked more questions or talked to my regular vet about the possibility of waiting. The vet did come every 6 months or so. But I felt like it was now she needed it to prevent pain. I wasn't a new dog mom but Tetley's problems were usually accidental, not chronic like Lexie's.

The cost of her surgery could have paid for a lot of alternative treatments. We may have stopped her sooner from too much activity. So many things we may have done differently and maybe I still would have chosen the surgery. We can't analyse the past knowing what we know now. We didn't know it then. Lexie had chronic health problems, and signs of bad or backyard breeding. Registered, reputable breeders do testing and breed quality dogs to ensure health.

Lexie was considered to be badly bred. Her health problems continued to mount. Chronic allergies, ear infections, eye infections, skin issues, focal seizures and bone and joint pain. No matter what we tried we just couldn't get away from her health problems. Over the last year and a bit, she hasn't had too much. She's hardly on any medications anymore.

In the summer of 2021, she had a vomiting incident and I took her to the vet where we saw a new vet. We got in on the walk-in clinic. He wanted to run x-rays in case she had eaten something. I told him she started a new pain medication they wanted us to try and a side effect was vomiting. I didn't think x-rays were needed because there was no evidence that she had eaten something. She had never done that before. Why would she now? Plus, the medication was the most likely suspect, why not start there?

Even though she was sick, she was happy and smiling, licking everyone and wagging. He gave her an anti-nausea injection and we went home to monitor her. By the time I got her home she was frothing from her mouth and had a seizure. Lexie's focal seizures were sad and scary. Her back would curl up, and her back legs didn't work properly, she scravelled to me where she would get in my lap, put her head on my shoulder and stay there, shaking and drooling, until it passed.

Then she would lay in my lap and stare at me, exhausted but smiling. She was always happy, even when she was sick and in pain. I returned to the vet with her and they again wanted to run x-rays and do all the things. I still didn't feel it was necessary. All of those things come with sedation and I didn't want to sedate my girls after 10 if it wasn't absolutely necessary. I normally always listened to the advice of the vet but this time my gut was telling me no. I felt he was off base this time.

I called Justin. I never consulted him on their care. I did what I wanted and what I felt was best. I was their primary caregiver so I made the decisions on their vet care. I sat with Lexie and talked to a couple of the staff who knew me but I just had to go with my gut. I closed my eyes, felt for the answer and I heard inside of me, take her home, take her off the medications and love her. She had been through so much in her life I knew I couldn't put her through anything else.

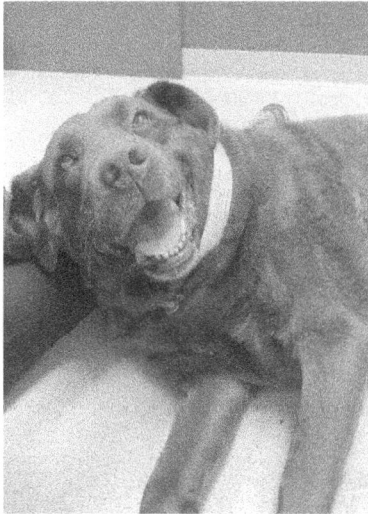

Lexie at the vet, vomiting and still smiling.

That's what I did. I took her home and loved her. She had a tough couple of days but she returned to herself. And since then she's been mostly fine. She's not had any seizures, her skin issues have resolved and her mobility has even improved a little. She still gets ear infections regularly but otherwise no considerable issues. She just keeps going, no matter what she is facing.

Tetley, though, had more paw cuts, emergency room visits and stitches than I can count. She had more sedation than is possible to remember and she has hardware inside of her keeping her hip attached to her leg and still she keeps getting up. Her drive to keep pushing and keep going is the thing I love the most about her and is the hardest part of living with her. It was easy when she was young, and we could just run it out or take an extra hike or throw a ball for twenty minutes and burn some high energy off.

She was surrounded by fitness, outside all the time and always had someone to throw a ball or a stick for her. It was easy then, but it's not been easy as she's aged and she cannot obtain the same level of energy expenditure. In the summer of 2021, I signed her up for a virtual challenge to hike Mount Everest with the Conquer Events.

She was slowing down and it felt right to take her on a final adventure as I didn't know how many we would have left. We finished Everest together and it was shortly after that she stopped walking. It was sudden. She went from our normal, senior, 2-3 kilometre, 2 times a day, walks to walking for about 5 minutes, and eventually, she stopped walking altogether except for around the house and yard. It was a hard day when she didn't want to go for her morning walk. I put her collar on, but she didn't make any attempt to leave the patio, she just stared at me.

I did take her swimming and she loved it. I guess it didn't hurt her body and there were no mobility issues in the pond. She still swims every day. I imagine that she feels unstoppable and young in the water. She still looks for her workout every day. She started doing a tapping thing with her front paws and she struggled to move from one room to another. She was restless at night and barked in the evenings. We assumed it was from the reduced activity and behaviours resulting from that.

I had just returned to university full-time, post-pandemic, and I couldn't have a zoom call, nor could I sleep much because she was up pacing and wanting to go outside throughout the night.

In January 2022 she lost the use of her back legs. One minute she was fine and the next she wasn't. Her mobility was declining but this was a "what the heck just happened" moment she was fine a minute ago. It was a bad day, maybe the worst of having her. She cried and barked and squealed with no end in sight. It was a Friday night, and my only option was the VSC.

I was scared to go there as I was worried they would tell me to put her down, and I wanted our regular vet's opinion on that decision plus I wanted to see if she had a soft tissue injury and if she would recover. I had already made up my mind that there wouldn't be any more invasive procedures for either of my girls at their ages. I waited to see our regular vet on Monday but it was a tough couple of days. I had CBD oil which wasn't helping at all, and I had leftover sedatives from her recent surgery to remove an infected lump from her foot.

I left the house for a drive at midnight because I needed a breather. I came back to find her under the kitchen table completely freaking out. I felt so guilty for leaving her that evening and it reminded me of why it's so important to have our emotions in check. It was the only time I left her when she was unwell or stressed and it would never happen again. I still thought this was behaviour related. I thought the loss of her exercise and now mobility was causing her to act out but it was now clear this was something else.

After a few days of using sedatives, we finally got in for our vet visit. I was shocked to hear that she had Canine Cognitive Dysfunction or dementia. She was sundowning and the loss of her mobility was caused by her brain not knowing where her feet were. We were given medication to try to manage the behaviour because nothing else would matter if we couldn't control that.

We went home and it was tough. I cried constantly, those deep, heart-wrenching sobs. I had so much guilt for being frustrated with her over the last couple of months. I cried all over the place, with other people, in business meetings and even in stores. I reconciled inside of myself, as I carried her around in a harness, that I wouldn't let her suffer.

Tetley, on her 14th birthday in 2022 swimming in the frigid ocean.

I prepared myself and was trying to buy enough time for Justin to get home from his turnaround shift at work. I wanted to hold on that long. She's our baby. He deserves to be here with her when it's time. We always know it's a risk, travelling with senior dogs, whether for pleasure or work so I wanted to hold off as long as we could. It was just a couple of weeks more.

The medication was a success within a few days of starting it and she bounced out of it. I felt as if I had aged a lifetime in a few days. While she was sundowning and crying the house flooded and I was knee-deep in water in the basement with friends and family helping me out while we could hear her upstairs crying and barking. Everyone who knew Tetley loved her, she was just so much, a big personality and to see her decline so incredibly fast was hard on everyone who knew her.

Lexie, though, was splashing through the water in the basement as if, finally, we had an indoor pool.

As she started sleeping again and returned to her normal bad mobility, eating, engaging and sleeping and being her mostly normal Tetley, life settled back into its normal chaotic flare. But it is there, creeping on me constantly, a living grief that I didn't know was possible. I don't think we acknowledge the challenges of facing the loss of a loved one enough, how much it weighs on us.

I didn't have human children. The girls are my children. I didn't have a normal job. Tetley and Lexie have been constants in my life, a 24/7 presence and even though she was old, and while I had a healthy fear of death it seemed we always escaped it. This was real, this was age, and this was nothing money or love could buy our way out of. The impending doom settled in and in place of her big personality a waking, constant grief would sit alongside me every day. How do you know? How do you really measure how to decide? It's a big responsibility, their life, in our hands.

For now, though, she was back. A little old lady but she was reminding me again not to live too far in the future, that today is what we have and if we can get up today then we get up.

I watched her determination with her mobility challenges and how much she refused to be supported. We tried a cart to take her on walks and I could imagine her internal dialogue to that situation as she tipped the cart sideways and flew out of it and as far away from it as she could get. As if to say you have lost your mind if you think I'd ever stay in that!

She struggled her way to her feet, fought any assistance we offered and pushed herself forward. I had to respect the fight in her. Sometimes I think I couldn't have birthed a child more like me with that same determination. But I don't know if I have it or if she gave it to me or I gave it to her, either way, we are cut from the same determined cloth.

She had a surgery at 13.5 that I really didn't want to do, and we did everything to avoid it, but a lump had come out on her foot and she wouldn't leave it alone, causing an infection. After several cultures and rounds of antibiotics with it being a resistant strain of bacteria, we had to use drugs that I couldn't touch or get on my hands. They were risky and they didn't end up helping.

I often wonder if those drugs started her mental decline or caused neurological issues. I can't remember the name of them to look up the side effects and I suppose it doesn't really matter. We are here and how we got here isn't that important. Torturing myself about the past won't help. We can't judge our past decisions and choices by what we know now.

We ended up doing the surgery because she either needed to wear a cone forever or she needed it removed. It wasn't a big surgery but any surgery at that age is big, in my opinion. She didn't wake up from the anesthesia properly. This was during the pandemic so when I was asked to come in the back with her as Tetley always did better with me by her side, I wasn't sure what to expect. For as fearless and independent as she was, she wanted her momma when she was sick.

She was pitiful and it was my fear manifested in real-time. It was why I didn't want to have surgeries or anything that would require sedation if we could avoid it. This was 6 months before the CCD diagnosis and she was her perfectly normal self, and it was right after this that we did the Everest virtual hike. Physically she was still fine, walking a couple of kilometres a day. She was slowing down, sure, but she was still herself, spinning, walking, hiking and fetching.

But in true Tetley style, the next day she was back to her full antics, she managed to prop her foot up, using her cone as a prop, and rip her stitches out, having to go back to be sedated, cleaned up and restitched. This time she woke up fine but had to be put on a full sedative for home use to keep her from tearing her stitches out.

Tetley refused to wear a cone, in spite of how many times she was prescribed one. She used the cone as a weapon by intentionally ramming into me with it and she walked along the wooden railing in the house, hauling it along it to be both irritating and trying to get it off. She did this each time she had to wear a cone and cones were a regular part of the wardrobe. Tetley would not be slowed down, so we had to sedate her to give the stitches time to heal.

She was pissed about that. She stared at me as the medications kicked in as if I were a traitor. I suppose I was. But she was a danger to herself in any recovery that was necessary. Downtime was not on her radar and had to be forced on her.

When it was over, she bounced back to her normal self. A couple of months later we had a camping trip to Frenchman's Cove on the Burin Peninsula and stayed in beautiful log cabins. It was late August and her walk was slowing then but we walked the trail by the cabins, even Lexie was joining us and they swam in the pond at the end of the trail.

The first night there, it was pouring torrential rains and she had what appeared to be a neurological incident. It seemed to mimic Lexie's focal seizures. We're not really sure. It could have been a stroke or something else. It was too dangerous for us to leave and make the drive back to St. John's for a vet clinic. I reached out to Amanda to talk about it. We figured it was a seizure from the video I had taken. A few moments later, she seemed to return to normal and I kept a close eye on her.

But she was never the same after that. I didn't see that at that time, though, only in looking back. I don't know if it was the medications, surgery, or the sedation after it or the combination of it all or not related to it at all, but I feel like it was all connected. It was a lot in a couple of months for an old lady. She started this sort of toe-tapping thing she does and stopped her daily walks within months.

It was only after her CCD diagnosis that I started to see the big picture emerging and wondered if there were connections to the neurological issues she had. But for now, she was bouncing out of this, as she had with so many other things in her life, showing me the power of always getting up when we've still got fight left.

She's always been that dog, the spirit of the wildness inside of her, the power to keep going no matter what she was facing. While Lexie eventually gave up, accepting her fate as a house dog, happily, I know Tetley will never accept that fate. When she stops swimming or adventuring, she will not want to be here. She wasn't born with the companionship and gentleness traits that Lexie was. She will ride or die and that is that.

She will never be happy in a kennel or taking safe road walks. She will never be happy to sleep in and get belly rubs on the couch. She will never be content to be alive and not living. Lexie aims to please, and Tetley aims to live. She lives big, and everything she does is full out or not at all.

The way she eats and drinks is a scene to behold with the noise, snorts, and gobbles. Everything was giant and we often remarked that she couldn't actually be tasting anything because of the way she was eating. When she finished her food she went to the couch and wiped her mouth on it or to the polar bear rug that we got from an Indigenous hunter in Nunavut. She used his claws to scratch behind her ears and wiped her mouth in his fur. Every day was a battle with her.

When you spoke to her or told her off she barked back. When she wanted a treat she slammed the pantry door with her paw and went to her bed, waiting. If you ignored her she growled with pursed lips. She went outside, faked peeing while looking over her shoulder, came in and expected a treat, at 13! Exasperating is an understatement.

Lexie, on the other hand, chewed her food and sniffed food you threw at her before she ate it. Tetley drank water as if inhaling the pond whereas Lexie sniffed the water bowl, only drank fresh water, and took her time. She enjoyed life, and Tetley devoured life.

Lexie never asked for a snack or treat. She didn't have to,

really. She got it because we always gave her one when Tetley got one. And Tetley asked for enough for 10 dogs. Lexie was easy, and Tetley was crazy.

I've learned that the spirit of that is within us all. Sure, a lot of people do learn their limitations and become like Lexie, content in the new world they have. As long as she is with her people, she is happy. And that is ok. Sometimes acceptance and being ok with where we are is a perfect life to live. But Tetley is like Snow White, even when she is hurt, injured, or impaired in any way she would rather die today than live another day of this death.

She is relentless in her pursuit of activity and her drive. I've had many friends tell me they've never met a dog like Tetley and that's the truth. I am biased of course because she is mine, but I can tell you that living with her and raising her has been the greatest blessing and the biggest challenge of my life.

Her determination is both her best asset and her worst trait because there are times we all need rest. But for Tetley, she just doesn't want to. There are balls to chase and sticks to chew and a bigness of life to live, whatever she was doing, she was doing full out. She is all in, there are no halves with her or sort of showing up. She was pure in her drive and that drive taught me so much over the years about the power of getting up, no matter what.

When I was going through a very difficult time and working on trauma recovery there were days I just didn't want to get up. I didn't want to do my normal activities. I didn't want to be here. But Tetley wouldn't let me stay in bed. She ripped the covers off me and made me go. For that, I am eternally grateful.

Her force and push were bigger than just about her, it was about her always knowing that wind, rain, water, trails and dirt could solve a lot of problems. Sometimes in our lowest moments staying down is what we think we need but she knew that one foot in front of the other every day, sticks in the back of your head, with the wind blowing in your face was the answer to what ails us. She gave me the gift of never giving up.

Lexie was calmer in her not giving up in an accepting way. There are different ways to not give up. Lex keeps going. She didn't stop fully. She comes on adventures but also knows when her body can't do it. She will lie down and rest or stay in the vehicle. Because she knows her limits she will hang out with people and still be able to do things but not the way she used to. She lives it in her own best way. More isn't always better and while Tetley drives herself to total exhaustion, Lex dawdles around and gets love and cuddles and snacks and it's her paradise.

Lexie's attitude while struggling every day is beautiful while Tetley's refusal to give up, ever, is beautiful. They are different but equally powerful lessons in how attitude determines our quality of life.

One thing I learned from all the vets and surgeries for my girls is what I'd do differently for them now. In hindsight, many things cleared up on their own or weren't necessary for emergency visits. I sometimes wonder if I always did the right thing in sedation, medications, surgeries, and tests.

As the girls aged, I became far more cautious and careful about tests and treatments. I don't do anything invasive if I can avoid it or don't feel it is necessary. I now have a check-up, do the least invasive thing and then work up from there.

For much of their lives, I felt like we started with the biggest things and then worked down. I learned as a dog mom to finally trust that I knew my girls. Testing, medications and surgeries are absolutely necessary but so is assessing the full picture and working up to ensure not only medical treatment but if that treatment is in the best interest of the dogs.

Hindsight is 20/20 and the best thing we can do is to learn. I rushed Tetley to the ER once when she was 6 months old for spots on her belly, thinking she was having an allergic reaction. It was fly bites. It took me too long to navigate what was an emergency and what wasn't. That's why I often asked Amanda because I didn't have clarity, I'm a helicopter dog mom. My girls went through a lot, some accidental and some chronic. I don't regret trying to give them the absolute best care possible but I did learn how to navigate doing the best for them. In their challenges, they taught me how to face adversity with the right attitude.

They taught me to keep going, in spite of it all. Lexie, with her chronic pain and chronic health problems and Tetley with her determination to overcome and beat the odds. In their own ways, they keep going and they teach me the value in the sheer force required to do so some days. That force is sometimes quiet like Lexie's and other days, ferocious like Tetley's.

CHAPTER 8
FOCUS

Lexie with her peanut butter tub. She was never distracted with this.

Tetley has a one-track mind. So does Lexie, but for different reasons. Lexie is food motivated; she always was. Tetley is movement-motivated. She would do anything for that stick. Lexie would do anything for the snack!

Tetley was relentless in getting her way. She still is! When she plays fetch, in the water or out, she goes out, gets it, and brings it back. Lexie would often intercept her, throwing her full weight behind her and body-check Tetley into the air. Lexie wanted to play and Tetley wanted to work.

Our trainer, Glenn, told us it's Tetley's job as a hunting dog to go out and retrieve. Lexie wasn't bred for that, and she wanted to play. While Tetley was swimming, making a beeline for the stick to bring it back, Lexie would jump on her back, steal the stick, and often hold her underwater. Tetley was just trying to get the stick and bring it back. The only time Tetley gave up her stick was when Lexie slammed into her. She knew Lexie would get it one way or another so she let her have it.

We called Lexie little Lolly but she wasn't little at all. She was short and stocky and outweighed Tetley by a good 15-20 pounds.

It is a sight to watch Tetley's intensity and focus on doing one thing. She had one job and that was what she was focused on. She never cared that Lexie was hanging off her, she just kept moving forward. She still swims and gets her stick and brings it back, no matter what. It's a relentless drive inside of her to do that. Lexie wanders around. She might be in the water causing Tetley issues or she might sometimes just sit there up to her neck staring off into space but at some point, she will wander off to the sides of the water or riverbank and chew on grass or sniff rocks. When she's done she'll wait by the car.

Tetley tore trees out of the ground, entire trees, with roots attached. If she couldn't find a stick or a ball and needed something, I would try to crack branches off but sometimes it was difficult with living trees. She would find trees and wrap her mouth around them and yank until she got the tree out of the ground. Once she started and was committed to getting it there was no stopping her. She planted her back legs and yanked until she got it.

Big sticks and logs were her specialty. She navigated bridges, narrow trails, trees, and people with giant logs in her mouth. Sometimes you'd see her running with a log that was almost impossible to pick up. She landed in front of me with this thing and expected me to throw it. Some of the sticks were too heavy for me to pick up, never mind throw for a game of fetch! She dropped it, backed up, butt and tail wagging as she stared sideways at me and the stick with a stream of drool running out of her mouth. There were just no limitations on her intensity or insanity.

Sometimes the stick was 8 feet long! Lexie often grabbed one end and the 2 of them would run down the trail with it. The only time they did teamwork. When they came to a bridge or narrow crossing, or she had to navigate the stick between trees, she wasn't leaving it behind, Tetley turned her head and dragged it through, sideways.

Head tilt, waiting for the throw.

Lexie does her thing and does several things, she chews grass and drinks pond water, sometimes at the same time, nearly choking. She coughs in the water, blowing bubbles and surprising herself, every time. Tetley does one thing. Only when she is finished fetching does she smell around, eat grass or check out whatever else is going on. She can focus on one task until it's over like no one else I've ever met. There is nothing else in the space with her when she is doing something.

She started her addiction to fetch in the hallway in West 40 as a puppy. An addiction that would span her life and still, at almost 15, she is relentlessly fetching every day. No ball or stick would go unreturned. She had to return with the exact same stick or ball. If it was washed away by the current or lost in a tree because of my terrible aim, she would not come back without it. She had to be enticed with a new one and even then, she wouldn't be happy about it. I cannot count how many hours of my life were spent with brooms, shovels, and ladders trying to shake tennis balls from trees because she refused any other ball. Sometimes on the old railroad tracks - she fetched the entire way- and I would throw a skew stick and end up crawling through woods, using sticks and shaking the trees relentlessly until the stick would fall out to her waiting pounce.

Even small trees are surprisingly hard to get enough force to shake a tennis ball out of. Who would have thought? Sometimes I just couldn't shake the tree hard enough to get that ball to drop so occasionally I had to use rocks to try to get the stick out of the tree. We had more than a couple of close calls with rocks nearly landing on her as she stretched her front paws up the trunk of the tree, tongue hanging out and desperately waiting for the ball to drop. She would look at me, look at the tree, and bark. Repeatedly. I had to get it because she wouldn't leave without it.

She became so obsessed with fetch that she put the ball in your hand or lap. She threw sticks at you, shoved them into your lap and I'm sure she thought since you have it in your hand you may as well throw it. Her ball would get so wet it was slippery and covered with foam. She drove people insane when they were just trying to hang out and rest. Everyone she met had a stick in the kneecaps or back of the legs or a dirty slobbery ball in their lap at one time or another. She even jumped into the fire pit after my father threw her stick in there because she was just relentless one evening at a family fire. Thankfully, he caught her before she landed in the flames.

We had to take all orange hockey balls from her because her insanity with them was next level. When we first moved into our home our basement was unfinished, the gym wasn't yet there. I had a small workout space set up in one room and would work out in the evenings.

I missed the gym but it was a 30-minute drive and I had to make do living so far away. The drive to and from work, then coming home to take care of Tetley meant I wasn't driving back to go to the gym. I tried to go on lunch breaks but it didn't always work out.

When I was in the basement doing my workout, Justin and Tetley were often downstairs too. The full unfinished basement became her playground, Justin would hit the orange ball with a hockey stick and she flew around the basement, frantic, drool flying everywhere.

She took so much pride in returning the ball. She loved all balls and sticks and whatever she was fetching but those orange balls became a severe obsession where she couldn't control herself. She was hyperfocused and fixated and eventually Justin had to take all the hockey balls because she went completely insane and wouldn't stop. It was the one time she wouldn't listen to her commands, at all.

She never slowed down, danger didn't matter, she didn't even know it was there until she was cut and bleeding or couldn't get up. I watched her do a double split once and kept going. We assumed she was fine only to discover later that she couldn't get off her bed. A vet visit showed that she had a double groin pull. Sliced pads, cut limbs and even a tooth knocked out were just par for the course, as were emergency vet visits and stitches. There was no shortage of either and the vet clinic became our second home to the point that it was a running joke I should have just been a vet or a tech.

Tetley's vet, Dr. Meister once told me that she was the only Lab she had ever seen with a full set of abs. Most Labs also love food so even if they're insane they eat a lot. Tetley ate enough but wasn't motivated by food, she was motivated by medals. She loved being rewarded with praise more than food. When she knocked her tooth out we were at the playground near Justin's mother's house in Cowan Heights. We were in Torbay for a wedding and we had taken the girls with us and stayed in the city. In between the service and the reception we went back to his mom's and took them to the playground nearby for a little fetch and playtime.

They were so excited to be there. I got on the swing, Tetley ran to me and I threw her ball. While Justin was calling out to her to bring it to him; she beelined it back to me, but I was midair at this point. She leapt through the air and I tried to move my legs around her but I missed and hit her square in the chest with my knees landing under her chin, slamming her mouth together. She started bleeding from her mouth and a check-out seemed superficial. Normally I would rush off to the vet in a panic, but this time she seemed ok so we let it be. In the coming days, though, we noticed a missing tooth in the bottom row of teeth, to which Justin has gotten much pleasure from saying I kicked her tooth out.

Focus is such a powerful thing and while Tetley's level of focus could be called fixation, most success takes a level of fixation on a single task. When we trained for Tough Mudder, touted as the toughest obstacle course in the world, we dedicated ourselves to the training.

We spent every Sunday in the woods, playgrounds, and

parks, even taking a dip in Topsail Beach in March! Sundays were play days but they were serious training events. I spent my time researching the obstacles and designing similar things for us to do to prepare.

We towed tires through the woods with ropes around our waist, intentionally bear-crawling through bog, mud and culverts to mimic the stations we would experience on the course.

We spent our time hiking and carrying logs on our shoulders, sometimes *up* mountains! Playgrounds with monkey bars became our favourite hang outs as we practiced going across. Skateparks helped us prepare for Everest - the slippery slope we had to scale. We built an outdoor gym on the top of one of the mountains, climbing up with power tools, wood and whatever else we needed to secure our stations.

A ladder was built in the woods to climb and go over, practicing for the nets and other climbing obstacles we might encounter. And for good measure, a javelin throw made of a piece of board with a bright orange blob spray painted in the middle of it. We built obstacle courses in the woods behind my house, with chains, ropes, tires, hooks in trees for the TRX and even a homemade monkey bar.

Sundays were sacred.

The dogs came, always, as we traipsed wherever our adventures took us. Not just mine. Carolyn brought her dog and Nancy brought her 2 dogs. The adventure wasn't complete without them.

We scaled mountain tops and one time did 2000 burpees for cardio. We crawled the mountains and dragged, hauled, kicked, jumped over, built and made tire mountains to prepare.

Sunday mornings were off limits to anything else. We made the time and focused on our goal to get there. Not only did we fly to Toronto for the Tough Mudder event but we nailed most of the stations because we focused and practiced.

Sundays were sacred. Tough Mudder Training in the woods.

We did most of the stations, skipping some of the water stations because it was 4 degrees Celsius when it was supposed to be 16! We were dressed for warmer temperatures and had to stop doing most of the water stations because it was too cold.

The arctic enema was the worst for me, triggering a panic attack! Nancy did all the stations, even the most dangerous ones. The one where you jump in an enclosed slide and get shot out of the bottom. She flew out of that like she was shot out of a cannon. She, like Tetley, wasn't going home without attempting all stations.

Goals require focus. If we are going to achieve anything we must be able to focus. Even writing a book. It's a dedicated project that people are always surprised by when I talk about the writing of it, how much work, tediousness, editing and reading and re-editing the work it becomes. It requires a lot of focus. The writing of the first draft is always the easiest, it's the tedious daily work, reworking sentences, and phrases, changing things around, and making sure it's not repetitive.

When we want something it requires us to dedicate ourselves

to getting it, which means putting in the work to get it. Focus becomes the only thing in the way of us getting what we want. What we focus on is what we achieve.

The dogs could focus. Different kinds of focus but they could focus. Tetley was driven and motivated for activity. She had total focus when she wanted to engage in a game of fetch. She wasn't going to relent. Lexie sure could focus on food. And cuddles and she didn't usually relent until she got what she wanted.

But it was Tetley's relentlessness that gave us activity and adventure, and ultimately the life we've lived. Her focus and energy became the focus and energy of the rest of us. When I work on a project, a new venture, a book or a new goal, it's my focus that gets me to the finish line.

Energy flows where focus goes. When we focus on where we want to go, and what we want to do, hold the goal in our mind, then work on it until we get the outcome we desire, we will get it. If we don't, we adjust course.

When Tetley doesn't get her own way, she adjusts course. She will get more strategic, and even take a break because she knows she's pushed people to the breaking point. Then she'll come back again.

Tetley brought her focus to everything she did. She loved finding baseballs at the ballpark. She still does. We go to CBS to the dog park regularly, but we don't go to the park, instead, we walk the dirt roads and paths that intersect around the park. There's a small river that runs through, between the baseball field and the rugby field. The girls get into the water, play fetch, and splash around.

We walk a makeshift trail under the rugby field to an old pit with a dirt road. I came across an amazing swimming hole one day by accident as we scaled over the big rocks blocking the way.

There was a small space for the girls to squeeze through but they could still jump over rocks when we found this place. It has a large culvert, a rope for people to swing from and it's rocked and dammed up to keep the water high enough in it.

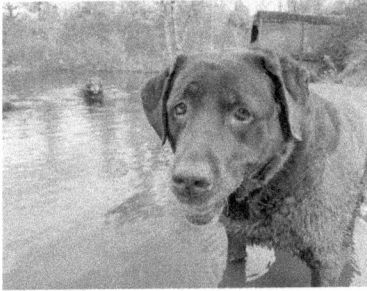

Tetley & Lexie in our favourite swimming place in CBS.

I felt like I found Shangrala. The heavens opened up and gave us a gift of this place. Finding places to go with dogs, in a not dog-friendly world, is challenging. We ask our dogs to be emotional, therapy and support dogs. They are drug dogs, cancer-sniffing dogs, and bomb detectors. They race into fires, collapsing buildings and raging seas to rescue people. But we barely let them walk on a city street.

Each time we find a great swimming location, we're usually chased out by people invading us. We used to do the railroad tracks in Holyrood. It was a perfect location with a pond but someone called the police on me one day and said I was there with my dog off-leash. It was basically the woods. When we came off the tracks, Carolyn, myself, our dogs and a few others with us that day, the police were waiting for us. The person who reported us was known to kick dogs and put out poison-spiked treats so we stopped going there.

We had a great place in cabin country, on the Salmonier Line and people moved in with trailers and campers. Not only did they leave garbage, and broken bottles and make it unsafe but they ruined the vibe. We have spent most of our time finding, losing and refinding places. This place in CBS became a staple for us. Just a 20 minute drive and no one ever seemed to be there. We could get a short walk and swim time for the girls. By the time we made it back to the car, they were tired, happy and mostly dry.

I liked places we could walk and swim so they would be mostly dry by the time we were leaving. When Tetley stopped walking much this past year, I started using the old pit road and drove into the swimming hole.

Sadly, it was discovered this year by people and it became a dumping ground, much like all places humans invade. Garbage, clothing, beer cans and bottles were left behind. It is still better than what Butterpot Pond in Holyrood has become, with human waste, drug paraphernalia, used condoms and take-out wrappers being the most common scene that greets us there.

I have to get out, check out the place for anything broken or dangerous, clean it up and then let the girls out for their swim. But the place in CBS remained relatively unknown and each time we arrived by the ballfield, where we parked, Tetley made a beeline for the bushes around the ballfield in search of balls she could fetch with.

They played softball there and the balls were bigger, usually bright pink or yellow. She would run through the bushes, and the sides of the banks of the river and come out with a ball. I'd then throw those balls for her and she would take them home with her when finished. Sometimes when she was finished swimming she would go collect more balls.

She did this for golf balls too. She has such a drive to retrieve. We went to the swim park in Holyrood, downriver from the golf course. We only went there when the girls were young and in the off-season. Pets weren't allowed there, either. Before they renovated it and it was still rough we went there for some swims. Tetley loved the place. She went insane when we pulled in there.

I always pulled in at the second entrance, crossed the bridge, went into the woods for a bit to the open field and played fetch and wandered around in the woods. Then we would walk back the trail to the river and let them swim.

One day Justin got Tetley to get a golf ball he saw in the river. She did. Then she started collecting them. They were all over the river as litter from the golf course. She brought him in a bucket full of golf balls! She was always focused, driven and intent on retrieving.

She loved St. Pat's ballpark. She smelled the balls anytime we went near the field. Justin played baseball at St. Pat's field for Holy Cross and our escapades at the ballpark were never about watching the game but finding the balls in the bushes outside the fence.

We had to take all the balls she found because Lexie chewed the leather off when she was young and we were afraid she would swallow them as we had to fish a couple of pieces from her. She couldn't be trusted with them so they were put into a crate and put away. When Lexie wasn't around or Tetley was alone with Justin she was allowed to have the baseballs or softballs she found.

She once ran onto the field when Justin took her to watch a game. It was shocking that it took as many years as it did for her to run on the field. She loved that ballpark. She loved the trail that ran along the Rennie's Mill River, the people, the noise and the excitement of the park. She was always in a frenzy.

She has a one-track mind and teaches me the power of focus and what it means to be driven by a single thought. Sometimes in life, there is only what we want and the only way to get it is to latch onto it and never let go. Tetley taught me that if you want something go for it and don't stop until you get it. There is power in doing one thing and doing it so well that you become the best in the world. There is something to be said for persistence, even when you piss people off, to get your own way and what you want.

It's cuter in dogs than people, but there's a lot of power in the persistence of chasing the ball, or the dream and never giving up on what you want. She didn't just enjoy getting the ball, she enjoyed chasing it, too. She will find a way to get you to do what she wants. Even Lexie would become her emotional support dog. If Tetley lost her ball under the patio Lexie would frantically run to the door and bring me to where Tetley was. Tetley would be maniacally tearing railings off and digging to get to the ball but Lex would just come to the door almost in a panic to show me that Tetley needed me.

I watch her with her focus and have thought about the difference between the 2 of them and how much more productive Tetley is in her pursuit, *then* enjoying things when she's finished. Whereas Lexie is the half-finished easily distracted type unless it comes to food. Tetley often doesn't finish her snacks, denta sticks, pizzle's, bones and treats. She enjoyed them occasionally but didn't care for them overall. Before Lexie, she could leave them and go back later if she wanted it.

The problem is if she doesn't eat it immediately, Lexie takes them. It became a game of Tetley's for many years. She lays with her treat, Lexie inhales her own as fast as she can, then sits in front of Tetley and waits for the scraps. Sometimes Tetley will hold it between her paws for a very long time and Lexie will stay there, drooling excessively until eventually, Tetley lets her have it. It's easier for Lexie to get extras now that Tetley isn't well. She doesn't have to wait, she walks up to her and takes it. Not long ago I was laying on the bed with Tetley and Lexie came in for her spooning session, edging closer and closer to Tetley. I thought it was cute until I realised she was going in for the uneaten treat between Tetley's paws.

Lexie's ability to wait for food is the same as Tetley's ability to focus on a ball. Tetley stood sideways with her ears cocked, the fuzz on her ears perked, nudging the ball toward you, backing up, wiggling, staring at you, then the ball and back again while she waited. Over and over she did this. We learned to break her fixation on the ball and reward her for looking at us.

This helped reduce her insanity at times. She always caught on quickly when she was rewarded. We learned to hold the ball away from us at arm's length and only when she looked us in the eye, would we throw the ball or stick. She picked it up quickly and it helped us control the sheer frenzy that was her drive for fetch.

Lexie was the same with peanut butter. When we needed Lexie to leave Tetley alone so she could fetch without the drama of having to fight Lexie for the ball or stick, we traded a peanut butter tub or peanut butter-filled kong for peace.

When Lexie got the toy or stick she wasn't giving it up easily. She never listened to give or drop commands. Tetley wanted to fetch and Lexie didn't want her to fetch. Sometimes she would take Tetley's ball and lay on it so she couldn't get it or she would chew up her stick, leaving it in shreds and tatters so there was nothing left to play with.

Lexie would not let go when she had it. Tetley was on one end begging for the toy and Lexie was on the other, withholding the toy. For my own sanity some days I placated Lexie with skims of peanut butter so Tetley could get an uninterrupted game of fetch so I could buy some work time. My life was a series of negotiations, which I was constantly losing.

When Lexie saw the peanut butter tub she dropped every-thing and ran. Justin says she's the only person who loves peanut butter more than me. It was the only joyful food I had when I was training for fitness competitions so it became a staple in my diet.

Lexie could lay on the ground with her Kong or peanut butter toy and stay there for hours. When I put her in the bath I distracted her with a splat of peanut butter on the tub surround wall, not that she needed it, Lexie was good and easy in the bath, but Tetley needed a catch pole and taser to be bathed. For a dog who loves to swim, the bath was a nightmare.

In the evenings I enjoy a cup of tea with a tablespoon of peanut butter, strange I know. The hot tea melts the natural peanut butter and gives it a little something extra. Lexie sits in front of me on the couch with drool dripping everywhere, begging for peanut butter.

I started taking 2 spoons of peanut butter so she can get some licks as well. She had a problem enjoying it and grabs the clump of peanut butter every chance she gets. I started putting it in a small dish and just took a tiny bit on the spoon and let her lick it, trying to get her to take her time with it.

The real problem is she thinks the couch snacks never run out. I have to show her empty spoons, bowls and even my hands and say "all gone" to get her to understand there's nothing left but she never believes me. She keeps staring up with her puppy dog eyes, pawing my leg or the couch and begging.

I usually have to leave the room to get her to understand there's nothing left. She can be focused when she wants the snacks and she will eventually get the snacks. Tetley is the same with fetch because she knows she will eventually get her way. Someone will eventually pick up the ball and throw it. Lexie will eventually get Tetley's snacks.

They developed an obsession with water bottles and popping the stoppers off the bottles. Tetley started it and Lexie always copied her. People nicknamed them copy and paste because of their colour but also their habits. Lexie did everything Tetley did!

Tetley started with water bottles in the studio because of the crinkling sound they made when she chewed them. She then started popping the stoppers off and spitting them out. She never swallowed them but loved to get them off.

Lexie caught on and started doing the same. They begged for the plastic water bottles at the end of class. Everyone guzzled their leftover water and handed over the bottles. Lexie would body-check Tetley to get the bottles from her. This was their end-of-class ritual for years. The good side is people drank all of their water and the girls had a pastime.

They sat and waited during each class for the water bottles and they knew the ones they could have. They never tried to get the refillable ones and some clients, like Mary Ann, brought extra ones from home. They could really wait and focus on something when they wanted it.

I can get hyper focused on tasks and let everything around me slide but Tetley always forced breaks for me.

It's a different kind of focus - tasks versus projects. I can lose myself for weeks in writing or project creation. Without Tetley to force me to take breaks I never would. I found the girls are great at task-based focus. They are doing one thing when they're doing one thing. They don't get distracted from the tasks at hand. Lexie is more easily distracted or gets bored if it's not about food, she moseys from thing to thing but each thing she's doing she's all in when she's doing it.

We can't get what we don't focus on. Lexie often steals Tetley's stick or ball when she returns with it. Lexie has very rarely chased a stick, but she has grabbed it when she gets the chance after Tetley has done the work. She wants Tetley to chase her but she never does.

When we create focus we can create unstoppable momentum in what we're doing. Perhaps the best thing the dog helped me focus on was routine. I'm variety driven, more like Lexie, while I can focus when I want to, especially on something I really want, I do like change and can also be found wandering around after too much routine.

Routine is critical for success. Tetley gave me that routine. Lexie never cared about what we did. Tetley has been like clockwork her entire life. She knows the days of the week and most importantly, the time. She knows how long my workouts are and when it's her turn.

Until the last couple of years, Tetley's rise time was 5 a.m. It didn't matter if it was winter or summer. She was up and that meant I had to get up too. If I tried to get a weight training session in or a spin session she would show up in the basement with minutes left to the workout.

As she aged and didn't do the stairs anymore she barked at the top of the stairs to let me know my time was up. I felt like I was always on a timer. Every day at 2:30 p.m. she started looking for her adventure. The time started because of my fitness work in the city. Before she was coming with me to work, she got a walk when I got home. This became habitual and was impossible to break, no matter how much I tried.

She always figured out Justin's schedule, even when it changed as he changed projects. About 15 minutes before he got home, she went outside and sat on the patio waiting for him. When he pulled in, her tail would wag and she ran to greet him.

Tetley created a schedule and lifestyle that we had to stick to and that lifestyle created focus. In our focus we created ritual and ritual is what made our lives what they became. Her ability to focus on routine gave us the daily need to get out and explore the world around us.

It also creates a fairly rigid schedule we could thrive in. While our adventure gave us the variety we craved so it wasn't all the same old road walks, river swims or forest walks, it was our routine that kept us focused on what was ultimately important.

I found the use of social media, work, and phones kept me more distracted than I care to admit. When I lost focus on my health it was because I was too distracted. Too often I am late because I wasted time online doing nothing important. I have lost hours to the scroll when I could have been making a nice dinner or getting a workout in, going for a walk or taking time for myself. Distracted is the easiest thing in the world to be. Tetley has such incredible routine and focus that it continues to remind me of the need to create routine. While adventure and variety and lollygagging are important, focus is the thing that will allow us time to lollygag without feeling guilty or not getting done what we need to get done.

Tetley forced me to become dependable. Our schedule had to account for her. My schedule had to become tighter for her. Dependability and commitment are the cornerstones of focus. In order to have focus we have to be dependable and committed. When we want something we need to focus on it to bring it to fruition. Wanting is simply not enough, we must take action.

Tetley has taught me the power of focus in achieving my goals. There is no way to get what we want except to focus on it and stay focused on it until we have it.

How much more would we be able to enjoy life if we learned to compartmentalise our goals - work hard and play hard? How much more effective could we be if we focused on one task at a time? So, if we're chasing the ball we're chasing the ball? Then when we're finished, we're chewing the grass but we're not chewing the grass while we're chasing the ball and choking on the grass while we're trying to catch the ball?

The power of focus allows us to bring ourselves fully to a task or a moment and gives us back our power at that moment. We feel alive and create core memories because we are fully there. How often have we all punched a full day and can't remember it? How often have we driven somewhere and can't remember the drive? How often have we walked the dogs, but weren't even there?

We always think we have time. We always think that after this or after that, things will settle, and we will focus on and spend more time with people. But it never comes, and we end up feeling guilt and shame about it. We want to be better, but we are too often distracted. We are living a nightmare instead of a dream.

I watch Tetley in the water, even today, and I see how determined and focused she is on that one task, and I wonder if I brought that into all aspects of my life, to be focused at that moment on what I am doing, how much better would my life be?

Focus isn't just about achievement, though there is great power in that, it's also about our lives and the lives we're living and how we want to live them. One thing that keeps me focused is my fear of regret. I always envision the end of my life, walking down the tunnel, and meeting the person I could have been. That drives me to focus and live the life I want to and not settle for one I don't.

Focus is perhaps the most underrated trait or quality we could learn from our dogs, whether it's the focus on getting a belly rub or a snack or the focus on chasing that stick until we can't go anymore. What we gain from focus is more time for things we want to spend time on. It also brings us presence and that brings us peace and alignment and makes us feel alive and connected to our lives.

CHAPTER 9
STUFF DOESN'T MATTER

Me & Tetley at my trash the dress shoot.

When we picked Lexie up we didn't have anything ready for her. We weren't expecting to get a dog that day so we used Tetley's kennel for her and steel baking bowls for food and water until we could get to the pet store to pick up things for Lexie.

We bought her a new kennel, bowls, leashes, collars and a new tag for her, with her name and our number. She was ours then. If she was lost, someone would call us. It's an odd thing, really, in retrospect, how we just go get an animal and call it ours, put a tag on it and that's that. We spend all of our time with them and we don't even speak the same language.

We learn to understand each other but they don't know the basic information about us, where we work, what we do, our names, how much money we make - not that they care. It's just interesting how we give so much of ourselves to each other when the stuff that matters between humans doesn't matter between dogs and us. Although, sometimes I'm sure they know when I have extra money because they always seem to need the vet when I'm planning something for myself!

We set up Lexie's kennel in my office, a converted bedroom. It was large and had a lot of room, with a view of the driveway and the front yard. Tetley had a bed in there as well and Lexie's kennel was put there so they could be with me when I was working. We took Tetley's old kennel and gave it to Lexie, and gave Tetley the new one.

I really thought that Tetley would like the new kennel, like a child almost, the oldest would get the new thing and the younger would get the hand-me-downs. Tetley was vicious.

She wouldn't use her new kennel and we kept finding her in Lexie's kennel. Tetley's kennel was in the spare bedroom and while she never used it, suddenly, she was all about the kennel Lexie was in.

We wondered if it was because it was hers, with her scent and smell. We switched them around, giving Tetley back her old one and Lexie the new one. Tetley went to her kennel in the spare room and Lexie went to her new kennel in the office.

After a couple of days, Tetley abandoned her kennel again, laying next to Lexie's kennel or on one of her several beds around the house, the couches or my bed. She was letting me know that the kennel was hers, even though it was older. Lexie never cared about what she had but Tetley was territorial.

It was a big lesson for me about the girls and what matters to them - not a whole lot. They want love, attention, affection, kindness, and food and that's about it. Nice things, fancy things, and new things don't really matter to them.

We spend so much of our time collecting and worrying about stuff instead of memories. We've been conditioned to a capitalist society of better and constantly upgrading our things. The dogs taught me, constantly, that stuff doesn't really matter.

Many years ago, I wanted the dog beds to be aesthetically pleasing and suit the decor of the house. I ordered beautiful brown wicker beds with burnt orange cushions from Pier One Imports. They had legs that brought the beds a couple of inches off the floor and had to be shipped to me because they weren't stocked in the local store. When they arrived, I fell in love with them. The girls hated them. I removed their $25 Costco beds and forced them into the beds, which they fought their way out of.

I tried giving them rewards for staying in the beds to no avail. I held out for a week, determined to get the upper hand and have something nice! All my furniture and accents were brown, and I was starting to feel like I was living in the 80s with the brown decor to match the fur and dirt they were trekking through the house constantly.

I lost. They lay by the beds, staring at me in defiance. They would go to their beds in the bedroom, my office and even their kennels before they would get into those wicker beds. I finally gave up, put them for sale on the local marketplace and brought the Costco beds back in from the garage.

It wasn't the last time I tried to get them in swanky beds,

either. I kept looking for something larger that they might like and closer to the floor. I wondered if the base didn't feel stable enough for them. I found beautiful large handcrafted wooden dog beds but was quickly dismayed when I realised it was $899 *and* in California. Shipping and exchange rate to Canada meant more than I wanted to spend to test out something that in all likelihood wouldn't work. I wasn't in *that* much denial.

I posted to social media asking if anyone knew of someone who could make one. A fitness client reached out to me and told me her husband made furniture but he had not done it for anyone outside of the family before.

He charged me less than half of the fancy store price in California and I commissioned it. Hopeful. It is incredibly beautiful and I ordered 1 to see if they would use it. It has a drawer in the bottom for their collars, hankies, and clothes. They refused it. I managed to get Tetley on it once and she stayed there for an hour or so. Lexie also spent an evening on it. But that was that.

That was the last time I tried to fit them into anything fancy or nice.

I like nice things, who doesn't? But my father used to say who needs enemies when you have children or pets, they'll destroy everything you own. They ruined 2 of our vehicles and a friend's husband's truck. Tetley ate saltfish from dad's flake one summer and threw up in the car on the way home. In the dead heat of summer, fish and throw-up were smashed into the carpet.

We didn't have air conditioning in the Saturn I was driving at the time and we ended up stopped in a traffic accident. We weren't stopped long but it was long enough for her to get sick. It would take months of vinegar and baking soda to remove the stench. We'd still get an occasional whiff of it from time to time when the weather was hot and I sometimes wonder if the new owners ever get the smell.

There was mud everywhere. It was ground into the fabric and even grooves in the door of the vehicle and seats. I traded in my Mazda protege for the Saturn because the protege had non-stop problems. It was second hand and I went through wheel bearings like most people go through underwear. I settled on the Saturn, second-hand, from a dealership. The ad said air conditioning. I bought it in April so I didn't immediately notice it didn't have it. As I was about to pull out of the parking lot, with everything completed, including payment, I realised there was no a/c button.

The dealer tried to convince me the sunroof was the same as a/c. I knew better but Justin told me if I wasn't happy with the vehicle he would take it and I could get a new one. So I took the refund he gave me and left in the Saturn. After the hot summer with no air conditioning, I upgraded to an SUV. Not only was I tired of Newfoundland winters in a car but I was done with 2 dogs and no a/c so Justin got the fish-smelling trashed Saturn.

I picked out a GMC Terrain, it was large enough for the girls, extra dogs, people and our hiking gear. Tetley used to stand on the armrest hanging out the window with her entire weight on the door, eventually ripping the entire side panel off the door.

You can imagine having to explain to GMC how the door panel was ripped off. We had it replaced but she did it again. I upgraded to a Mazda SUV a few years later, traded in the Terrain, and left the door in shambles. The Mazda salesmen had a good laugh at it, especially when they knew it was the second time. He suggested I might need an army tank and Justin always told me an old Astrovan, converted, was what I needed. He felt it was all we should have, given the state we usually returned in.

Justin got so mad at us for how reckless we were. He would go on and on about how hard we work for things and why would I let the dogs destroy them. It's good to keep your things in good shape. We work hard and should take pride in it. While I normally give it as good as I get it, in these instances, I would just take it because he was right. Carolyn listened to the same things at home with her husband's vehicle. I mean they were right, but they just had no idea what it was like out on those trails with a bunch of wild animals. We did eventually start taking buckets of water, but the damage was done and ultimately, we knew that one day we'd have new shiny vehicles that we would only wish for their dirt and hair to be filling them.

I tried to keep my perspective on the bigger picture that yes, we work hard for our things, and it's good to keep them in good condition, but we also are living and using things to add to our lives and not just keep them in showroom quality while living perfect lives. At least that's what I kept saying to get out of trouble!

There was the one time I purchased a back rack for the SUV and committed to putting them in the hatch, blocking them from the vehicle so they would be safe and my vehicle would stay clean. I mean, I didn't *love* a dirty vehicle but twice-daily adventures meant it was hard to keep clean. Plus, wet dogs have been my eau de perfume for years.

All that happened is they ripped the rack down on top of themselves and I had to pull over on the highway to take the rack off them as they pinned themselves under it. I put it back in place but then they knew it was moveable, so they just kept doing it and eventually, they won and got access back to the entire vehicle.

We have a big bog ditch on our property. Bog is a really dirty smelly sort of rotten mud. Tetley discovered this hole when we moved here and it became her favourite place to go... she loved that bog hole. She played fetch until her tongue was almost touching her toes. She would beeline it to the bog hole to slam her belly in and cool off. She rolled in it and would grind her head and face into it. It stank to high heavens and she loved it.

She came out of it looking like something coming out of the depths of hell. She only stopped going there last year when her mobility or dementia, or both, took over.

I cannot count the times I had to hose her off, sometimes two and three times a day, or how many times during workouts she would come out of the bog looking like a black lab and run to people with her ball, shaking bog and dirt everywhere, sending people running and screaming.

Anytime I had an appointment or somewhere to be you could be assured she got in that bog hole and I would be standing in the driveway, dressed in stilettos, hosing off a rotten dog, or 2, while swearing like a sailor.

I would text or tell Justin about it later, venting my frustration with that bog hole asking him to put a fence around it so they couldn't get in it. One day he stood staring at me asking if I was "for real?" "Yes, I am, you're not the one who has to deal with it every day" I retorted.

"Where do you think she gets it?" He asked. I stared back silently as he reminded me of the days of Tough Mudder training and him having to hose off a yard full of women who were crawling through the bog holes in the woods, or the culverts at the playground. "She gets it from you. When you stop crawling through bog, maybe she will too".

I hate it when he's right.

Tetley introduced Lexie to the bog hole almost as soon as she moved in. It was their favourite pastime. If they went missing from your sight, you could be sure they were in the bog hole. We might be having a chat or a workout outside then you'd hear the splashing. Lexie loved it as much as Tetley, maybe more.

I was cleaning my vehicle one day and per normal, Tetley brought me her ball and I would throw it while cleaning and vacuuming. Lexie was either next to me, trying to intercept the ball or otherwise dawdling around.

I knew they had gone to the bog hole and planned to walk to the river and let them swim the dirt out of their fur. When I finished cleaning and was putting everything away, I called them only to discover that Lexie was nowhere to be found. I panicked because she never left my side. After checking the road, and the neighbours' houses, I returned to get in my vehicle to broaden my search, only to notice the back door was ajar. I must have not closed it all the way.

As I walked onto the patio I saw the muddy paw prints. I hesitantly walked into the house and followed the paw prints through the kitchen and into the hallway, directly into the spare bedroom and there she was, in the bed. She had shaken off before she lay down, of course, so for good measure, the bog was from one end of the room to the other and onto the ceiling. She was four paws to the wind and couldn't understand why I started screaming 'get out!".

I spent an entire day cleaning it off and I'm sure it was only covered up fully when it was repainted. They loved to be dirty more than they loved anything else. There was always something to get into.

They regularly went missing and not because we let them roam or weren't on a leash. We fenced 10,000 square feet for them and put locks and gates in after we adopted Lexie because we quickly discovered that two dogs on clotheslines was a serious safety issue. Lexie would get tangled in Tetley's tie out and often end up clotheslined when someone threw the ball for Tetley as she would take off, wiping Lexie out. Lexie would crawl under the patio and walk, tightrope style, on the basement concrete wall... thankfully she never fell and hung herself but it was a risk, so we installed fencing.

But Tetley learned how to open the gate, of course, because a fence is still a cage. They made the NTV news with their video of her popping the lock and using her paw to open the gate. We had to change the locks to the outside so she couldn't open them. She used her nose to nudge the hook out of the lock, then she hit the gate, which opened inward, to get it to bounce back then she used her paw and nose to push open the gate door. Lexie, always at the ready, ran out first and Tetley followed.

We kept wondering why the gate was open and thinking we weren't locking it or even blaming each other for leaving it open accidentally or not closing it all the way. We started to notice her picking at it. She watched the windows and patio doors to see if we were watching her. If we stayed there, she lay down so we had to hide in the corner of the door, where she couldn't see us, but we could see her. We knew she was smart but this was next level.

When she got out she lay in the yard watching the house, most times not going anywhere but letting us know cages or gates wouldn't stop her. She wasn't going to be kennelled when she was 7 weeks old, and she certainly wasn't going to be locked in as an adult.

This wasn't a big deal when we were nearby and able to watch them, but I often had online calls or was working on something in my office, only to see them running out the driveway or check on them, see the gate open and they were nowhere to be seen.

Thankfully they rarely went far, usually just to the neighbours around us or in the woods somewhere or checking out something they heard or smelled but one day I couldn't find them anywhere. It was a normal occurrence for me to panic text Justin and say "I can't find Tetley" and she would turn up a few minutes later covered in dirt and bog having gone somewhere nearby through the woods. She was never remorseful or apologetic.

One day they were gone longer than normal and there were no signs of them in a couple of places they usually went. My fear started to rise, especially as Lexie very rarely left. I was getting close to 25 minutes of searching when I finally found them. I was walking the road, having checked the neighbours and in the woods behind the house to no avail.

Suddenly, I could hear them, and I followed a little dirt road to a piece of land that had been for sale for a long time. Sometimes on our walks, we went in there and through the woods behind it. There wasn't a path we hadn't combed over.

I couldn't see them but I could hear them. When I came into a clearing in the woods, I saw them inside a dead moose. The moose must have been hit by a car and died, a frequent thing in our area because it was a whole moose. Lexie was inside its rib cage rolling around and Tetley was tearing its leg off, with her back legs planted and the full force of her weight tearing at it. She's pulled entire trees out of the ground so getting its leg was just a challenge.

I was horrified. My worst nightmare was in front of me. Mud and dirt are one thing but a rotting animal? Tetley was yanking with everything in her and Lexie was rolling with everything in her. I have never been so violently ill, horrified and relieved at the same time. I dragged them home calling them dirtbags. They were not sorry. If someone who didn't have the full picture heard or saw me that day they'd think I was a horrible dog owner. Lexie had maggots in her eyebrows and Tetley had blood everywhere, embedded in her fur.

I walked to the river and let them swim off the maggots and blood. When we got home I took out the purple elephant kiddie pool, put on gloves, used the dog shampoo and scrubbed and scrubbed while I retched, dry heaving at the smell. They still stunk. I put them in the hatch of the SUV and went to the river, again, armed with shampoo. It took over a week, and a groomer, to get the stench off them.

And that wasn't the only time for a stinky roll. My friend Alex and I took her 2 dogs, Molly and Tulo, and Tetley and Lexie to Cupids for a hike. It was late summer and the capelin had rolled a month or so before. There was a fairly inaccessible beach on this hike, with a steep scale down to the beach. It was possible but tricky to get down unless you had 4 legs and a desire for rotting stuff.

As we rounded a corner we smelled the rotting capelin. On most beaches where the capelin rolls people collect it. It still stinks but there's far less of it as people take most of it. I avoid the oceans after the capelin rolls.

This beach was covered in rotting capelin. Lexie and Molly bolted to the beach, down over the bank and started rolling in it. Tetley was a little behind and I managed to catch her, leashing her, as Alex scaled the bank to the beach, chasing the dogs while screaming bloody murder.

Lexie was in her glee, and Tetley was rotted that I had caught her. Alex had caught Tulo so he didn't get in. She manhandled them back up the bank. Lexie was covered in slimy rotting capelin and maggots, as was Molly.

I was urging from the stench of her. We found a cleaner beach to try to scrub her off but it was useless. We made our way back to my SUV where the 2 clean ones were put in the backseat and the dirty ones were put in the hatch. I tied them down so they couldn't get capelin on the fabric or roof of the vehicle.

I felt bad but I'd need to burn my vehicle if they got rotting capelin in it. I covered them with towels to contain the debris.

I stopped at a store in Brigus and bought fishermen's gloves and soap. All they had was Irish Spring. I didn't think of dish liquid at the time, which may have been better. We headed to the same beach I've taken the girls many times, with the picnic area and lookout, next to the cave. I picked up a couple of cans of beer, too. I felt we deserved a drink.

I got into the water up to my waist, scrubbing and urging. The stink wouldn't come off but at the least the capelin pieces did. It was a hot summer day so Brigus was alive with tourists, including a wedding party, getting their pictures, and watching me scrub the dogs with soap. I dried them off, headed to the grassy picnic area, stayed for a while, and had a beer and some takeout while we relaxed. It took a few baths to get her clean that day. I'm not sure how I managed to save the vehicle but I did.

Through it all, they taught me to care less about stuff and know that things are replaceable. Money can always be made, and things can always be replaced but time, dogs or people cannot. The best way of living is to be in the moment with stuff. It's good to take care of our things but not put things above the quality of life or the relationships in our lives.

Dog beds are replaced every couple of months because they

are dirty, wet and smelly. I replaced the bed sheets on our bed every 6 months because someone was always digging in the sheets and ripping them open. I started buying the cheap bamboo ones for $30. Meanwhile, they turned out to be more comfortable.

Lexie popped all the buttons off just about everything. She had a sleepover with Mary Ann and Mark, and she ripped the eyes out of the doorstops and several decorative teddy bears. She loved to get into the blankets and suck on them. She still does this. She stuffs her mouth full and rocks back and forth as she sucks the blankets. We assume it is a soothing exercise or that she was taken from her mom too young.

She ripped open the duvet covers and the decorative pillowcases. It was a favourite pastime to the point we stopped putting stuff on the spare bed and just put a protective mattress cover and old sheets and only did the bed up when people were coming to stay.

They dove into the shower and ripped the curtain to pieces, several times each, and they grabbed the ends of the towel when I was trying to dry myself, or them off, and would do the death shake, what we called it, where they would intentionally tear it to bits. If they heard it rip it was like music to their soul and they couldn't wait to leave it in shreds. The same with their toys. Before Lexie came, Tetley had all sorts of toys that she kept, she tore them open occasionally, but she mostly destroyed herself with fetch and playing. She loved the squeaking and relentlessly squeaked her toys.

Justin named her toys, and she knew each one. We would ask for Peter the skeeter and she would run and get her green mosquito toy. Marsha the moose was another one. She could have a basket of them and always go get the ones we asked for. When Lexie moved in they just destroyed everything. Tetley had her indoor and outdoor toys but Lexie dragged everything outside and back inside. She never listened so the toys made their way in and out. She'd take them out, then back in, and I would toss them back again.

They each got on one end of a toy and dug in their back legs and used their whole body to rip it into shreds. Stuffing went everywhere. Justin tried to stuff them back together and tell them to stop but I enjoyed watching them just bust out their energy and see how much joy they had in tearing something to pieces. He said they got their spite from me.

They were the same in the woods. Mornings were usually my free time because I taught fitness classes in the evenings. I often didn't start seeing clients until 10 a.m. and some days a little later. That made our mornings the time for adventures.

I took my time in the mornings and brought my workout gear on a forest walk. Justin built a makeshift bench in the woods for us so we could bring tea or a place I could sit and enjoy meditation or a morning without rushing. We nicknamed it Fred Penners. They always joined us and, in the clearing where we spent our time was a giant dead tree that had branches bigger than me. It was enormous. Within a few months, they had ripped all the branches off and even ate away at most of the tree itself.

Just this week I went to Fred Penners and laughed about how they cleared the area because they cracked and ripped branches off the trees. Lexie would lie down and chew on the stick, destroying it and Tetley would drop hers for a game of fetch. She eventually gave in to the destruction desire and lay with Lexie and shredded her stick, too. We often wondered how many splinters they had. Once, Lexie cracked a tooth off and required surgery to remove the base and pulp and so that ended the days of letting them chew sticks.

Vanessa and I were working out one morning, doing an outdoor workout, early in the pandemic. The girls joined us for tire flips and running sprints in the driveway. Tetley was playing fetch with Lexie intercepting her, body-checking and throwing her in the air. An otherwise normal day in my house.

They eventually both got sticks from the fire pit pile and lay down chewing. That evening Lexie showed signs of pain with excessive drooling. I checked her mouth and it looked like she was a missing tooth. I gave her pain medication and a vet check the next morning showed it was cracked with the pulp exposed. She needed surgery.

Lexie chewing a stick.

No more sticks. Our lessons were usually hard learned and expensive. They taught me to care less about money and things. I had no choice! Lexie lost everything. She came out of the woods without her clothes, coats, collars, tags and even her safety jacket once.

Because of the hunting close by I put orange safety vests on them in the fall during hunting season. Technically we were too close to houses for hunting but that didn't always stop people. Once we heard a gunshot very close and saw smoke rising up from the trees just across the marsh. I bought safety vests that day. Everything for large dogs is expensive and Lex always needed extra large. Hers was $59 and she promptly lost it.

We were in the woods for our morning trek and she vanished. I heard her whimpering so I called her but I couldn't see her. She showed up a minute later with no vest. I said, "Lexie! How do you do this!". She reminded me of myself as a child, losing my lunch money every single day.

They have dozens of collars for all sorts of occasions with matching tags. Or at least Tetley still does. Lexie lost every tag she had. We managed to keep 3 in the last couple of years but that's only because she doesn't go anywhere anymore.

Justin had to go to the woods and crawl through the brush to find her safety jacket. He did. He said it was caught on a twig. The velcro strap was broken so she pulled enough to get loose. Oh, Lexie!

Stuff is meant to be used. People often remark that I wear good brand-name clothing in the woods, and I always reply "I bought good gear to wear on an adventure and the purpose for which I bought it". What's the good of great gear in the closet?

Stuff has become synonymous with who we are as people, and we often reflect more on the things we have than the love or people or beauty we have around us. In the end, what will matter? Stuff or how that stuff helped us live the most amazing life? Would teddy bears and collars and the seat of my car be better in perfect condition which I could proudly display in a museum, or would a chunk ripped down to the steel of the steering wheel be a funny core memory as we incredulously wondered which one did it?

Who needs enemies right? We're almost certain Tetley did it out of spite. And she had plenty of that. We called it the spite bite because she would get so over-excited she would chew in a certain way on her toys, snorting and gnawing while doing it. We started playing puppets with her with the remnants of her toys as a baby. The ones she did destroy I would put my hand in and play puppets, changing my voice and talking to her with it. She would bite just hard enough because she knew it was my hand, but she would dive into that with all the spite she could muster. She loved the game of puppets.

When they stopped destroying their toys in their senior years we just played with the teddy bears that were intact and she still loved them. She nudges her teddies to let us know she wants to play. She attacks their faces with spite, biting their eyes and nose. She "gets them in the guts" when we tell her, biting their bellies for the squeaker.

Lexie never really got into the puppets game. She was a bit freaked out by it. I'm not sure if she understood the game or if she thought the toys were coming to life in those moments, either way, she wasn't into the game. Or perhaps Lexie was more intelligent than we realised? We always said she was the pretty one while Tetley was the smart one but perhaps she had us all fooled with her do de do de do behaviour. She licked the floors, and windows in the car and house, chased mosquitoes in the windows and lay on the back of the couch, while Tetley stared judgementally at her.

Lexie didn't like many of our games, thinking they were serious. Tetley always loved the intensity and had a game where we would tap the sides of her face and she growled and snarled and snapped, all in jest, we knew it, she knew it but Lexie didn't know it. She always gets in the middle of the game to break what she thinks is a fight.

When Tetley and I run around the island and play hide and seek in the house and she vocalises, Lexie body checks her, stopping it. We try to get her involved but she just doesn't like it. We call her the referee.

I suppose it's a bit different for Tetley, not only was she raised knowing the difference in play, and when to start and stop, she also was raised in wildness. Stuff wasn't something I cared about in the pursuit of adventure. After our wedding I hired a photographer, took Tetley with me and had a trash-the-dress photoshoot. We swam in a river, played fetched and lay in the middle of the road in my dress. Sure, I could have sold it and got some money for it. I could have left it in the closet in perfect condition. But what fun would be had in that?

Justin is right. They get it from me.

The girls might have destroyed a lot of stuff but in that destruction was a lot of living, fun and joy. They knew how to celebrate. They were always the first ones to know my good news. Because they were my coworkers I always told them my news and then threw on music for us to have dance parties. They loved dance parties. When we turned the music up and played hide and seek around the island and the house, they really loved to tear stuff up. Parties always ended in the destruction of something. But they are always ready for a party. They don't know why but they're here for it.

The floors have scratch marks, the cabinets have stain missing, the door frame is scratched up from toenails, the wooden bed frame has nail grooves in it and there's been more mud dragged along the walls than I care to think about. My vehicle is destroyed, so the 3rd one really, and I don't care. There are scratch marks on the leather sofa and I clean up paw prints, fur and mud constantly.

When I look at them I think of the life we've lived instead of the stuff we've lost. Stuff is to be used in living not to keep in perfect condition. And if it could help us live more and enjoy the moment more, we were willing to sacrifice a toy or a coat or even a vehicle in the pursuit of living in the moment and enjoying ourselves.

CHAPTER 10
FRIENDSHIP

Tetley. Chloe. Lexie on the East Coast Trail.

L iving in the moment meant having a lot of friends because we were always adventuring, we met people who wanted to adventure. Tetley and Lexie are very social creatures, not just with humans, but they have had many dog friends over the years. Only a couple of them are still alive, most of them having crossed the bridge, some many years younger than was fair and others into their old age.

I'm not sure that Tetley knew she was a dog. She went to the dog park sometimes and the dogs would jump all over her and she would seek out anyone with hands who could throw the ball. Lexie blended in with packs, she fit right in. Tetley hated dogs that took her ball or stick. Lexie was always doing that and she hated it.

That's why Chloe and Tetley got along so well. Chloe is Carolyn's Golden Retriever. She minded her own business and they peacefully coexisted, hiking, running, and walking many thousands of kilometres together. And Carolyn and I got along so well because we committed and followed through. We never cancelled. The first time Carolyn asked to join me I told her where I would be the next morning. She and Chloe showed up and I was surprised. Over the years many people had asked to join me but rarely committed. Carolyn and I committed.

I wouldn't be able to count the kilometres we drove or the amount we walked together. Because Lexie had elbow surgery when she was 2, she missed out on a lot of hikes and walks as that was the year we completed the East Coast Trail. The only hike Tetley and Chloe missed was The Spout Path to Petty Harbour. It was 34 km and while we wanted to take them we knew the path was rough terrain and we didn't want an injury.

We were glad we left them home that day because it was hot and gruelling. It was the first and only hike in my life I didn't think I would finish. I had to dig deep that day and overcome the mental blocks that were tearing me down. Several times I almost cried and at the 22 kilometer mark I had to sit for a bit. I looked at my phone and saw there was no cell service and I told myself "girl, get it together, there's only one way out and it's your feet!".

The day was gruelling. Normally the coast is cold and often foggy. Whatever the forecast is, it's usually much colder on the trails. The weather turned out hotter than forecast and I was sweating at 6 a.m. when we started the hike. The sky was cloudless and I would have paid good money for a snow bank that day. It was an incredible day until about kilometre 20 when the sun was at its peak. The whales were breaching the entire way and it felt magical until we went into a cliff that seemed like it would never end.

Despite filling up on water, and carrying plenty with us, we ran out. I found a sketchy stream but figured I could deal with the after-effects of getting sick instead of not making it out because of dehydration. I had 6 litres of water and we knew the river was clean. I had drunk more than 10 litres of water by the time we got off the trail and my arms were blistering in spite of sunscreen. I kept putting on and taking off my shirt. Too hot with it on and burning with it off.

By the time I finished, I could have cried when I landed my butt on someone's deck in Petty Harbour at the end of the hike. The hike literally ends on someone's property. He came out and offered me a ride and I turned him down. I said "no, I can make it that far ". Forgetting it was another 2 kilometres to my vehicle.

We had our driveway paved that day and I had to park in the neighbour's drive across the street. Justin had to come over and get me, carry my pack and walk me in a straight line, to get home. That night I showered on my knees and can't remember eating my supper, so I was grateful for having the sense to leave Tetley home for once.

As we were eating supper my parents showed up. My mother, who drove me to choose my own life, still worries endlessly about me and says "what is wrong with you?". Dad then proceeded to tell me about his rowing crew walking their boat to St. John's from Placentia to commemorate the 100th anniversary of the Placentia Giants rowing crew. They walked until the skin came off their feet. They rowed in between walking and made it to St. John's in 5 days. They took home the Triple Crown championship that year, the first crew to ever do it.

I looked at mom and said, "that's your answer to what's wrong with me. It's genetic. You married him so I come by this honestly".

Tetley trained for several Tely 10s, Tough Mudder, other road races and mud runs as well as just our daily walking and running. Lexie did some of them. I always took their photos with

the medals because they worked as hard as I did! If I was registered, they were training and so were Carolyn and Chloe.

From sunrise runs on the old railroad tracks to icy winter
hikes in Lamanche, from mountain tops and beach adventures,
we did it all together. The dogs got excited when they saw each
other's vehicle. Carolyn and I took 2 vehicles so we could park
on either end of the hikes. We met at the top of the Salmonier
line, Holyrood Access road or the Witless Bay line turn off and
drove together to the trail heads, dropped a vehicle and moved
bags and dogs from one vehicle to the other. Then we headed to
the start of the trailhead, fully loaded down with dogs, food and
gear with adventure running through all of our veins.

Chloe is mostly a normal dog. She didn't like to get wet and
her hair would blow in the wind like she was in a shampoo
commercial. She was a good girl unless you broke out chicken on
the trail and then it was all bets off. She turned into a wild
animal, forgetting her well-bred, well-raised manners and her
sheer prettiness. She liked to smile with her full teeth when
you'd see her and she liked you. I got her smiling teeth often,
and still do when I get to see her. She is a calm energy dog and
enjoyed the hikes and trails. Much like Lexie. She loved the
squirrels and gave chase, and she liked rolling in crap, to which
Carolyn would fill the air with profanities as she chased Chloe.

Chloe on the East Coast Trail.

We rarely saw anyone on the trails when we were out,

starting at daybreak and finishing by noon. It's a good thing too because we were like a bunch of wild animals out there. We can judge the dogs but they came by it honestly.

Where Chloe was calm and mostly well-behaved Tetley was insane. She ran through the bushes whacking the back of our legs with her stick. Because she was always covered in mud, so were the bushes she ran through, leaving us streaked full of mud too.

She slammed into me over and over again and the entire hike she would drop a stick in front of me, hiking and fetching 30 kilometres sometimes. I would occasionally have enough, it was frustrating sometimes, and I would grab her, sit her down in front of me, take her by the face, look her dead in her yellow eyeballs, and tell her all the reasons she had to be a good girl. Carolyn was always shocked when she listened. It was clear she did know the difference, she just didn't care. The talking to lasted about 30 minutes and I would have to do it all over again.

She flew down over banks into the ocean and I scaled down after her. I shoved her up the hills and cliffs where Carolyn grabbed her collar to help her back up. Lexie was usually here too but Tetley instigated and Lexie followed. Lexie missed a lot of those hikes because of her surgery.

On the Freshwater Path Trail in Fort Amherst, the last hike we did on the ECT we lost the path and scaled a small cliff, straight up the face of it. Carolyn got up first and I boosted the dogs up to her one at a time. Lexie was recovered at this time and was on the trail with us.

I propped each dog on my knee and hoisted them up. Carolyn grabbed harnesses and collars and I kept my hands on their hindquarters to boost them safely. Once we were at the top we saw a footpath that went around the cliff. That's how we did things. None of us looked for the easy way, usually, we only found it after we had already scaled the hard way.

Chloe and Tetley had magnificent adventures and their eyes shone when they saw the vehicles pull into our meeting places. I can still see Chloe's eyes and her long-haired tail standing straight out and see Tetley hanging out the window squealing and jumping because she knew it meant adventure.

All over the Avalon, they traipsed together. I've brought Tetley and Lexie over to visit Chloe a couple of times this year because they are all aging and Chloe is struggling as well. We haven't hiked together in years so we took them for a final adventure together last year to Salmon Cove Sands. It was a beautiful fall day, the sun was shining, and it was a great final adventure for them.

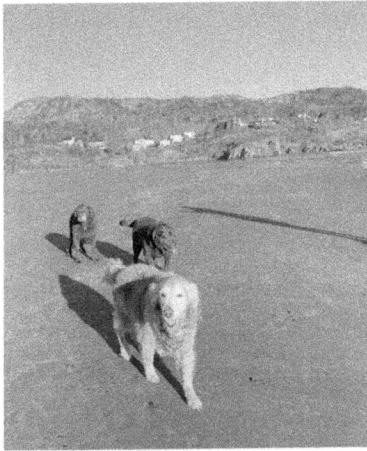

Tetley. Lexie. Chloe on their final adventure in Salmon Cove Sands.

Tetley was struggling with her mobility by then and while Lexie had been the one to normally struggle, she was now the better of the three. They had an incredible day, and we knew it would be their last adventure before it was impossible to take them. It was bittersweet because no one ever wants it to end. We never want it to be over and we never want it to be the last time. But we're glad we did it. It was good for all of our souls.

That's the thing about it being so good, we never want it to end. Sometimes we have a last walk, but we don't know it will be the last walk. We have an adventure, and we don't know it will be the last adventure. We take them for granted, and even when we don't, we still think there's tomorrow. One thing about age is that we can also plan and create those final adventures, even when they're hard for us, they can be those beautifully hard moments that fill our hearts while breaking them at the same time.

They loved all their dog friends and had many over the years but none like Chloe. It was just different with them. They had so many adventures together and they respected the differences and needs of each other. They gave each other the space they needed and Carolyn, Chloe, Tetley, Lexie and I became a fivesome.

My friend Kelsey's dogs, Daisy, Sydney and Harley, were part of their lives as well for many years. Daisy and Harley crossed the bridge a couple of years ago. Daisy is the face of the senior dog rescue, Furever Young. They had many play dates in the fields of Mount Pearl and the Southlands over the years whenever I was running errands and shopping, I would stop by for a visit and a walk with all of the dogs. Kelsey is always happiest surrounded by a pack of dogs. There's no one in my life that welcomes dogs quite like Kelsey does.

Kelsey in her happy place with Daisy,
Harley, Sydney, Tetley & Lexie.

It was her place we spent that one good New Year's Eve when Lexie was still reasonable to get out before her fear got too bad. She was scared so we wrapped her in blankets and all the other dogs were trying to comfort her. Not Tetley though. She was outside with Justin watching the fireworks.

Pepper was my parent's pit bull. She went to live with them after my brother moved away. Teddy was still alive, and Sailor, so they ended up with 3 dogs. Pepper was a brindle pit and she was a great dog. Tetley and Lexie loved to see Pepper and she loved to come to our house. As soon as Mom & Dad took the Salmonier Line turn off she sat up and got excited. We welcome dogs into our home. They were and are part of our lives and the people we loved too. Our home was always open to them. When we had socials there were as many dogs as people sometimes!

Pepper.

Pepper died at 16. The girls loved to go to Pepper's house, as we called it, and loved being in the bay at Mom and Dad's. Tetley was obsessed because there was always someone there to throw a ball for her. She loved the Boxing Day kitchen party at my parents' house. Kitchen parties are a Newfoundland tradition of our Irish roots, where people play music, eat and drink in the kitchen until all hours.

She stayed up with all the drunk people throwing a ball for her until 5 a.m. There were times we had to physically put her in a kennel to force a break.

Mom and Dad's house is like Grand Central Station. The

door is always open and there is always food on the stove and a crowd around. Friendship was a norm growing up for me and whether that friendship and sense of community included dogs or people it's one of the greatest pleasures in life - to have great friends.

Lexie was a little more sheepish, finding her security under the table at Mom and Dad's, or under a bed when it was time to ring in the New Year or it got too much for her. Tetley, on the other hand, had to be kept on a leash during those times because she loved the fireworks and the intensity of a Point Verde New Year. We stopped going to all the places because of how scared Lexie got and made our own New Year's Eve traditions at home.

There were a lot of dogs in their lives, including Dewy, my brother's dog who was the child of Pepper and Sailor. Let's not dive into that one. Tetley and Dewy lived together when we moved back to St. John's from Nunavut. We weren't sure about Dewy at first but he turned out to be a great dog friend. Sometimes I would think Dewy was being a jerk but my brother Craig told me once that he thought Tetley was setting him up. And sure enough, she was. After we moved into our house, I often pet-sit Dewy. He came on hikes and thoroughly lived his life. We nicknamed him Searl Snear because of his ears.

He walked as if a human wasn't attached to him and would almost dislocate my arm from my shoulder. He loved the bay life but was a city dog. He would go insane for the first couple of days and blow off his pent-up energy. When we went to the river he cannonballed in. I've never seen anything like that before or since. He would jump and go vertical and tuck his knees in and land straight down, sending up a massive splash. He didn't care about fetch, he just kept diving.

When he stayed with us Tetley would come running to me, acting as if Dewy was up to no good. One day I walked into the room and sat on the bed facing away from her but there was a mirror where I could see her. Dewy was scared to come into the room because Tetley was silently showing her teeth. I looked at her and she acted as if she feared Dewy! I looked away and she did it to him again! What a little skeet. She was busted! She did this to Lexie for many years as well. Lexie looks in the bedroom before she goes in, ears pinned back and eyes sideways to assess Tetley's mood.

Dewy died at home as a senior. He had just spent a few days with us and seemed ok then he went home and died in his sleep. Then there was my sister's dog Baylee, a Bernese Mountain dog who was such a good girl. We had a few sleepovers here and Tetley and Lexie would visit there often, and Baylee always came to our family events. She just recently passed a few months ago and was a great dog. Tetley loved to hump her and we're not exactly sure why. It's the only dog beside Lexie that she did it to. She did it to Lexie often!

Then there was Sailor of course, whom Tetley did get to meet. He was in his very senior years at that time and crossed the bridge just a couple of months after we moved to Newfoundland. And Hunter who was Lexie's BFF as my brother, Kevin and his wife Alyssa, got Hunter at the same time we got Lexie. He is an enormous Yellow Lab who is the family's claim to fame in his Air Lab commercial.

He and Lexie would play nonstop but Hunter grew into an extra large dog and Lexie stopped playing when she couldn't get the upper hand. Hunter is obsessed with Tetley though. He drools on her, follows her constantly and is always at her. We're not sure as she's spayed but he has a loving sight set on her and she never seems to mind, she puts him in his place when she's done with his antics.

There was Kuma, my sister's dog who was tragically killed by a car. And my friend Amber's dog Bandit who came on hikes and workouts to play with the girls. He passed away a couple of years ago. And Tetley's old friend Suze, Chad's dog. They loved each other. Tetley loved to go to Suze's house. She was a Jack Russel mix and she passed away a couple of years ago. She loved to push rocks around with her nose. Some of the rocks were twice the size of her!

And Eddy, of course, Christine's black lab who sends his Christmas card each year, in his full pose of a man who knows his value.

And there was Simon, who lived next door, a yellow lab. Simon was a spaz of a dog that loved Tetley and she loved him back. Lexie hated him. Or at least she didn't want him here for whatever reason. We thought it might be related to the foster dogs we had. It seemed that Lexie was scared dogs were going to come home and move in with us. She wasn't ok with that. Simon was bouncy and she was long out of the bounce stage by the time he arrived on the scene.

He loved Tetley though and he came over every day. Tetley and Simon had a relationship. She went there every morning at 8:00 a.m. She left every morning and walked out the driveway to visit him. Simon would come to our place every day too. I had to watch the food when he was around because he had a condition where he had to eat in a Bailey Chair. He couldn't swallow his food properly. He was a rescue and for a very long time we didn't know the neighbours' names, we just called them Simon's parents.

Simon was much younger than Tetley, but they loved each other. He often slipped his collar and came over. Other times he was dragging his tie out behind him, after breaking loose. His mom was always at our place looking for him and I was at theirs looking for Tetley. It was really pitiful when he couldn't get away but he could see us.

One day I noticed Tetley didn't go over to Simon's house. Initially, this was around the time she was struggling to get around, but she was still going over there every morning. I wondered at first if she couldn't do it anymore but after a couple of days, I noticed that Simon wasn't coming here either. The neighbours were away so I thought it might be just that Simon wasn't home. But when they arrived home from their holiday, still she didn't go over and he didn't come here, I knew something was wrong.

I reached out to them, and they told me he had passed suddenly. It was related to his condition. A few weeks later they told me that the morning after he died Tetley went over, stood in the yard, smelled around with her nose in the air, checked out the patio, left and never came back. She knew.

Simon & Tetley

I've watched the dogs have their friends over the years and seeing their excitement as well as their concern or acknowledgement when they're gone or hurt or not themselves is a powerful lesson about how important it is for us to cultivate friendships. Watching them excitedly welcome dogs and people was a joy to witness.

Dogs don't hold back. And not just for their dog friends. My girls get very excited when their people friends come to visit. It reminds me to be happier when I see my friends. It's ok to be real and honest but I try to remember less complaining and more laughing. We all need to do better at making each other feel as special as dogs make us feel.

I struggled with close friendships for much of my life, finding where I fit in and accepting myself and even being able and encouraged to be myself. Thankfully I have found incredible friendship in my life by being myself and doing what I love. The dogs brought me incredible connections as well...so many people I met because of the dogs.

Friendship is one of the most important aspects of our lives. People who have well-rounded lives have strong communities. As a Sociologist, I study society and how it impacts human behaviour. We know that people who are embedded in their communities and have solid friendships and trusting relationships are more grounded and happier.

People who don't have that put undue stress and pressure on their intimate relationships and it becomes their entire trust relationship. It's why when intimate relationships fail they are much harder for people who do not have a bigger network or community.

Me. Carolyn. Chloe. Tetley & Lexie. As usual my girls would not look at the camera.

The power of friendship cannot be underestimated and friendship that's developed in the woods is even more powerful than other friendships. I feel there's something deeply truthful about people who go into the woods together. And even more true when we involve dogs. Dogs bring out the best in us and when we let our guard down for others to see it, it creates a different type of friendship.

It's been my experience that a day in the woods with human friends and fur friends can take care of so much. A shaman I once worked with said there is something sacred about a walk in the woods, each step we take lets go of stress and problems and opens up our energy field.

The dogs gave me the woods. I had never really gone outside until I got them. The woods gave me friends, deep friends, real friends. The woods gave me my writing and the content for my work. It gave me fitness and hiking and retreats. It gave me adventure and soul.

There's not much in my life that I have that didn't come from the dogs in one way or another. I'm not sure that if I had gotten any dog other than Tetley that I would have created the life I did or found the true friendships that I did. Lexie isn't the type of dog who would have pushed that. She would have gone for walks, maybe, but she wouldn't have been the catalyst for adventure because she was always content. It was Tetley's lack of contentment that forced us to find adventure.

I grew up in a house where my parents valued friendship. They had many friends, and our house was always open. My brothers and my sister and I have grown up to be similar people who value people around us and we love good friends. Friendship is the thing that gets us through life both for the good and bad. Friends add to our lives, but they also hold us up when we need them.

The circle I cultivated became the most supportive people I knew. It didn't happen by chance, it happened by choice. My girls helped me be myself and because of that, I found amazing people. When we aren't authentic we won't find authentic friends.

My friends are the first to buy my books, support my work, share my blogs and my words, and support my business, but more than that they are there for the hard times.

It's amazing to have people who are there for you. Like Nancy. She is my ride or die friend. Nancy is the friend I can say "Wanna go to Peru this week?" and she says "Heck, yes!". Nancy and I went to a Madonna concert in Toronto a few years back, getting there to discover the hotel gave away our room. It was the Toronto International Film Festival and several massive concerts were playing.

The hotel found us a single room well out of town and we took it - for $450 a night. Our hotel had been booked months in advance at a $150 rate. We got a taxi and kept saying "It's just money". That's become our motto. Life is happening. Sometimes it goes sideways and we just gotta go with it. Nancy is the friend who booked her trip to Nashville as soon as she found out my book launch for "Unchained" was happening there and flew to Newfoundland for the book launch here. She said, "I invited myself". Friends who make us feel like we matter are special. The people who remind us that we are a big deal are the friends we need to keep close.

We need ride or dies. We need friends who we can call and say "let's go" and they say yes. Tetley is my ride-or-die in dog form. Nancy is my ride-or-die in people form. But it's not all just about the good times. Life is a balance of amazing and awful and we need to have friends and people who can be with us in the valleys and not just at the peaks.

Friendship is critical for everyone; community is the thing that makes us whole and offers a place where we can give and receive. To see the dogs light up when they see each other and how excited they are is proof that dogs too have friends. To see them light up when they see people they like or like Chloe to give a full tooth smile is all the reward we need for the selfless-ness of the dogs in our lives.

Friends in our lives should be the same way. They should support us, lift us up, help us, and clap when we're winning. If they're not, then we need new friends.

I have found incredible friends that are with me during the

good and bad in life. I've found, as I've gotten older, that quantity is less important than quality. The people who can be with you at your lowest are the ones who you need to foster relationships with. The people who lean in when you're down, the people who let you cry, sob and even scream when you need to are golden souls that are hard to find.

I've discovered that true friendship is about accepting people for who they are and not becoming who they want you to be. When we can be our whole selves, like Lexie who sprawls off for a full belly rub, or Tetley who throws a dirty stick in your face, the faster we show people who we are, the faster we can get on with choosing.

Lexie never made Simon feel welcome. She didn't put on a show for him, act ok with him being here, nor did she stay outside with him. She just got up and went into the house. If he tried to go in, she blocked his way. She let me know what she liked and didn't like.

It's taken me a long time in life to discover true friendship isn't always about those that are at your mountaintops. I've found that real friends are the ones who can sit with you in the depths of the darkness. And they are the ones who deserve to be at the mountaintop with you.

Many of my friends really showed themselves this year, as I've punched one of the hardest years of my life. Justin's been away most of the year, working, Tetley has been sick, and I've struggled with keeping on top of everything. Our property is large and our life was set up for 2 people.

I lost the bulk of my business during the pandemic and had to start over. I had made a rash decision to go back to school so my workload was high but so was my drive. I made it all work but it was a fine balance and nothing could go wrong or I would drown. Then our house flooded. Tetley got sick. And I was alone. Or so I thought.

But the amazing people in my life showed up. They came with buckets, shop vacs and pumps. I was surrounded by people. My father came with a heavy-duty pump, but my friends, Justin's dad Gord, and others showed up in the midst of it. Chrissy and her husband Dennis came and bailed water out of the basement all day. Vanessa shop vac'd with my mother all day, while my father pumped out the basement. Amber and her husband, Jerry, spent the day rigging up hoses and pumps. My uncle Kenny made a pump to bring to me. We had a winter storm that landed over 300 millimetres of rain. The frozen ground couldn't absorb it.

Tetley wasn't sleeping and I was exhausted. I was having nightmares of the house flooding and the roof collapsing and being churned into the ground like a vortex was pulling us into the mud as I was frantically trying to find the dogs. I was waking up with panic attacks constantly.

I was up all night with Tetley. I wasn't sleeping. Lexie was the constant, calm, presence getting me through it. Once Tetley's medication kicked in and started working, Vanessa and her daughter Sarah came to help me out, to let me get out of the house for a break, to go shopping, for a hike and they took care of Tetley and Lexie. Vanessa has been my biggest supporter this year, coming to work from my house so I can leave for work meetings when I have to go out, providing support that few would. She gave up her time and came so I could get out and not worry about Tetley while I was gone.

Chrissy and Vanessa stayed with the girls so we could sneak off for a quick long weekend to New York City. We really needed a vacation after the pandemic and the year we've had. Our travel is on hold because of the girls. They're just too old for us to leave now. If something happened we wouldn't forgive ourselves and we wouldn't want them to be without us if something happened.

Friendship isn't just about the good days when everything is amazing. It's also about the hard days. When the cards are down you get to see who people really are. My friend Jamie-Lynn, one of my best friends and the biggest supporters of my work and I spent many days walking around Topsail Beach and Manuals River, talking business, with the dogs running around, splashing in and out of every puddle we could.

We sometimes skirt into the woods on topsail beach, have a fire, and burn things. Or Jamie would stay over for sleepovers as we chatted business, and planned for the future with Lexie jammed between us, sneaking licks.

My life motto is more friends, fires and fur bags will make us all happier. The thing about the woods is it opens us up to ideas, creativity, and adventure. We become someone else, or more of who we really are in these environments. I've found more innovation in the woods with friends than I ever have in a board room.

Vanessa and I spent a lot of mornings hiking to the lighthouse in Harbour Main. It's a hidden gem of a hike with a little bit of everything. On beautiful, and not-so-beautiful mornings, we hiked out, sat and drank our coffee or had a workout followed by a morning coffee.

My friend Chrissy has been a massive help this year, with Justin away. I am not handy at all. In fact, I'm the complete opposite of handy. She rescued me when my dishwasher gave out and flooded the kitchen. She taught me how to paint as we stayed up late too many late nights drinking Prosecco and painting the house during the pandemic.

She also taught me how to use a plunger and fixed my sink when the drain plug got stuck. She gave me the confidence to try things, giving me more independence. I have never used a lawn mower before and now I even use the snow plow.

I wouldn't have survived this past year without my friends. They were the backbone who taught me what I didn't know because men had always done it for me. They helped me when I desperately needed it and they companioned me in one of the hardest years of my life. They are companioning me still as I face the most devastating losses yet to come.

All of these women are in my life because of the woods and

dogs. We bonded over fitness, hiking, adventure, business and unconventional ways of living. We have been driven by the same desire - living more. All of us have dogs, love nature and find new ways to be more of ourselves instead of who the world told us to be.

These women have carried me this past year when I desperately needed support. They didn't ask me to be something I couldn't. They didn't tell me how to navigate it. They just stood by me while I had to carry what seemed to be an unreasonably difficult year.

I think friendship can be pretty easy if we take a page from the dogs. Be ourselves and be there for each other, good, bad and ugly. Walk away from the ones you don't connect with. Spend more time with the ones you do. That's the journey of life. It's not all sunshine and roses and the real test of who we are is how we show up when the going gets tough.

Dogs are there for the dance parties and the darkness. We need friends who are too. And we need to be those friends for others.

CHAPTER 11
FOLLOW YOUR INSTINCTS

Tetley in all her glory. Photo by Ken Reid Photography.

nimals have instincts. So do humans but humans' instinctual nature has been conditioned out of us. How often have we ignored red flags, gaslighting ourselves into thinking that we are insane or wrong or making it up? How often have we thought we are the problem, or we convince ourselves to go down a path that initially didn't feel good?

How often have we overthought something to the point of exhaustion only to end up not deciding anything at all? Animals don't do this. They have instincts that are far more in tune with nature and instincts than humans do. I've often yelled at the girls to stop barking only to discover a cat on the patio or a moose in the yard. Tetley hated a male fitness client I trained. She wouldn't let him near me. She stood between him and me with her tail between her legs and wouldn't let him get close.

She showed her teeth and vocalised her feelings. She didn't do this to other men so it wasn't just a stranger or a man thing. She had met hundreds of clients by that point and this was the first time this happened.

I had to kennel her and eventually stopped bringing her to the sessions because she made it impossible for me to do my job. I never forgot her reaction to him as it was so out of character for her. I trusted her reaction to him so I never let my guard down. He didn't renew his sessions so the problem worked itself out, but he kept saying how strange her reaction was, he said he loved dogs and dogs loved him. But I trusted her vibe.

If I have change in my console or in my pocket I give it to homeless people. It's not my place to judge someone's experience. Having worked in the homeless community in Nunavut and Newfoundland, I know there were some pretty heavy stories behind people who find themselves on the streets. Giving them a few coins or even bills might not change a lot for me but I know it can change a lot for them.

When I stopped at the lights if someone was asking for money, I'd wave them over and empty my change into their hand or bucket.

Tetley and Lexie put their heads out the window, getting petted by the men I was giving money to. As a man approached one day, I started putting my window down but Tetley came on top of the console, while Lexie was in the passenger seat, with her teeth barred and foam dripping from her mouth. She was freaking out. She startled me. Lexie was more likely to be scared and bark and this wasn't a bark, this was a message.

Tetley leaned across me, stepping onto my lap and she hit the driver's side window, snarling. Even Lexie was startled. The man backed up and I drove off, shaken by her behaviour but understanding that she was telling me something in that encounter.

She often ran to men on the trails and anyone who approached her, she was excited to meet them. In those 2 encounters, I trusted her instincts.

Tetley's instincts are strong. She saved me from burning the house down once. I was in the shower and heard her barking incessantly. She was at the bathroom door that I kept closed because the smoke detector is outside the door and the hot steam always sets it off, leaving me running, soaking wet to turn off the alarm and wait for the call from the alarm company.

This morning she was at the bathroom door barking nonstop. I shut the water off, grabbed my towel, and opened the door, where she ran back out the hallway. Dripping water, I followed her, to discover a melting cutting board laid on a burner I left on low.

I knew she was smart but I was impressed that she knew to get me and bring me to it. She got extra love and a visit to the pet store that day! They had regular pet store visits for toys and treats but sometimes they got extra when they went to the vet or were extra special or sick.

Tetley also saved Lexie, sort of, from the river one day. As we went to the river and they both jumped in, the river was rushing more than normal after a big storm. I called them back and Tetley came to the side and got out. But Lexie kept swimming straight up, like an endless pool, where she was swimming hard but didn't get anywhere.

I kept calling to her but she didn't even look at me, staring straight ahead, fixated. Tetley started barking and she looked to the side but kept going forward. I thought "I'm gonna have to go in for her if she doesn't come out soon". But, Tetley jumped in the river and swam out to her, breaking her trance, and Lexie followed her back to the shore. After that, I called them back before letting them in so I could assess the flow of the river.

Lexie is a dog with mixed-up instincts because of her traumatic background. She and I have that in common, trauma. Lexie was always easily fooled. She's finally caught on now but we use her lack of instincts when we need her to leave Tetley alone in the water if she was on her back. I'll say "who's there?" and she barks and runs to see who is there. She falls for it every time.

She is more likely to stay in the house and bark while Tetley puts herself on the patio in the direct line of fire. In fact, Tetley regularly chased moose and was not the least bit scared, well, except that morning when she was a baby.

One morning, I was having my morning coffee and doing final prep for an upcoming women's retreat and noticed Tetley backing up the stairs leading into the yard. All the fur on her back was raised as she walked backwards. I knew something had to be there. Tetley did not back away from anything.

I went outside, with Lexie following. I walked into the fenced woods area. When we fenced our property we used goat fencing for a portion of it to give them more room without the need to excavate. This way they could have both manicured and wild sections. It was early fall so the growth was still ample. As I walked into the wilder section, Tetley ran ahead, all the fur on her back was up and she was barking incessantly.

It took me a while to see it as it blended into the background but suddenly I saw the moose, camouflaged in the bushes, chewing away, staring at me. Tetley ran towards it, confidence increased with me there, I suppose. As if I could do anything! Lexie stayed behind me doing her normal poof poof poof barking as if she was providing backup somehow.

The moose moved away from us towards the road in front of our property. It walked around the fence and came out into an open section where its full frame was visible. Tetley charged it, full out, and I grabbed her by the collar and was heading back to the house with her. "Leave it alone," I said.

We got out of the wild part and back to the lawn and the moose kept following the fence. He ended up at the end of the lawn in full view. Lexie bolted to the patio as Tetley bolted to the moose. It was on the outside of the fence and somehow I wasn't worried, I just wanted her to leave it alone. I called her back, intending to put her in the house.

I heard the school bus coming and thought to myself "don't run in front of the bus" at the same time the airbrakes hissed when the bus came to a stop, Tetley charged it at that very moment and instead of running to the street, it hopped the fence, heading straight for Tetley and me.

I was standing in the narrow part between the house and the bank and it came straight for me. Lexie was on the patio steps and she ran closer to the house. Tetley got out of its way and I turned sideways to avoid a collision and sure death. The moose kept going, its fur brushing my face as it passed me, where it hopped onto the patio, over the fence on the other side and headed for the woods behind the house.

Tetley's eyes were wide that day as she realised that she had met her match. My adrenaline was pumping and Lexie was beside herself to get back in the house. She was dancing with her toenails clicking. I didn't need to finish my coffee anymore as I was pumped and we headed out for a walk to reset ourselves.

Lexie didn't like men with hats or sunglasses in general. She barked when anyone approached the house, or me, but quickly settled when she realised they were good people. She then attacked with full-on body contact, belly up and licking! Lexie dances when she's excited. Her whole body wags while she scuffles her feet.

She would almost come out of her fur with thunder but on the trails, she climbed rocks and cliffs and stood way too close to the edges. She was fearless in the woods but terrified in the house. Although she craned her neck to look around the turns on the trails instead of using her nose. She looks versus using her instincts.

When she's with people, she always knows who needs her. She knows how to snuggle, cuddle and get people to open up. She always seems to know who needs a little extra love and attention.

There is a house on one of our walks that Lexie would not walk past, no matter what I did she would sit as soon as we got there. I turned back there because there was just no way she was going past that house. Lexie is like a tank when she doesn't want to do something. She plants herself and that's that.

I always told Justin "There's something about that place". He laughed at me but I was firm, she would not walk past it for a reason. Something was going on there and one day we would find out. Several years later, we found out someone had died by suicide and I believe Lexie was feeling what someone was going through in that house.

It's harder for people to do what she does. What dogs are so inherently great at doing - they lean in but we have lost that ability to lean into each other's pain. I mean, how could I ever walk up to a house and say "my dog is tripped out, what's going on?" I also didn't know if she was scared and sending me messages like Tetley had done in the past with those men.

While dogs have a knack for this, it's a little weirder and scarier for people, in some ways. Maybe that's why we have dogs, to bridge the gap between humans, and to be good at what we're not.

When I taught morning fitness classes at Topsail Beach, I got there at 5:30 a.m. to set up. The dogs were out running around while I was building and setting up my stations. The sun would rise over the bluff and it was incredible. When the weather was bad we went into the trees for protection against the elements. One morning, when I got out of the vehicle, I noticed a woman sitting on a bench. Immediately I felt something was off but I minded my own business.

Lexie ran over to her. I watched her pet Lexie, who then ran off chasing Tetley and her stick. As I set up, I kept my eyes on the dogs and stole glances at the woman. I realised she had a baby with her. I told myself she might have been up all night with the baby. She was probably out driving around to get the child to sleep. I told myself there were a million things I couldn't possibly know about why she was on that bench. I pushed my gut feelings aside.

Then Lexie ran back to her again, and sat directly in front of her, with the tip of her tail wagging. This is a sign from Lexie when just the tip of her tail wags. She reached out and petted Lexie again. I took it as an opportunity, at the very least, to speak to her. As I walked up I said, "I hope she's not bothering you". She replied, "not at all, she's so sweet". As she turned toward me I saw the tears in her eyes and I asked if she was ok. She said, "I am now, just a hard night". I understood. Not as a mother of human children, but as a human being who knew some dark days.

The workout group started showing up but we talked about the sun rising and how good of a day it would be. She left but I've often wondered if she was ok. I wasn't as good back then as I am today at addressing things directly with people. Years of working with women and working on communication, real conversations and deep work of unravelling our conditioning have made me better.

I'll never be as good as Lexie though. Because I'm sure she wanted me to go up to that house and I never have.

I started hosting Women's Empowerment Retreats in 2016, until the pandemic shut them down, where I take women on deep experiences where we get out of our conditioning and into our authentic power. I hosted many retreats at my house and while Tetley used everyone to throw sticks for her, Lexie was a natural emotional therapy dog. She really thrived in this environment. She always let me know who had something going on by whom she chose to sit with. She always picked the person who needed the most help but would be less likely to ask for it. She inherently knew, in a way that people just don't pick up on, because we're too in our heads and not enough in our world.

We are all born with instincts but most of us have lost touch with them. Tetley's instinct to hunt was alive in her drive for fetch. She had it from that day Justin threw her toy down the hallway and gave her a treat for bringing it back. I'm not sure she would have needed more than praise. Tetley loved retrieving. Her whole being vibrated on bringing it back. It was bred into her to be a hunter. We didn't hunt so she hunted sticks, toys and balls. Her instincts to do what she was born to do were very much alive in her and were never trained or conditioned out of her. I'm not sure it was even possible with her.

Lexie is a retriever but did not come from hunting stock, she was not trained for anything other than companionship and most likely neither were her ancestors. Dogs are bred for specific traits. Reputable breeders breed for standards. We don't know where Lexie came from. The people we got her from told us she was from Marystown, in Newfoundland, but we never found any breeders in that area when we searched.

Lexie is more in tune with emotional needs, being a part of the family and being a good girl. Her instinct is to be a good family pet. She is domesticated. Now, she sure loves a good roll in a dead moose or whatever she found dead but otherwise she is mostly an amazing family dog who is focused on giving to those around her.

Tetley was all about performance and she loved the attention being a performer gave her. She got her first frisbee, a rubber Kong, during her first winter in Newfoundland. She was born in March but came to us in May. While it was still winter in Nunavut and there was snow until June and even patches in July, it would be the next winter in Newfoundland that I considered her first one. After we moved into our house I gave her a frisbee and we walked down the road with her playing with it.

Tetley liked to tear the centre out of her frisbees, especially when the spite hit her. She ate the centre out of the frisbee and started throwing it in the air and catching it around her head. I don't know if my squeals of delight or her own pleasure was the thing that helped it catch on, but it became known as circus tricks. I would ask for a circus trick and she would happily oblige.

She started performing those tricks with the frisbee and eventually moved onto sticks. She put it on the bushes and used her nose to flick it into the air and catch it. She loved doing those. Lexie hated her getting the attention from it and would body slam her for doing it, sending Tetley flying into the air. It didn't stop her, every chance she got she did those circus tricks.

Tetley with her kong frisbee doing circus tricks.

It was instinct for her to perform as if she was a natural show dog but not the kind for inside arenas or doing what she was told, more like doing what other dogs couldn't do. She sat with her chest up, always, taking pride in how she sat, how she carried herself, in who she was. That is instinct. When we carry ourselves with confidence it's because we know who we are. If we're honest with ourselves how much do we need to learn about sitting tall and being confident in ourselves?

Even now, with her very old age and all of her challenges, she sits tall with her paws crossed. Even as a little old lady, she exudes pride.

She taught me a lot about being myself. Watching her never give up no matter how many hardships or challenges she faced, to never hold onto the past, to relentlessly pursue what she wanted and how powerful a one-track mind is. She wasn't inclined to be afraid of us. She wasn't beaten, hit or caged into submission. Instead, she was allowed to flourish as her whole wild self, never tamed, caged or contained.

Lexie didn't have the same start in her life, coming from neglect and abuse, she worked hard to please people, less confident in her place in the world or our home. It took nursing her back to health and helping her find safety with us to help her become who she could be.

She became attached to me, becoming my shadow, her safe place and her safe person. She became more confident, but we had to help her do that. She was afraid of the world because her instincts were taken from her, she was likely removed from her mom too young and couldn't learn what she needed to learn, then she lived in a house where she was confined to the porch, and I can only imagine what else she experienced.

Her instincts were damaged. Lexie had some strange behaviours, like ducking under light poles as we drove the highways. With each one we passed she started ducking. She eventually stopped this behaviour but she flinched when we passed under bridges and overpasses. It was as if she couldn't see properly or had depth perception issues.

She always eats from Tetley's leftover bowl instead of finishing her own. She pushes blankets on her bowl and dances around the food bowl before she eats the food. We aren't sure what she's doing, or why, but we wondered if it's putting her scent on the food.

Instincts are something we all have but the world around us reinforces healthy or harmful ones. Imagine if we were all given the opportunity that Tetley was to be wholly ourselves? How could we thrive and live? Or even to be like Lexie and find our best qualities despite it? Lexie had every right to never trust people again. She had every right to snarl and bite to protect herself when she felt scared. She certainly had every right to be reserved but she wasn't. She became more loving, kinder, more compassionate and more giving. Lexie had an eye injury that left a calcification on her eye, it formed in the shape of a heart. We say it's because she can only see love. The eye specialist told us that it's like having a spot on your glasses. It's annoying but there is nothing we could do about it. People always ask "Oh my god is that a heart?"

Yes, yes it is.

How can we listen to our own instincts and learn to trust them, so we know who to avoid and what tricks or gifts we inherently have within us?

Instincts come to us when we are exposed to the proper stimulus. Tetley learned to swim when my friend Catherine threw her in the pond, she did what Labradors do - she swam. When Justin threw a toy, she brought it back and he rewarded her for it, she tapped into ancient traits and instincts of her breed to do what she was born and bred to do. When Lexie sees someone in trouble, be it a human or Tetley, she immediately rushes in to make it better. She has that instinct.

Lexie sitting on my lap while I was working. I regularly did office work like this.

What instincts would we have if we had not been conditioned to be good and pleasing and how to work and live and what is good and bad and what we should do, be, say and have? What would be different for us if we weren't conditioned to be fearful instead of having only the two we're born with? Heights and loud noises - 2 survival instincts are the only fears humans are born with. The other fears we have are manufactured and conditioned to the modern world we live in.

One morning as we, as Carolyn and I, headed out for a hike I had a weird feeling we shouldn't go. Back then I never backed down, I never said no or that I couldn't or wouldn't do something, especially if we had shown up for it.

We got out of the vehicle by the pit on the old railroad bed off Woodford Station in the pitch dark at 5 a.m. on a bitterly cold winter morning. The barricades weren't up then so we could drive into the pit from the main road without having to drive around the pond. This was our regular meeting place. It was the blackest of mornings with heavy cloud cover, no stars or moon visible in the sky or lighting the path.

As we got out and put on our ice grips, the frigid winter air hit me. I pulled my balaclava up over my nose and we laughed about how cold and dark it was. The dogs were already on the move and they had flashers and glow-in-the-dark tags so we could see them.

The feeling came over me again to call it and say it didn't feel safe, but I pushed it aside and off we went. We were about 5 minutes into our walk when I lost my footing, the ice was thick and everywhere, and with a light dusting of snow and the darkness, it was hard to pick the way. My foot landed on an icy snow-covered patch, and even with my grips, I was on my back with the sound of my head hitting the ice reverberating through the dark before I even knew I was falling.

Lexie jumped on top of me, followed by Tetley. Lexie was frantically licking my face while Tetley was throwing a stick at me. This was the norm when I fell down and falling down was something I did regularly. When Justin comes into the woods with us he asks if I fall this much when I'm alone. I don't know why but I find leaves to trip on. I seem to trip on air sometimes.

And the girls do their normal, one licking me and one throwing sticks at me.

Chloe came over and got involved. Carolyn yelled "are you ok" and all I remember saying was "get the dogs off me". She had to hold Lexie back while I sat up, fearing the worst with my head. My head went back so far that an egg-sized lump formed on the top part of the crown, almost on the top of my head. I took my hat off, feeling through my hair, fully expecting to pull away bloody fingers.

I didn't feel anything other than the lump. I felt fine. Nothing hurt and nothing appeared broken. I got to my feet and headed back to the car. I knew I couldn't continue on and had to get home to ensure nothing was wrong or broken. It was just too dangerous to continue that morning.

Carolyn told me later that she was sure my head was split open and she could hear the sound of my head hitting the ice for weeks later. I put the girls in the back seat and climbed into the driver's seat. When I opened the door there was a dime on the seat. I didn't see that when I was getting my ice grips on. I had an eerie feeling come over me as if I should have listened to that apprehension and not gone. That was instinct. And I didn't listen to it.

I had an instinct problem. I often pushed through to get what I wanted, not realising there were feelings, knowing, and sometimes blatant signs to not push forward. I always believed that quitting was a bad thing and that I would never be that person.

That was the first time I knew that I was ignoring my own instincts. Sometimes going back isn't a weakness, it's power. Since I had my appendix out I didn't take my health for granted. Had I gone when something was first wrong I could have had laparoscopic surgery and prevented such a massive surgery with a long recovery. Because of this, I headed to the emergency room to get checked out. I wasn't hurting but that was scary enough. I felt the smack was hard enough that I *should* have been hurting.

After a check-up, I was diagnosed with a grade 3 concussion and whiplash.

In the days following the accident, I developed trigeminal neuralgia, as my skull and face shifted from the impact. Even the heaviest painkillers at the doctor didn't work and I was scheduled for a neurology consult, with a 2-year waitlist. There was no way I was going to make it 2 years.

I was in agony.

I found a chiropractor with a craniosacral specialty who adjusted my jaw and neck and did myofascial release inside of my mouth in the muscles around my jaw. It was horrible. I gagged on the taste of latex gloves in my mouth while excruciating pain shot through me. It isn't something I'll soon forget. I went for several weeks and my pain finally subsided as my skull, muscles and neck were realigned.

All because I didn't listen to that inner voice, that instinct, to turn back. It was a painful lesson. I've learned to honour that feeling, to trust it, as the dogs do with theirs.

We had this motto of "We don't go back!" We laugh about it now because it sure gave us many wild adventures. It happened on one particular hike in Middle Cove as Michelle, Carolyn and myself were crossing over a river. It wasn't really deep and there were rocks to cross on. Carolyn and I had done similar many times, the dogs went through fine but Michelle was a bit apprehensive and wanted to go back.

As I was coaxing her across the river I exclaimed "We don't go back!" This is good and bad. That day it wasn't necessary to go back. Sometimes we need to face our fears and overcome them. But there are times when we need to acknowledge those inner voices or go back because the conditions aren't good, dangerous even.

Like Tetley, this attitude has been one to keep me moving, never giving up, but there are times we need to check in and ask if going back is the right thing to do. We always joke now that we're not as crazy or stupid as we used to be. Experience and pain are great teachers.

Imagine if we had the confidence to just be ourselves like our dogs do. Imagine if we could know our gifts and talents and purpose and just follow it like they follow their nose?

What if we could listen to our heart and follow it and believe in ourselves to create the life we want instead of the one we're supposed to want?

Imagine if we knew ourselves so well that we didn't worry about tomorrow because we trust who we are instead of who the world told us to be. Imagine if we could sit in our power like Tetley sits with her chest out and her head high, fully confident in who she is.

That's what she taught me about being wild and free. Watching her helped me become more of myself and helped me redefine who I am, and what I wanted for my life and even helped me embrace my own wildish nature. Being with Lexie opened me to love and taught me that it really is the most important thing. Because what is life without love?

While dogs don't have mortgages or bills to worry about they do have deep conditioning in our world. They aren't allowed to be free to run or roam or play. Everywhere we go, "dogs on leash" signs exist. Newfoundland is one of the only places where there are no off-leash-friendly hikes or trails. While people do it, and I sure did, there is a constant backlash for it. I don't mean the city trails, parks, streets or inside towns, obviously, dogs should be leashed in those places, but I mean dogs in the woods or having a trail to run free in the safety of the woods or a dog-friendly beach. Dog owners understand they need to be free in their souls as much as we need to be free in ours.

Dogs and people have been overly conditioned in this too-modern world that hasn't left room for who we are. Tetley is one step from the wolf. She is the closest thing to wild any of us will ever know and while she always enjoyed a hot towel from the dryer, after a cold ocean swim, in her warm bed, she was only content after she ran wild in the woods.

I know the woods healed Lexie's soul as much as it did mine. It's instinct to run free. Justin always hated to chain Tetley on, he didn't want that for her and neither did I. There is a time for fences and collars and leashes for safety and protection, just like a seatbelt in our cars for us, but there's also a time for wildness and freedom and rolling in the mud.

When we trained for the Tough Mudder obstacle course and crawled through the bog and culverts it was the happiest the dogs were. They loved joining us on those adventures as if they had finally convinced us this was the way to live!

I don't ever recall feeling bad after a hike or a run or a good slog through dirt and bushes. Even Lexie, as domesticated, calm and kind, as she is, was a result of her wilding in the woods with Tetley. She was calm because she had the chance and the opportunity to go wild whenever she wanted. All of us sleep soundly every night because we are tired, the good kind of tiredness that comes from fresh air and dirt.

The problem with most of us today is that we are holed up inside and not drinking enough pond water. We are unfulfilled because we are chasing money and stuff instead of sunsets and adventure. But when we are wild, we are whole and in our wholeness, we don't need to chase anything. It chases us. Happiness and wildness are contagious. I learned that from the girls. They are happy and content and sleep soundly between adventures because they are free.

There's a lot we can't change about our world but a good splash in the mud with fresh air on our skin can bring alive what lies dormant in our psyche, like the instincts in the dogs, we can find our way best when we stop frantically searching for it and instead start living for it.

CHAPTER 12
NEVER GROW OLD

Lexie in her favourite place - the console wearing her sunglasses.

G rowing up is mandatory, getting old is a choice. My grandfather often said, "I don't know how old I am, but I know how many years I've been alive". He never let age define him. He challenged me to a race up Regatta Grounds hill in Bonds Path and I lost. He was 78 and I was 15.

Pop defied the odds. He never had a driver's license, but it never stopped him, he went everywhere, by boat or by foot. He never seemed afraid of anything, and he lived with hardship through the depression, raised a large family in pretty hard times in Newfoundland, moved from a small town on the Burin Penin-sula to the bustling centre of Placentia and worked on the American Naval Base as a bartender. He fished and hunted, and he drank. He got sober in 1980 - the year I was born.

I never knew my grandfather to drink or to be any other way than filled with the wisdom he had. He took us to AA dances when we were kids and we loved those dances. We loved being included. He spent most evenings in our house, snoring while we tried to watch TV over the noise. When he sat on the couch he fell into it, slamming it into the wall so hard that sometimes dad would say he was going to land in the driveway if he wasn't careful.

Pop was pop. He was unapologetic and he was a storyteller. I come by it honestly as my father is a storyteller too. It's in our blood and our bones, it's *our* instinctual nature. He fished and cut wood, towing it out with his 3 Wheeler, and he checked himself into the hospital the week before he died. In admitting, he got assurance from the nurses and doctors that he wasn't there for treatment but was there to die and get help doing it. In his words "every time I open my eyes some fool is staring at me". So, he went to the hospital to die in peace. He was active until the end.

My grandfather Whittle.

Tetley reminds me of him in her refusal to grow old. She is old, has mobility issues, has outlived her expected age, has survived a car accident and has more ailments than I can name lately. But she refuses to just lay around the house as if there aren't still ponds to swim in or sticks to chase. She has no intention of being an old house dog. She doesn't want to provide or receive comfort in her old age. That's Lexie's job. Her job is to be the kind of girl whom the devil himself is scared of when she wakes up every morning.

My shaman, Regina, told me that old women were often called hags because they had outgrown the desire to please people. They did what they wanted and were called hags for it. Old women have an attitude because they are beyond the pleasing requirements younger women are held to.

She says Tetley has been an old hag her whole life and now has really stepped into her hag energy. She calls it *hagitude*. It makes me laugh because she's even harder to handle the older she gets. When I say anything to her she now looks at me as if to say "how dare you!". When she gets really out of hand Lexie hides in my closet.

Tetley will never be content to be old. She will never be ok to lay around with no purpose other than to be alive. Even today I took her for a swim, and she comes fully alive when she is in the water, slicing through and chasing her stick as if she is 2. I put a life jacket on her these days because she had an ear infection recently where she rolled around in the water, and it was a little scary. I had to go out to my waist to grab her and bring her in.

Given her age, we use a vest for her safety. We thought she'd hate it but she loves it. It was Justin's idea to buy it for her. She gets buoyancy from it and can stay out longer.

I have taken cold water therapy and am prepared should I have to go out for her. In fact, I've had my fair share of dips with her in the winter, not because of her, but because of our adventures. A few years back we hiked the loop around the Butter Pot Pond, not the Provincial Park, but the road in Holyrood. There isn't really a trail there, but people partially connect to the pole line and eventually come out nearly in someone's yard. As we were exploring there one late winter day, the ice skimming the top of some of those big bog holes was frail. It was still frigid in early March and Tetley went through the ice into a bog hole. It wasn't the dangerous kind of going through the ice on a pond, it was more like a ditch with a covering of ice we didn't know was there because of the bog. The sides were steep but the water was not deep.

I gave her a few minutes while calling her to see if she could get up on her own, she's scaled much steeper on the East Coast Trail Hikes! But it was clear she couldn't get out as the sides were just too steep. I used the ice safety training from the course I took… spreading myself out trying to reach for her collar and bring her up on my side instead of having to go in the water if I could avoid it. Carolyn was with Lexie and Chloe, and I inched myself across the ice, just at the moment I touched her collar, the ice broke, and I went into the gulch with her, face down.

I grabbed her by the collar and tossed her up the bank and off she ran, with her stick in her mouth, happy as a lark as if nothing had happened. I was soaked through on the front of my body. By the time we made it back to the vehicle, my mittens were frozen to my jacket and my jacket was frozen to my pants and my boot laces were frozen together.

That wasn't our first time for that either. There is a wilderness hike Carolyn and I used to do that connects from the pole line to the swim park in Holyrood. It is a rough-cut trail with just some ribbons on trees. We heard about it and went in search of it. Once we had the path figured out, we did it regularly, taking the dogs with us, of course. We often took spray paint and extra ribbons to keep the trail from being lost to blow down. In the winter it could be hard to see the paint on the trees so we tagged the trees with bright pink ribbons.

It's a beautiful trail that would be lovely if developed but it's also nice to have secret locations where we can be alone in the woods with the dogs. It has everything from hills and over-growth to ponds and eagles nesting. Sometimes we went in the early mornings to do a portion of it to get a good hill hike in.

We hadn't been on that hike for some time and Vanessa and I

decided to do it. We got to the part where we had to turn to find the path to the park, but the ribbon was gone and so were the other markers that were always there. At the top of one of the hills was an old chair and a cutout to an ATV path that led to a footpath at the top of the park. It had snowed that morning so there was a lot of cover-ups but there was also a lot of blow-downs. It had been years since we had been there so the trail seemed to be lost.

Our only option was to turn back and that was a 7 kilometer trek back. We were only half a kilometre from the park but we just couldn't find it. I knew there was a giant river and a steep cliff if we went straight so we couldn't just beat our way through the bush to the other side. I decided to make one more attempt to find the ribbons indicating the path. I was looking around the blowdown and stepped onto a piece of ice with nothing underneath it.

I went up to my armpits in a bog hole. Lexie, per usual, was all over me licking and squealing, as I tried to claw my way out of the bog hole. Vanessa had to peel her off me so I could get out. Because of my cold exposure training, I was ok but I still knew from my instincts and training that I had a short time in the freezing temperatures and had to get moving.

The path back was clear so we started jogging. I was in the front with Vanessa staying in the back, with Tetley and Lexie in between to make sure they didn't veer off. Vanessa was on our heels as we all ran to keep warm. I called Justin from the trail and told him I had fallen into the water up to my armpits and asked him to meet me by my car with a change of clothes.

He showed up on the trail when I had run about 5 kilometres and had 2 left to go. He brought food for my energy and a change of clothes. We soon discovered that I couldn't change my clothes as my laces and boots were frozen onto me. We raced back to the cars where he took Vanessa to hers, which was parked at the other end of the trail where we should have come out, while I drove home. He met me at the house, with the dogs, cleaned them off and put a hair dryer on my boots to start removing clothes.

With each piece that came off, blood and bruises were exposed, and my legs were red and numb from the cold and slamming into sticks and stumps while running and falling down. The dog's fur was frozen on their chests, something that regularly occurred because they swam all winter. The ice would melt in moments in the house. Justin didn't say a word and neither did I. The dogs plowed around the house gobbling food, water and snacks in their wake. They were dried off and I was put in the rec room in front of the fire with a cup of tea.

I sat in front of the fire waiting for it. I knew it was coming. The dogs came downstairs and lay in front of the stove warming up. It was almost a hallmark movie, but Justin was ready to burst the bubble reminding me of my reckless behaviour and how I was not going to stop until I die and why do I think he worries about me or asks me about my safety plans. I took it. As I deserved it, I suppose.

Adventure comes with risks, and it also comes with owning our own stupidity or where we went too far. I mean, I would like to defend myself that I didn't know there was ice there but reckless behaviour *is* when you don't know where you are and how fast things can change. One thing I do know though is never go on those adventures alone, and I don't, and never give up.

The thing about adventurous souls is that we will always wander. Yes, I learned over the years what to do and not to do, like hiking the Lamanche trail and needing to use tow ropes to navigate the ice to using dog leashes to get up Murray's Peak. I've learned winter is treacherous and ice cleats and picks are necessary. I also learned that if you don't know the ground around you, you check it *before* you step. There are lessons to be learned from our mishaps. And that's not to go home and never have a mishap, it's to do better each time. Learn from our mistakes and do better.

My grandfather had a lot of mishaps in his life, but it didn't stop him from living fully to the end. He embedded a cod jigger in his face and cut it out himself when my uncle refused to cut it out for him, insisting he go to the hospital. He refused and took it out himself. He said he was not going back to the wharf with a jigger in his face! He bandaged it up and treated it at home. Now I don't recommend these things. He was a different breed of man, even for that time. I remember him having a lot of mishaps and I can't really say he learned much from them because he often just kept having the same ones. Maybe the apple doesn't fall too far from the tree, after all.

Tetley has had a lot of mishaps in her life but she's still pushing to the end and squeezing every drop out of life. When we have mishaps and instead of learning from them, quit, we grow old far before our time and we miss out on living.

When we have accidents or make mistakes it's easy to stay home or be scared or let other people's fear or judgment make us play small with our own lives. We stay alive but never really live.

For me, I want to live with the spirit of Tetley, the spirit of my grandfather, and the spirit of the wild living inside of me for as long as I can. I want to be the old woman, like Tetley, who frustrates everyone around me while I'm up to antics and no old age home will keep me because I'm just too much to handle. I want hagitude when I'm old. Maybe even a little right now.

I can only hope to be like my grandfather, doing what he loved and making him feel free until the end. I hope that when the end comes, I'll accept it as well as he did, and I hope when the end comes for Tetley that she can accept it. I think when she's ready for it, she will, but not a second before. It will be on her terms, like my grandfather's, and I hope, mine.

When we grow old, we lose ourselves. There is a time to grow up but there is never a time to grow old. Tetley nor my grandfather ever got the message about age being a limitation and I think we can all learn that lesson. Never let our age define what we can do or who we are.

Lexie has a playful personality, she always has. I feel she came to us to give us an attitude adjustment. We have always been so serious about our goals and achievements but Lexie turned everything into an adventure. Justin always says that I make Lexie out to be an angel who never did anything wrong. It's not true, entirely. I know she was a handful but she stopped being a handful so it feels different than Tetley. She is still a handful.

Viktor Frankl says that one can be stripped of everything except one's attitude in hardship. I know my grandfather had this attitude. He certainly had his share of hardships. Growing up in the depression in Newfoundland, at a time when the Merchants owned the people, he took a job on the ships heading to the Grand Banks at 13 years old. At that age, he would actually get the money, not just credit. The way the merchants worked in Newfoundland at the time was that men fished for the merchant's vessels and then got their pay in credit at the merchant-owned store in their town.

Many of the fishermen couldn't read or write so had no way of knowing if they were ripped off or not, but most were. He told me that when his season was over he went to get his pay and the merchant told him that his father didn't earn enough to cover his debt so they were taking it from his earnings. He reported it to the constable at the time, as he felt it was wrong but the merchants doubled down and said his father had taken him on board so they could take his share to go towards his father's debt. That was that.

He told me that he might have only been 13 but he knew that was wrong. Pop was in his 80s when he told me that story. He told me so many stories about his life. He loved to talk. Nan would say he could talk the head off a brass monkey and when he was dying he told me as many stories as he could. He told me I would be the one to do the talking for him and tell his stories. I was in my early 20s when he died. But I loved his stories and his death changed me. The way he faced it shifted how I viewed death.

He told me he had worried a lot about me because I was too withdrawn but he also knew that I would come around and he knew I would be ok. He faced life's adversities with a positive attitude. He didn't have much but he had that. Pop had his yellow dory and on the Cape Shore, in St. Bride's, they said it sounded like the devil's chains hitting the bottom of the ocean when he was out in it, with his old make-and-break engine. He went everywhere in that dory. He couldn't drive a car but he could drive that thing. His dog, Snuggles, would follow him to the dory every day.

And every Sunday he got dressed up in his best clothes and went to visit people in the old age home and attached hospital. He made time for people, to see the people no one else visited. Snuggles followed him to the end of the driveway those days and stayed. She knew she couldn't go where he was going when he had those clothes on.

Pop sure could laugh. And he couldn't remember anyone's name. He was notorious for forgetting names. He often called us every name in the book and then finished with "you know who I mean", to which we would burst into laughter. One time he called my brother Kevin, Snuggles, while coxing their rowing crew. He yelled "row, snuggles row". They couldn't keep it together and the boat, and pop, descended into laughter.

He taught us to play 45s and like all the old people, he was serious about his cards. He called clubs crubs and when he laid his cards down he hit the table with his knuckles. Pop was not a small man and there were times the wooden table shook.

Pop saved a lot of lives when he joined AA. I didn't know until he died, the impact he had. They couldn't close the church doors, it was filled to capacity and people were overflowing outdoors. Placentia had a very large church, the upper level was filled, the hallways, walkways and outdoors onto the church steps. They filled 5 guest books at the funeral home and we had a true Irish wake for him.

With songs, step dancing and a lot of tears, we entertained people who said it was the best funeral they ever attended. We honoured pop's life in the way he lived, with song and dance, friends and family. And we listened to hundreds of stories of how pop saved people's lives. So many people came to speak to me and I'm sure others in my family, shaking my hand and telling me how incredible of a man he was.

Pop was a sponsor. That I did not know until he died. He was just pop to me. Pop once invited a man doing a cross-Canada bike tour in for lunch. He ended up staying for 3 days, where Nan fed him because she thought he was too skinny. He left to finish his tour saying he wouldn't be able to ride his bike if he didn't leave soon. They were those people. Salt of the earth people.

So when he died and the stories poured in, it wasn't surprising and yet the magnitude of his impact, a man who couldn't read or write much, read the bible, loved watching wrestling on his small black and white TV with Nan and listening to tapes of what I now realise were motivational speeches.

Nan and Pop faced loss, childhood infant loss, SIDs, miscar-riages, alcoholism, children with mental illnesses and more. It took me becoming an adult to fully realise the hardships they faced and yet how well they faced them. How they stayed kind and good and true to themselves, how they continued to help others and didn't let those experiences turn them away from each other or people.

They aged in body but not in spirit. For Pop, it wasn't just about being able to work but he also knew how to live. One would never think he had the hardships he did and to know that he used those experiences to help others, showed that he not only learned but he paid it forward, in spades, not crubs.

Lexie is like that. In spite of her 11 years, a senior by all accounts, she neither looks nor acts like a senior. She is a silly goose and no one believes she is a senior, except she walks very slowly because of her pain, has significant health issues and still she is happy every day of her life. She is always a joy. When she came out of surgery, her eyes glistened and she couldn't stop licking, so happy to see you after she woke up.

Even when she was vomiting and at the vet undergoing tests and needles, she was happy. Her vet tech, Matt, cuts her nails, gives her needles and does unspeakable things to her, and she is still so excited to see him every time. She licks his face and each time I can hear him laughing from outside the room. I know she is up to her antics. They take her in the back sometimes when she won't let Tetley be examined and she runs through the place, on her slow little legs, going as fast as she can to see as many people as she can.

They always say no dogs are happy going in the back, but Lexie is always a goofball in the back. Tetley was always dramatic at the vet. On one of the first visits we had at Paradise Animal before we knew most of the staff on a first-name basis, Tetley was being extra, playing up not wanting to go in the back.

She used her back legs to crawl up my body, hooking my pants and flesh as she did. She wrapped her back legs around my waist and her front arms around my neck, clinging to me. She was a big girl then! Matt, who we didn't know at the time, took her from my arms but she managed to get away and got on top of the reception desk.

She crawled into the lap of one of the receptionists where Matt had to take Tetley off her and carry her in the back with her flailing about.

He came back to tell me that when the door closed behind her, Tetley walked in the back fine once I was out of sight. He let me know she was playing her Momma. Tetley fought everyone and everything at the vet. She never let anything be easy. Sometimes getting blood work required several people to hold her down and sometimes it had to be abandoned because she fought so hard. She faced the corner, hyperventilating, even when it was Lexie's appointment.

Lexie is not dramatic in that way. She's dramatic in her flopping on the floor getting pets and rubs. If you stop she will let you know to keep going by pawing at you. She is easy. She goes into the back, never acting out or scared. Even when she had to go in alone, during the pandemic, she walked off with the staff and was totally fine, scravelling and wagging when she came back to the car, so proud of herself for having a big girl appointment without her mom.

Attitude is about all we can control in our lives. Lexie, less dramatic than Tetley, sure makes life easier and more joyful with her attitude and her antics. Tetley's go attitude is admirable but her demanding attitude is a lot to handle some days. Lexie makes up for it with her pure joy and fun attitude. She takes it as a personal mission to get you in a good mood or lay with you in a bad mood.

Lexie always makes us laugh, even when she isn't listening. Lexie didn't always do a good job of listening. She did her own thing. Justin always says "Let her sniff the bushes, she's going to anyway, there's no point in fighting her". She never did a command, gave a paw or a kiss. She wasn't really trainable and we spent more time making her safe than caring about her training and tricks. Plus, Tetley's tricks were exhausting and who needed another one full of tricks?

Not us.

She turns her head when you try to kiss her but sneak attacks with her giant tongue when you turn away or aren't expecting it. Lexie stood at the wrong side of the door to come into the house her whole life. Tetley does that now, which is dementia, but Lexie always did it. When she would leave the gym to go upstairs she stood at the wrong side of the door. The vets remarked at times that Lex might have had a little something else going on because of how she didn't seem to have the capacity to be upset, angry, or anything other than happy.

Lexie never gave kisses but always sneak
attacked when you weren't expecting it.

We couldn't leave a coffee cup around, or in the car, when we came back the lid was off and she would have inhaled an entire cup of tea or coffee. When we ran errands we put our coffee cups on the top of the vehicle or took them with us.

She would get in the front seat and refuse to leave it. When we grocery shopped or took them on any errands, they got in the front seats when we got out of the car. When we returned Tetley jumped in the back but Lexie wasn't going anywhere.

She sat with her back fully against the seat, preventing you from moving her. She flopped to the side, making it impossible to push her to the back. It would result in sitting in the car on top of her, trying to get her to concede, which she never did. Sometimes as I pushed my way into the seat she would jump to the other front seat, which resulted in the other person dealing with her.

It always ended with her needing to be carried out of the vehicle by Justin and manhandled into the back. Sometimes when I'd stay in the car for a quick errand he would remind me not to let her jump into his seat, but I'd often miss it and she made her way to the front, resulting in the same issue over and over again. It only stopped when she had her knee surgery in 2019 and couldn't get up in the front as easily.

Often when we were driving she got in the front on my lap. If

Justin was driving and I was in the passenger seat she climbed over the console and no matter how we tried to stop her, it never worked.

We drove, then, with her in my lap, all 90 plus pounds of lapdog in the front, jammed onto the dash, trying to drink my coffee and leaning across to lick Justin, with Tetley in the back, alone, sprawled off.

Attitude is everything and both my girls have had attitudes in various ways. Tetley, while insane in drive, was also very well trained. She knew all of her commands, gave a kiss as a pass-word, knew all sorts of tricks and generally did listen, except when fetch was involved. Even then when you yelled "break" she would stop, for a minute. While she was well-behaved and generally good we see her as a devil because of her drive.

Lexie never really listened and yet we see her as a little angel because of her joyful attitude in not listening. Because she is so loveable it's easy to forget that she doesn't listen.

Lexie did grow into herself these last few years and espe-cially this last year with Tetley. Our lives are easier and slower and with everyone older, it's easier to forget how insane it all was. But in the midst of the mayhem, the leading attitude was love. Always love. We make some kind of imperfect family filled with medical problems, accidents and general chaos but we are always filled with a deep love for each other and the life we are choosing.

CHAPTER 13
SLOWING DOWN IS OK

Lexie in the gym.

While relentless is about pushing forward and finding our deepest potential that wouldn't be complete without talking about the need to slow down. We can't and shouldn't always be on, that's the toxicity that leads us to burn out. While Tetley has a lot of drive she also rests between those driven moments. We joke that she sleeps so she can get up and go again.

When she was on, she was dialled all the way in. But when

she was off, she was all off. When she was tired and we tried to cuddle, it was not happening. She moved her head if we tried to pet her or if we lay down with her for a cuddle she was having no part of it.

She huffed, puffed and left. Justin would say "don't touch her or she'll leave".

The only time we could get a good snuggle with Tetley is when she got to be about 11 and started sleeping a little later in the morning. She did spend her evenings on the couch with us, always ready for a drive and before Lexie she was the front-seat girl. She always found it hard to get the same out-the-window experience in the front so she preferred the back seat.

Tetley did lay next to us on the couches and in bed but she never wanted to be petted. Lexie loved being petted. She wanted to be touched all the time. Tetley wanted to be with us, but our equal, not our pet. With Lexie, life was easy but with Tetley it was adventurous.

After her accident getting in and out of the bed was harder. We put a bench by the bed and she used that to get up and down but eventually, she stopped coming to the bed. She used to sleep between my legs for most of her life or snuggled into the crook of my bent legs. Lexie would sleep in between us with her back toes on our pillows.

While Tetley had a high drive she also knew how to sleep and recover. Lexie, on the other hand, knew how to chill out. Lexie is the kind of dog that could shop with me in stores and would have made a great support dog for hospitals and homes. She is perfection in dog form, and she brought the yin to the yang in this family. There were times I thought of training her as an official therapy dog but our lives were really full, with a busy business and keeping active, so it never happened. Plus, an enormous amount of time and money was spent at vets so often time for other things was lost in caring for them.

For as much as Justin could give me a tongue lashing for my behaviour, he's just as bad with his cuts, bruises and sometimes how he just stretches with a scream and fires himself into whatever he is working on.

Lexie arrived unlike any of us and forced us to change who we were for her. We couldn't work at the same pace we always had because she couldn't or didn't want to. Either way, we had to find a balance between sonic speed and snail mode. We had to find patience in sniffing the bushes and even more patience in getting her out of bed in the morning to do her business and get breakfast before we could leave the house.

I spent much of my life with them on leashes in opposite directions. Tetley pulled in one direction and Lexie was stopped in another.

Lexie knew how to slow down and without her, I'm not sure I would have ever found the grace to find, and enjoy, the slow moments in life. She frustrated me when I first adopted her. Why couldn't she pick up the pace? Why did she need to be so slow or take so long to do everything? That frustration helped me ask myself bigger questions. Why did I get so frustrated and always feel like we were supposed to be doing something more productive? Why did I always think faster was better? Why were we always so busy that everything had to be regimented, including our walks?

Lexie came to me just months before I faced my trauma and the way I was living my life. Perhaps some of these questions I was forced to ask because of the way Lexie came into my life, damaged, broken, needing a softness that I did not have nor the ability to slow down. I had to change for her.

When I was sick, Lexie lay on top of me and when I was in trauma recovery she lay on top of me as if her weight could absorb my pain. She knew the presence of her weight was all a soul needed to heal. She is like a blanket full of healing and she pours whatever she has into you to help you feel better.

Lexie created the balance we desperately needed that we didn't even know we needed. We learned to appreciate her love and how she operated. She was the caregiver for the rest of us.

She washes Tetley's face and cries to wake us up when Tetley needs something. She snuggles us when we are sad or hurt and she lies with us, content to be there, not needing anything else other than us.

She woke me up one night by licking my arm. She needed to go outside. She had a bad belly but she still woke me gently. Tetley woke us up, and still does, by flipping out.

Lexie didn't need anything other than love. She does not need to be taken anywhere and is content to sleep in or go if we see fit. She is happy to get snacks but never begs for food nor asks for treats after she learned not to jump on the table! She is content to just be as if all we are, and all we have, is enough.

The rest of us were always striving and moving toward some goal and had varying levels of stress because of it. Lexie is never stressed unless there are storms, fireworks or yelling. She is happy. Whether she was truly born that way or developed it, she is just happy, and I believe it is because she's been happy where she is with what she has. I think that's the difference with rescues, they seem to appreciate it more.

Today, at this moment, whatever is in it is fine. Tetley is always about the next adventure and while I love every ounce of her being it's a lot to live with, even for an adventure-driven enthusiast who lives for it. When there is no off button, it gets really overwhelming some days.

Lexie is never overwhelming. She is only overwhelming when everyone around her is rushing, and she isn't. But in that she taught me to accept it, I cannot change it, I cannot change her, and I would not want to. Sometimes we just must wait. Sometimes we must adjust our lives for them or other people in our lives. And it's ok. We are the centre of our own story but we're not the centre of everyone else's story. Lexie has been the best-supporting actress for most of everything in our lives. She has been ok to blend in, be in the background and let Tetley be in the lead in many ways.

While Tetley drove our adventures, routines and our daily

schedules were built around keeping her happy, Lexie thrived in the attention and cuddles she got with us and the hundreds of people she met. She is happy that Tetley never wanted that kind of attention, more love for her!

She's been ok to be the quieter, easier, less demanding one. She's been the best dog in the best ways with the best personality. It's less demanding than Tetley's but that's needed in life, too. All demands never make for a balanced experience. Lexie brought the only balance we had in our lives. I found a deeper ability to rest, relax, cuddle, and enjoy wasting time.

Sometimes while Tetley was snoring after a big run or swim, Lexie and I would lay on the floor, or in bed, with her in the crook of my arm, snuggled into my body with her head on my chest and we would stay that way for a while. Now she gets far more of this because Tetley sleeps more so Lexie gets even more cuddles.

Sometimes when the weather is nice, we do the same on the patio. I would work out outside and Tetley used to fetch the entire time. Lexie lay on my mat with me, or next to me or really, she takes my mat and I lay on the pavement, Tetley would fetch until her tongue was hanging to her feet and she would go take a break under a tree or in a bog hole and Lexie and I would snuggle.

There is nothing like her snuggles. Lexie could be a professional cuddler. It's her life purpose to just make people feel loved and accepted and as if this moment is just perfect as it is.

The first night Lexie stayed with us I put her in her kennel at bedtime. Tetley got in bed with us and we went to sleep. None of us are sleepers so I was shocked to wake up hours later than normal the next morning. Even Tetley had slept in. I remembered we had another dog and I jumped out of bed to check on her. She had been in there for 10 hours without a sound!

She wagged her tail when I went to her kennel. She was awake but quiet. I was sad because I wondered how she had lived for her to just stay there for 10 hours. And no doubt she had it rough early in her life but she sure loved to sleep. When I pulled shift work at a shelter I worked on call and more often than not I got the night shifts. Justin got up and left for work around 6:00 a.m. and I got home about 8:00 a.m. on those mornings. Tetley hit the patio in full force. I took her for a walk, fed her and Lexie and then Lexie and I crawled back into bed.

If I had a morning where I worked a night shift and Justin was off the next day, I got in bed and he got up but Lexie stayed in. She knew how to relax! Over the last year and a half, since Tetley has struggled with mobility, Lexie gets to relax a lot more, which she enjoys. It's easy to forget she's old now too. Tetley is ancient and Lexie is old.

This past year we've gotten to sleep in, and snuggle every morning without needing to go somewhere. I spent every morning last summer with Lexie on the patio at my feet, with my feet sweeping across her body while sipping my coffee. There are times I feel Lexie's needs get pushed to the side because she's so easy and Tetley has to be placated before anyone else can relax. Which is a little true but Lexie always got her cuddles, no matter what.

She spends her evenings on the couch next to us, hangs out with me all day in my office, and sits in the console of the car and this year has really soaked up the downtime. The pandemic took a lot of what we did with other people. The fires I hosted at the beach, retreats and even workouts were brought to a halt. They got all of me as my career, and travel, ground to a stop.

That was also when the girls really started to age. Tetley turned 13, then 14 in the pandemic. Lexie turned 10, then 11 during the pandemic. Before that, I travelled more. While I was home most of the time, I hosted weeks-long retreats. During their very senior years, it's been nice to have the time when we didn't go anywhere. I wasn't working and really couldn't worry about much. There was nothing I could do about it. When things opened up I no longer felt comfortable leaving them.

We spent days lazing around, walking and hiking before

Tetley couldn't anymore, trips to the beaches, ponds and swimming holes but mostly enjoying our time together at home, cooking fun meals, and simply hanging out together with much less to worry about or stress about.

Justin has been working away from home so it's been me and the girls. Sometimes it's been hard as Tetley's struggle mounted and the world reopened but I feel like we're still cocooned here. For fun and social activity, I started hosting workouts again for a group of friends. This way we could have friends and fun again, like we always had and I feel it's been good for them, especially Lexie. She really loves all the attention.

As people come for the workouts she meets them, gets on the mat, and takes every opportunity for a cuddle she can get. She's really milking it. Every morning I take my thyroid medication and get back in bed waiting to have my morning coffee. I roll over and put my hand on Lexie', singing her favourite songs, listening to her tail thump, with her half rolling over and shoving her gut closer.

I used to make myself go for a run or a walk but this year I gave myself the downtime. As the world opened up, I returned to University full time, resumed much of my work that was delayed, and was generally busier than the past couple of years, but I still make sure we have lots of downtime and I account for the extra time we need for adventures these days. They are still my number 1 priority.

I know I won't have this forever and it's been nice to give this time to Lexie in the mornings. Mornings were always Tetley's forte. Lexie got cuddled throughout the day and most evenings. But now she also gets the mornings.

I really enjoy our days on the patio. Lexie gets in the shade of the umbrella, and I write, read or work from there, with her at my feet, while Tetley is settled from her swim and we just get to enjoy the slow pace of life that I believe Lexie came to give me.

Without her, I don't think I would have ever learned the value of doing nothing.

While we've always been the driven type, we did always make time for vacations. We weren't great at slowing down in our day-to-day life without Lexie forcing us to. But each year we take a staycation with the girls to a place in Newfoundland. We started doing staycations before we knew they were called staycations.

The first summer we had Lexie, in 2012, Justin booked us a weekend away. We stayed in Swift Current in the cabin rentals because they allowed pets. The girls had so much fun, hiking, checking out the place, fighting and ramping in the cabin. We spent the days driving to locations, some hiking and finding cute eateries and enjoying time off. There was no cell service in the area so it forced us to be off.

The girls in one of their ramping fests.

That began our yearly commitment to a summer staycation. While we travelled to Europe, Jamaica, Dominican Republic, Florida, New York and other places we loved our staycations with the girls. We only went places they could go. We haven't made it to Fogo Island, the only place in Newfoundland we haven't been yet, because we always struggled to find dog-friendly places. This year we found 2 places but the bedrooms were on the second floor and it's too difficult to navigate for them now.

We don't go if they can't go.

These vacations became our family trips. Justin painstakingly searches for locations that are easily accessible, near fresh water, with limited people around so we could have freedom and relax and enjoy them.

We pack up the vehicles, with their dog beds, tie-outs, toys, and food taking up more space than we had for our stuff. They jumped into the back with Lexie in the console and Tetley hanging out the windows as we made our way to the destination. We have many stops for food, pee breaks, fetch and swimming. With the playlist loaded, coffees, and pockets filled with treats, we went off.

Getting there was stressful, especially when we had long distances to drive, but once we were there we relaxed. Our days were spent bringing them places, swimming, and driving around to see sights and towns and they came with us. Always. They were never left in the cabin unless we had to go in somewhere they weren't allowed.

These long weekends and weeks-long vacations gave us time to connect as a family with no household or work obligations. Sometimes I would do a little writing but otherwise, it was just about relaxation. Well, the relaxation came after the road trip, of course, with Tetley's usual insanity starting when Justin was packing the car. I took her for a run in the morning but it never mattered, she was a raving lunatic. We always had a pit stop at the Clarenville dog park, which we were grateful opened because before it opened, we often ended up in arguments trying to find a safe place to stop. Tetley's lunacy in the car knew no bounds.

One of my favourite trips was Sandy Cove and Gros Morne. We stayed in Lomond, and rented log cabins on the Salmon River. The living room and kitchen were smaller than our apartment in Iqaluit but the bedrooms were huge. The girls had a bed each in the spare room but slept with us, jamming us all into the small double bed.

On one of our staycations. We slept like this every night, even at home. I was in there too, somehow.

We always rented 2 bedrooms for the extra space as we found the 1 bedroom usually really tiny. We spent the days there hiking and exploring the area. The girls swam in every pond and ocean we could find. They put off a performance in Rocky Harbour one day, drawing a crowd as Tetley fetched relentlessly but Lexie was determined to get the stick. Lexie was always a fast swimmer and she could motor through the water back then, slamming into Tetley, grabbing the stick and then terrorising her with it.

The people on shore were cheering them on while I was having a slight panic attack that Lexie would really drown Tetley this time.

Our day in Cow Head at the Shallow Bay Beach was a special bonus when we found it empty. This was always such a bonus for us with dogs. There was a slight breeze and the day was one of those Newfoundland days that make you love the place more than you already do. The grass was vibrant green and the sky a clear blue. I set up our picnic while Justin took the girls on a fetch photoshoot. He was always great at getting amazing photos of them. They played in the long grass and Lexie ate some of it.

We had a picnic with them devouring food. They always ate heartily when they were on adventures. We sat at the picnic table with me feeding them and us having a snack. We spent a few hours there and went back to our cabin rested and tired. We had an outdoor fire in our pit that night, while the girls dozed in their beds. It was cold on that trip and we froze by the fire while the girls snuggled warmly in bed.

We stopped in Sandy Cove on our way home. It was such a long trip we decided to break it up and spent a night in Sandy Cove Cabins. We rented a 2-bedroom cabin, which was huge! It was nice to see a cabin set up that gave us proper living and kitchen space. The cabins had staircase access to the sandy beach below. After we unpacked we headed to the beach for some fun. Dogs are welcome on the beach, another bonus on the trip!

Sandy beaches are rare in Newfoundland, especially on the east coast, so the girls really enjoyed their time. Lexie was extra wild on top of Tetley but the waves had enough surf to scare her back to shore. She waited each time Tetley came back with the stick, grabbed it and attacked her with it, running off then back and slamming into her with it.

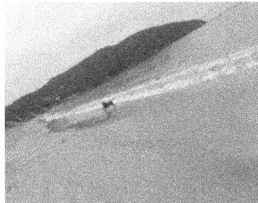

Lexie running from the waves in Sandy Cove.

Each time the wave crashed Lexie bolted. She was so out of control that day I had to leash her and take her on a beach walk.

We always gave Lexie her own stick to play with but she never wanted it. She always wanted the one Tetley had.

We tried to play fetch with her but it hit her in the face more than she caught it. The same with snacks and treats. She rarely caught it and instead flinched as it slapped her in the face. I did help her learn to fetch over the years but she wasn't really interested in it. She just wanted to intercept Tetley's game.

We went back to the beach for sunset and again for sunrise the next morning. I can still feel the calm that morning as we watched the sky turn bright pink. It was peaceful, even though they were gallivanting wildly down the beach. All of our vacations were special because of the trips we took. The girls were our priority and because of the adventures we took them on we experienced more of what Newfoundland, and life, had to offer.

Our second staycation was in Ratting Brook. We rented cabins and when we pulled in there was giant caribou in the yard. The girls gave chase and we followed. We didn't see the caribou again but followed the trail to the Rattling Brook Falls and hiked in.

The next morning we hit the Alexander Murray Hiking Trail. It was scheduled to be hot that day but the hike had rivers and 3 waterfalls along it so we knew we would be ok. We packed snacks and extra water and headed to the trailhead. It has 2200 main stairs but more if you hike to the waterfalls.

This was before Lexie's elbow dysplasia diagnosis.

We stopped to give the girls water regularly as we came across dried-up rivers. When we reached the top the girls found a bog hole and got in. Tetley covered herself in bog, rolling and grinding her face in it.

We had them shaved close that summer, not intending to go as close as they were, but the groomer went too close given they have undercoats. Tetley was more of a pale milk chocolate at that time, bleached from the sun but when they came out of the bog hole they were black labs. Tetley always turns burnt orange to blond in the summer and dark chocolate in the winter. Lexie's coat is the same all year.

We continued on, finding the waterfalls and getting them in the freshwater, cooling off and playing. We stayed there enjoying the day for a while, letting them rest and refresh in the water.

We explored the entire area, walking on a sea glass beach in Harry's Harbour, hiking through old woods paths and tall grassy fields, visiting all the towns and enjoying the area. We walked the streets with the girls running down the road in the middle of it, lazy towns with no traffic, and stopping at the fishing stages and letting them swim in the ocean.

We went back to Rattling Brook several years later. The girls weren't hiking much then so we did some short ones and spent more of our time visiting the towns we hadn't yet seen.

Back Harbour, In Twillingate became another favourite location, which we visited twice, staying at Net Loft Cottage. We couldn't use the loft because it had a ladder and Lexie wouldn't have been ok if we were up there and she wasn't.

We spent our days walking to the beaches, having evening fires at the beach, hiking all the trails and checking out the surrounding towns. One evening we had a fire at the beach, I took a bottle of wine, and the girls happily ate their treats.

We loved those getaways where it was about us, as a family, making memories and enjoying downtime. Slowing down was critical for us. These are the times we loved the most with our busy, hectic lives.

Perhaps one of my favourite trips was the one we took to Red Island with my parents. Justin gets seasick so he went in the speed boat with my brother, Kevin. It was a rough sea but the weather was going to be nice on land. I went with Mom and Dad in Dad's longliner, taking Lexie with me in the big boat. Pepper was with us too. The girls had been in the boat and on several trips to the island but this time it was just my parents and us.

With a large family of 5 siblings, it's not often we get to do something alone with my parents. Tetley went in the speedboat with Justin and Kevin. It was rough. The kind of rough where I stood in the doorway of the wheelhouse, Lexie was behind me under my feet, shivering as the boat went up and down with the swells. The fish tub cover flew off and I didn't see it, even though I was looking right at it, because I was just trying to survive.

Kevin was hanging back, alongside Dad and I could see the nose of the speedboat go up and hit back down. They later said Tetley was sprawled across the floor covered in salt water while Justin was praying. It was his idea to go in the speedboat, even though he was warned it would be rough going.

We made it to the island, docking at the old Government wharf. The tide was low so Dad threw the dogs overboard and they swam to shore, climbing the slipway. We unloaded the boat and made the short trek to the cabin, which is off to itself, not in the harbour with the other cabins.

We had amazing weather that weekend. We walked to Sand Pond and Wild Cove. Wild Cove became my favourite place in Newfoundland. No longer a community, nothing even remaining from resettlement, but an expansive beach with tall grass and beautiful cliffs. We sat in the grass while the dogs ran around. Pepper was young enough then to join us on the hike.

Justin headed to the beach and the dogs ran along with him, diving in and out of the water, chasing each other and playing fetch as I watched from the grassy cliff. Mom and Dad walked ahead and we found a place to sit and enjoy the view.

The island was filled that weekend with cabin goers. We visited people like in the old days and had a fire and a few drinks in people's cabins. The next morning Mom and I went back to Sand Pond. She told me about growing up in Red Island, shearing sheep and how they swam in Sand Pond, a red sandy bottom pond.

When we got back to the harbour I saw Lexie grab something and start chewing. I gave chase because I knew it wasn't anything good. As I caught her she clamped her mouth shut. I pried her jaw open to find a dead rotten rabbit. I hauled it out of her mouth, urging and dry heaving with Mom behind me saying "ah, Jesus get it from her". Someone in one of the cabins came out to see the commotion. She gave me a plastic bag to throw up in and discard the dead rabbit. My arm was covered to the elbow in slobber and dead rabbit.

We headed home a couple of days later, with the seas still raging. We had to get back for work so we faced them anyway. This time I felt better and enjoyed the ride as the dolphins joined us and put off a show. Justin was in the longliner this time too. The sea rose to 5-meter waves as the dogs huddled under the chairs on the deck and in the wheelhouse with Dad. They slept for nearly 2 days when we got home from that trip.

There's a lot of value in taking time off. Not only did I make incredible memories with my girls but we got to spend invaluable time with my parents. That's the thing about slowing down. In it, we find not only peace but we create memories that last a lifetime.

I've strived my entire life to find meaning, purpose and to matter. I've struggled for success and to make a difference in the world. I've had goals and dreams that I've chased at the cost of my life, my family, my relationship, my friends and even that success itself.

I couldn't enjoy any level I reached, and I found ways to sabotage my own success at each new level. Lexie taught me that sometimes the answer is not striving and struggling or pushing or wanting anything other than what we have right now. This moment is all that matters because we are never promised a single breath past the ones we have right now.

We all know this, but we don't always practice it. We have experiences where we tell ourselves that we will change our ways because someone close to us dies or we have a close call with death and we promise we'll do better, that we'll spend more time with those we love, that we'll read more or enjoy more sunsets and we rarely do.

We change temporarily but not long-term. We go back to our busyness and distraction and before we know it we've forgotten our promise to ourselves. Lexie taught me that slowing down isn't optional, it's necessary. There is a lot to be found in the wasted moments of life and the places where we could be finding productivity. When we allow ourselves to unravel from the conditioning that every moment must be sellable or monetisable or that we can't do something just for the joy of doing it, even if that's nothing but staring at the clouds.

Lexie brings that joy to everything, the ability to let you waste time and slow down and for time not to matter and stress to melt away. Nothing matters except her in those moments when you snuggle in and stroke her fur. You can tell she lives for the feeling of that touch and the slowness of life in those moments, and she makes you crave more of it.

That sense of deep peace, even in the brief stolen moments between the chaos of life, business, marriage and Tetley. In the bigness of it all, there is Lexie who offers solace in the storms, a soft place to land, and an inviting bear hug with a constant tail wag. She embodies the happiness of someone who is here, now, in the moment and helping the rest of us be the same. She is a constant invitation to slow down.

We all need this balance but some of us don't have it inside of us. Tetley and Lexie have provided a perfect balance of yang and yin energy. Tetley is the doer and the pusher and the driver. She is determined and fierce. She sometimes must be given something to chill her out so we can all have a rest. I struggled with the guilt of this for a while, but I realised sometimes we all need a little help. I don't hesitate to give her dementia medication or to take my thyroid pills.

We don't think twice about Justin's insulin so why would we hold back a medication that she needs to give her and all of us the energy break we need? Since Tetley got old, she can't get the same workout to blow off the energy that she was used to. Her brain still wants to go and with dementia, she often feels younger than she is or that her body can handle. Swimming lets her glide pain-free, but she still wants more. So, we help her relax with CBD oil and anti-anxiety medications, which she tries to flick off her tongue, and that increases her and our quality of life and surely Lexie really gets to enjoy those quiet moments when Tetley is sleeping and she is the snuggle monster.

It's ok to do what we need to do. It's ok to take time off. It's ok to help ourselves and those we love with medication. It's also ok to be ourselves and find joy in the moment and acceptance of what is.

Sometimes life is hard, and we can't always wave a wand and think it away or change our circumstances. Whether it's our aging dogs that we're facing the loss of or any other challenge in our life, it's easier to check out and distance ourselves from it, to close our heart and try to emotionally turn off or stay hypervigilant to avoid the pain we know we'll face but when we do that, we turn off the beauty too.

We can't experience the good without the bad. When we shut down, we think we're blocking only the hard stuff but when we close our hearts we close the good stuff too. That's not how to live in the moment. Opening our hearts to the pain too allows us to not repress or suppress ourselves and it opens us to the full experience of life.

When we slow down, that comes up. It shows up for us. Maybe that's why we struggle with slowing down. We might not always like what we find when we're not busy. But Lexie, through slowness, taught me that it's there in the sweetness of life that we often find the greatest of gifts. Relentlessness in moving is not always the answer. Many of our gifts will also be in the slow down, in the soft moments, in the down moments. Sometimes the best views are from the ground and not the peaks at all.

Dogs know how to do this, and we can learn from them. Like dogs, some people will be happy to be in the background and be supportive and other people will need the limelight. It's ok to be either of those as long as it's authentic to you.

The key to a balanced life is to know when to push and when to slow. Lexie taught us how to slow down and enjoy the quiet moments of life. She taught me the beauty of coffee in bed on a Sunday morning or waking up and rolling over for a full-body cuddle with snorts and stretches. There is something powerful in the medicine of a dog.

CHAPTER 14
BE WHO YOU ARE

Tetley in all her intensity focusing on fetch. Photo by Ken Reid Photography.

When I got a dog I had this romantic notion that we would do really fun things together, and we did, but I also wanted to do things like hang out at the beach and read a book while my dog dozed next to me. I had a movie-worthy image in my head and I tried to make that image come to life for many years!

Lexie is the type of dog that could do this. She is used to being a wandering little gypsy so she might want to wander off sniffing something but she could be placated with an empty peanut butter tub or if she was tied onto something she would lay down and chill out. She could also be happy with a belly rub and next to me.

I really thought I could negotiate this with Tetley; a relaxing day at the beach. I packed the vehicle, snacks, books, and umbrellas and headed to Topsail Beach or sometimes Salmon Cove Sands, those were my go-to destinations to make this dream come true. Once, I attempted to go to a private park in Brigus Junction and another time we tried to take a family day at Northern Bay Sands. When we did our summer vacations we would also attempt to sit on docks and decks and in fields for some of these movie-worthy images that live in my head of what it's like to have a dog. I'm sure it's the same for people who have children. There's the idea of what it's going to be like and the reality of what it is.

This is where trying to make reality something other than it is and trying to make people something other than they are, collide and cause frustration. Topsail Beach was a place we hiked and worked out. Tetley did not simmer down at all, she escalated as we drove closer to places that could be a potential adventure. Her paws would hit the ground and we would let her run and swim in the water and on these relaxation days we had planned, we would take our peg to put in the ground so we could tie them out while we laid out our blanket.

I spread it all out, Justin took Tetley and Lexie to the water and after 30 minutes of fetching and swimming, we felt it was safe to relax. We gave them water and snacks, those giant pizzle's from the pet store that cost $20 each. I was prepared. Lexie happily lay on the blanket in the sun, chewing her pizzle. Tetley took a break for about 20 minutes. She then started to move around, in and out of the trees, wrapping her tie out around the trees and having to be rescued constantly as she tangled herself up and started barking

I found the perfect place where they could get into the trees for shade and our blanket was on the grass in the sun, just to the left of the brick building that housed the washrooms. It was the perfect location because it was grassy and flat and it was a shock it was available when we arrived.

I was committed to this working out. After 20 minutes of Tetley deciding she wanted to be free, doing circus tricks with her pizzle, trying to tear trees out of the ground and flicking sticks, balls, and toys at us on the bed, drooling all over us, humping Lexie and pacing so much she hog tied Lexie with her tie out.

Justin took her for another swim to buy us a little more time and see if she would settle this time. I untangled Lexie, moved their tie-outs and tied Tetley's to a tree and put Lexie back on the blanket with hers tied to the peg. She stole Tetley's uneaten pizzle and happily lay next to me chewing on it. I settled back into my book.

Justin brought her back after 30 minutes and said she had a fan club by the water and was putting off a show, this was par for the course for Tetley, she really knew how to perform for people and how to show just how powerful, strong and smart she was. She was already doing it but an audience just increased the chances of getting more throws. She always managed to get an audience because she was so intense and so good at what she was doing that she attracted people.

Most people's dogs chase it but don't bring it back. She really is a sight to behold in the water and certainly during these times when she was in her prime. She dove into waves and water and would send it flying over her head.

When she came back this time her tongue was nearly at her knees. She rested for about 10 minutes and then it was back on. This time we packed up the vehicle and left. She had enough exercise and we knew home was the only way she'd relax.

I didn't give up on this dream though. I packed us up, minus Justin, many days to go to Topsail Beach or Salmon Cove Sands. Sometimes I'd even try out the little grassy park area at Butterpot Road in Holyrood. On the rare occasion, Tetley would lay down with a stick and destroy it so I would get a few minutes here and there in between her flicking sticks on me to throw for her. The negotiation for relaxation was how long it would take her to find her stick or ball, usually seconds. I'll admit that a time or two I lay on the grass, face up, listening to her bark into a tree for a ball or stick that went astray. I'd give myself a couple of minutes, and let out a big sigh, before getting up to help her.

There were times I felt like Charlotte in the pantry from *Sex and The City*. My god can you just effing stop?

When we attempted Northern Bay Sands, Justin had checked the website and it didn't say anything about pets so we assumed they could go there. They could not. After driving all the way there with Tetley losing her mind the entire 90 minute drive, head out the window, squealing, up and down the console, stepping on Lexie and doing 360 spins around the backseat of the car, there was no way we could head home without an adventure. We didn't know about Salmon Cove Sands at this point, otherwise, we would have gone there. Instead, we found some alcove for the derelicts in the woods, above Northern Bay Sands and we set up there.

Tetley was wilder than normal, just insane and Justin was pretty frustrated by this time. As was I. He likes to research things and for things to go right so the fact that everything was going wrong was a little intense for him. We found this woodsy area that seemed like a place teenagers might go to drink on the weekends, it was a good swimming hole so we set up there. I even got in the water with the girls. I made the best of it.

Lexie and I had a great swim together while Tetley played fetch. Lexie always enjoyed it when I was in with her. It also distracted her from Tetley's game of fetch and trying to stop her.

It took a good 30 minutes for Tetley to calm down that day. Constant fetch, tearing up trees, eating snacks, and creating anarchy. We ended up spending a couple of hours there and while it was initially one of those days where you just want to go home but since you went through the trouble of getting there, you're staying, good time or not! It worked out in the end.

All of us ended up calming down and having a great time but it was another big X on the relaxing beach day I had mental images of in my mind. That was the day I started to wonder if we could ever do it, actually make it happen.

I would go into the woods in Topsail Beach and the woods behind my house with them and have those relaxing moments I desired. I started taking some things with me, a blanket, or having a fire, Tetley was calmer there. She still didn't stop and constantly brought something to throw but occasionally she would wander around and smell things or lay down and chew on a stick. I started to get the message that maybe beaches are for terrorising and woods are for chilling.

Now, don't get me wrong, there wasn't much chilling in the woods but instead of 110% at the beach I would get an occasional 80% in the woods. Whatever I was working on I learned how to keep doing it while also throwing the ball or stick. I could write entire blog posts and articles, do whole workouts, have coaching sessions while throwing a ball consistently with one hand and not miss a beat.

I took them to festivals and even the Royal St. John's Regatta, lying to myself every time that this time Tetley would be a good girl. More people meant more opportunities for showing off. She was completely insane in those places and eventually, I stopped taking her.

I stopped trying to take her to the beach to relax and accepted that she would never be that dog. She let me cuddle her when she was tired and when she got in bed she liked to be curled behind my legs or in between my legs. In the mornings, she still enjoys a little cuddle, but typically she likes to be on the go or sleeping and when she's focused on sleeping she wants to sleep. It was the same when she wanted food. She usually only begged for steak and if you tried to pet her she moved her head constantly. Focused only on getting what she wanted.

We built an addition to the patio and bought nice wicker furniture and stayed home. We had a beautiful backyard and she had all the freedom in the world and we had peace. So we just stayed home more often instead of always going somewhere else to enjoy what we already had. Maybe there was a lesson in that too. I got to relax and she got to be free and wild. Lexie got to lay under the umbrella and chill by my side. The best of all worlds for all of us. It took too many years to have that realisation.

Letting her be who she was was a gift to all of us. I stopped trying to jam us and them into experiences that were never going to happen the way I wanted them to. It became a big realisation in other areas of my life, as well. How many times had I wanted people to be who I wanted them to be?

How many disappointing experiences had I had with people in my life because I wouldn't accept who they were? How many red flags, and emotional destruction did I suffer because I didn't accept who people were and wanted them to be better than they were or nicer than they were?

How often have I wished that people would be there for me? Show up for me? Believe in me? Far too often to count. I realised that this was a trait I had to let go of, trying to make people, even dogs, who I wanted them to be.

When I accepted Tetley for who she was, Lexie for who she was, and myself for who I am, I could start to recognise who other people were too. Instead of trying to make people who they aren't, when we can accept people for who they are, we make all of our lives easier. Sometimes people just can't be what we need them to be and that's ok. It's not that what we want or need is wrong, it's that we're trying to get it where we can't.

That becomes the problem. When we don't accept people for who they are, it's sort of an interesting catch-22 of emotional upset. We want them to be who we need them to be and yet, we don't accept them for who they are. Everyone ends up frustrated and disappointed. We need to stop living in hope that people will change, recognise them for who they are, and accept them for that but still allow ourselves to meet our needs, guilt-free.

What I learned from the dogs is that the sooner we stop trying to make people who they are not, the faster we can go find it in the places it does exist or we can give it to ourselves. I do regret not taking more time for myself over the years. I wish I had given myself more of those beach days but I didn't want to go to those places and leave the girl's home. I wanted them to be able to come with me. So I ended up staying home or going on adventures that did work for all of us.

I could have left Tetley home sometimes and taken Lexie or I could have left them home and Justin and I could have gone together and had an enjoyable day. But I tried to make us into something we weren't sometimes instead of accepting this. Justin would occasionally say to me "why can't we leave them home" and I would get so mad that he wanted to leave them home and he would just say "so we can relax and enjoy ourselves". I always enjoyed myself more with them. But what I really enjoyed was the idea of who I wanted us to be.

In the end, I learned the lesson, but it took a long time and a lot of stubbornness on my end to make Tetley into something she wasn't. Eventually, I started taking evenings at the beach or having a fire and left them at home. Sometimes I popped the hatch of the SUV and read a book while the sun was setting. It took a long time to start doing this for myself, to create something for me in a way that filled me up and gave back to myself so I had, even more, to give to them.

It takes time to find our way, to overcome the guilt of parenting, whether it's human or fur children or to overcome the guilt and shame we feel for wanting something other than what we're told to want, for needing time for ourselves, or to leave them home so we can relax and enjoy ourselves. Whether it's people or dogs, we need to accept people for who they are and recognise that we can still have the things we want, just maybe not from those people.

It's a hard lesson in life but one that's so important for us to learn so we can create boundaries and balance in our lives.

After her CCD diagnosis I drove to the places we had always gone; Topsail Beach, various places in CBS, Witless Bay to the beach, Salmon Cove Sands, Bay Roberts, Harbour Main, Butterpot Road and Brigus, she gave me what I always wanted, a moment together. I had to go to the places where I could drive and easily access water and parks because she couldn't walk far anymore. It was a mild winter and I was grateful for that.

One day in Brigus, she got out with me for a swim. We tried to swim but the tide was too low and the beach too rocky. Lexie stayed in the car and Tetley and I went to the grassy lookout by the tunnel and sat together. We stayed that way for 45 minutes. She lay next to my legs, leaning on me, looking out at the water and I was looking at her and thinking about our journey together. That day I didn't expect to get another year with her. I thought it was over then or soon.

She gave me that, I know she did. I felt it. A gift from her to create that core memory I had always wanted with her to just sit together peacefully in public and not need to do but just be. Lexie refused to get out of the car that day and I feel it was somehow meant to be. She would have sat next to me easily and effortlessly but I know she stayed behind so we could have that one moment. I'll never forget it. She couldn't ever be who she wasn't but in this way she could give me the one thing I always wanted for us, to have a moment, just a moment where we truly appreciated each other and the incredible journey we've had.

I still hold that moment in my heart. I have had many of those moments with Lexie over the years but not many with Tetley. She was always paws on the ground and my go-girl. She saved my life during my trauma recovery because of that. Lexie would let me stay in the bed and die, but Tetley refused to do that. She hauled sheets off me and barked for me to get up. She did the same when I had been working too much. She never let me stay at my desk for too long.

In Brigus. That day.

Lexie would let me stay at my laptop forever but Tetley wouldn't leave me alone for more than a few hours. Lexie is good and Tetley is wild. It's that wildness that's both a gift and a curse. In my life, it was mostly a gift.

In spite of their breed and their copy-and-paste nickname, Tetley and Lexie couldn't be more different than if they were completely different breeds. Tetley is relentless and exhausting, and Lexie is loving and easy, for the most part.

Lexie has a lot of quirks that are unexplainable. Partly because we didn't know where she came from and partly because we didn't know how she was raised. We had our suspicions and ideas but nothing concrete. We thought for sure she was raised by or with cats.

She chased leaves until she was 9. When a leaf blew down the road she chased it, using her paws like a cat. Every fall we watched her chase the red maple leaves out the driveway. If we were walking on a trail or the road and a leaf blew she yanked your arm as she gave chase to it. The more leaves the more she changed directions.

She cleaned herself by licking inside her paws and washing her ears and face. She doesn't do this anymore but she did it for many years leaving us wondering if she was in fact exposed to cats early on. We have no idea but we do tell her she's part cat.

She "hunted" Tetley while she was swimming and hiking, hiding in the bushes and wiggling her butt like a cat before pouncing as Tetley got closer to her.

Giving chase to leaves or Tetley wasn't the only thing she did. She loved to chase the stability balls in the gym. Lexie would run at the balls and bounce off them. Tetley had learned to do burpee push-ups, stability ball planks and other workouts before we got Lexie so she often put her paws on the stability ball after backing it against the wall.

Lexie would run at it, sending her and Tetley flying, bouncing off it. Then she would attack it with her mouth, dragging it around, trying to bring it places only to see it deflate after she bit into it.

I had mini green balls for classes and she destroyed all of them. She grabbed the balls, threw them in the air, pinched them between her teeth and flicked them around until they deflated. She seemed surprised every time, yet she managed to deflate all 30 of them.

She and Tetley would grab the ends of bands, gliders and skipping ropes and chase each other around the studio, often ending up in a pile of vocal noises, kicking and biting each other.

It was chaos. They were obsessed with destroying things, especially Lexie. She ripped up yoga mats, bands, balls and toys. You couldn't turn your back on her and she was off with something.

I did discipline them but I also let them be who they were. We don't get a lot of permission to be who we are. Maybe I wouldn't have had as much damage or destruction but I wouldn't have had as much fun either!

Once they had their crazy burned off they settled into who they were. Tetley was wild but reserved. Lexie was loving but needy. We didn't force Lexie to learn tricks or do commands. We didn't medicate Tetley or kennel her to be good. We didn't use choke chains or shock collars to control them.

We didn't put Tetley down when she needed a major surgery. We didn't put Lexie down when she bit. Instead, we helped her be better. We didn't change who they were at their core, instead, we met their needs and let them be who they were. We brought out the best qualities in them by meeting their needs and letting them run the crazy out.

Because of this, they became who they were. I made Lexie into the loving dog she was. I struggle to own my own great qualities sometimes and I shrink away from taking credit. But the reality is Lexie was a lot of work in her younger years. She was always into something. She bit me and my nephew. She didn't listen. She wasn't trained. She had non-stop medical problems. I dedicated myself to her. I made her safe. I loved her. I cared for her. I didn't force her to learn tricks or commands and instead focused on letting her come out of her shell.

She became love because of that. I can't say for sure what would have happened to her if someone else had gotten her. I don't want to know. I cannot imagine my life without Lexie now. I cannot imagine if we didn't go back or if we rehomed her. I don't think Lexie would have thrived in many homes.

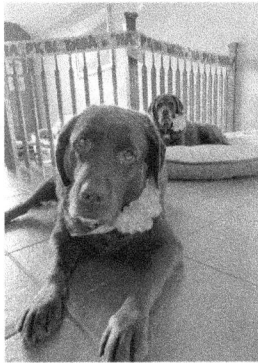

Lexie in the front being cute and adorable.
Tetley in the back being judgemental.

The wrong home would have hurt her. Well, she had the wrong home initially but I know another wrong home may have been the nail in her coffin. I cannot imagine Lexie not being her loving self.

My friends and clients who didn't know her when she was younger are always shocked when I say she tried to drown Tetley all the time or that she was into the garbage, wasn't good, and bit people. No one can believe it.

Lexie became that because of me, my dedication and devotion to her, to creating a safe and loving environment, not giving up, following through on training, and keeping her medical needs tended to. That's what happens when dogs, or people, are cared for. When we are allowed to be who we are, we thrive, and we grow into the versions of ourselves that are the best ones.

When we aren't treated well, our defence mechanisms come out in full. If we all had the opportunity to grow into who we are, not conditioned into who we are supposed to be pleasing, what a different outcome for so many of us.

From the dogs, I learned just how important it is to accept people in my life for who they are, not try to make them who I want them to be. Sometimes that might even mean leaving them where they are. If I accept people for who they are, I'm less disappointed because I have fewer expectations.

When I accept people for who they are, don't try to blame or shame them, but truly accept them for who they are, we can move on and find what we're looking for. In my work, I have this conversation regularly with clients. It's not that what we need is wrong, it's that we can often try to get it from the wrong people.

If I wanted Lexie to be a relentlessly driven dog I would be constantly frustrated. If I wanted Tetley to be a calm dog, like I sometimes did, I would always be frustrated and sometimes was. Until I accepted them for who they are, their individual personalities, different capacities, different mobilities and abilities, I was frustrated with someone all the time.

When I accepted who we all were I created peace in our environment. That often means we have to be open to getting our needs met in different ways. It also means we need to let go of expectations and instead create standards for our lives.

I decided that I no longer wanted to fight with Tetley. I accepted her for who she was. I created ways to meet her needs while also giving us relaxation time. I accepted that Lexie would never be a driven, focused dog. She wouldn't be the girl who would get me out of bed but she would help me through the darkest days in other ways.

The same boiling water that hardens an egg softens a potato. We are who we are, and even in the same circumstances, we will be different. Tetley loves praise and worked hard for it. Lexie loves affection and works hard for it. Different work, different motivation, different dogs. It's really that simple.

Where Tetley was an early riser, loved to blow off her energy, and then relax, Lexie loved to sleep in, often needing to be dragged out of bed when we had places to be.

They both spent most of their time in bed or on the couches with us, even Tetley. Because she's been old for so long now it's easy to forget that she loved to be with us as much as Lexie, just in a different way. Tetley loved to be on the couch with us and being scratched but never petted. Lexie loved being touched, she didn't care what you were doing with her, even clipping her toenails, she was just always happy to be touched.

It's easy to forget that Tetley, too, spent her rest time sleeping in my office with me, next to Lexie or Lexie was the one in another room while Tetley dominated my space. It was only when Tetley got over 11 that Lexie completely took over the spaces. Tetley's been an old lady for so long but her energy and drive make you forget she's old. But looking back we can see changes in her for nearly 3 years.

Tetley had to be harnessed for grooming where Lexie sat quietly. Tetley usually had to be taken in the back for blood work, whereas Lexie just quietly let them take her blood work. Tetley had to be held down. Once, the vets and techs tried to do it in the exam room with me there but Tetley fought them so hard they had to stop. Her eyes bugged out of her head and she pursed her lips and she did everything to get away from the needle.

3 vet techs and a vet and me. I called it. I said we'd come back another time, I wouldn't put her through that. She happily bopped out of the room. Tetley knew she could fight her way out of anything. Lexie never tried fighting it. She was always easy.

Except when she didn't want Tetley to have attention. She

pulled her bandanas off, hockey fight style, and ripped her flowers off from the groomers. She kept hers on while Tetley's were pulled off. She hated Tetley looking good.

When she was fed up with Tetley's fetch, she took her sticks or toys and lay on them. We all appreciated this. Where Tetley fought being hosed off and even dried off, Lexie sat and took it all. Grooming was a wild experience, with Lexie sitting quietly being groomed but Tetley fighting it every step of the way.

Their first groomer told us that Lexie would try to eat Tetley's fur so they had to put her in a kennel while Tetley was being groomed. She also freaked out when Tetley was in the tub or on the table. She stood at the base crying and scravelling around wanting her to get down.

She did the same with me when I climbed trees in the woods or Justin got on the roof of the house. She stood there, crying as if to say "get down!"

We're not all the same. Dogs or people. There are people in our lives the same way. We need to accept their limitations. It doesn't mean we have to be limited because they are but we need to learn to move on and get our needs met in the way they need to be.

We need to embrace the differences we each bring to the table and create a well-rounded approach through friendships, work and relationships that allow us to have ways to meet our needs.

We also need people in our lives that accept us for who we are. We need to be able to be ourselves and not have to be something for others. By finding this, even if it's with our dog, it creates a place of self-acceptance. The more we accept ourselves for who we are the less we want to wear masks and be conditioned to be something we're not.

When we can be ourselves we can allow others to be themselves. There is no greater gift or lesson than to be wholly who we are. And to honour how we change over time. We're supposed to change. We're supposed to go through early, middle and later life phases where we are different versions of ourselves in different stages.

Like in our dogs. This is easier to see because their lives and phases are so short. We have different needs and are different versions of ourselves in different phases. We're supposed to change. Life is supposed to change us. We're not supposed to cling to phases we've outgrown. When we are able to be ourselves we can embrace these life phases and let them shape us.

CHAPTER 15
LOYALTY

Lexie on her bed in my meditation and journalling space.
She never left my side.

We joke that Tetley is loyal to us and Lexie is loyal to her gut but that's not true. Lexie is the epitome of love and she is very loyal to me and she needs to be loved and cared for all the time. Sometimes I feel like Lexie is the human baby I never had. Lexie is not a dog that does well on her own. It was a long time before anyone told me she cried the entire time I was out of the house. She had to be with me all the time.

This year I got a live stream camera for them because of Tetley's illness, so I could make sure she was safe when I was away. After the night I left her alone and found her under the table, I didn't want a repeat and in order for me to leave the house I needed to know she was ok or that I needed to go back. What I found was Lexie by the door waiting for me and Tetley asleep in her bed.

A few years ago, as we were leaving for a trip to Jamaica, our pet sitter told me she was crying for me by the door after we left. I hadn't even made it off my street. Justin was not happy about this because he knew I would worry about her more than I already do. I had no idea she was so addicted to me. We haven't been apart hardly at all. She came to me in 2012 and other than the few times she was left because of surgeries or trips she was never without me.

Tetley, on the other hand, had a couple of years in her early life where she was left alone for the day when I worked corporate and had to be away. I also rented studio space in St. John's for part of my career so she had to stay home. Lexie never had to develop the skill of being independent or alone. She also had Tetley when we left them at home.

I am her safe person and she adores me. But at the same time, Lexie is an opportunist. She regularly throws herself at people. She really dislikes Tetley having any attention and she uses her charm, her puppy dog eyes and her happiness to get anyone on the ground with her. And everyone does, from Amazon drivers to handymen and all of my friends and clients have had a cuddle fest with Lexie.

Anyone who has slept in my house has slept with Lexie. Tetley is more standoffish, even polite with people. We taught her that. She waited for people to invite her to them and she never slept with anyone other than us. We were her people and that's that. She still waits for people to approach her when they come inside but Lexie rushes to the door and flings herself at people.

I have clients who come, get out of their vehicle and immediately lay on the ground with Lex, in any weather. She half rolls over, shoves her belly up and immediately starts pawing if you dare to stop. She is everyone's best friend. She throws herself at people, relentlessly. She doesn't care if you like dogs, you will love her when she's done with you. She doesn't care that her fur will be in your tonsils and you will choke for hours after a love fest with her, she will crawl into your neck, your arms and your heart.

Lexie is a little bully of love. She wants to be loved and wants you to feel loved, whether you know it or you don't. Everyone thinks they're her favourite person but it's not exactly like that and she has been caught in some difficult situations when several people who think they're her best friends are at our at the same time.

Lexie has to process who she goes to. She still goes to everyone and everyone obliges because there is just something about her that makes you fall so deeply in love that it's virtually impossible to say no, even when you know she's using you. My friend Chrissy, who legit calls Lexie her bestie, thinks she is her bestie. She believed that Lexie only cuddled and snuggled with her the way she does. While Chrissy had known Tetley and Lex for a long time, it wasn't until the pandemic that we spent time together in my house.

She was helping me with work projects and she got to see Lexie in full action. I had some personal training clients at the time who would come back and forth and one day Chrissy and Jessica overlapped.

They both soon understood that they weren't really as special as they thought they were. I mean, Lexie did absolutely love them and knew it would be a cuddle fest. But she wasn't going to be particular about who got on the ground with her.

She's like the perfect little bully who looks so innocent and cute, that body slams Tetley out of the way and wanders from person to person to get her needs met, while at the same time making you think she's the most adorable thing you've ever met. And she is.

However, we've often had to remind pet sitters and even ourselves that Lexie's need for constant attention and her inability to share attention with Tetley isn't always so cute and has left Tetley out on more than one occasion. Now, Tetley really loved her balls and fetch and she had no problem with Lexie wanting to snuggle and not bother her while playing fetch, yet, Tetley still loved attention, sleeping in bed with us, getting kisses and being greeted and paid attention to by others.

We often returned from trips with Tetley desperate for attention. You could see in her eyes that she was emotionally neglected and was desperate to see us. Without being here, we 100% knew that Lexie cuddled her pet sitters and threw herself at them. Tetley is the type you have to work for her love and attention but Lexie just flings it at you full force. It's nearly impossible to see Tetley because Lexie is in your face all the time.

When I travelled for work I would FaceTime the girls and Lexie was always so happy to see me but Tetley would intentionally get up and leave the room or turn her back. When I arrived home she would rummage through my suitcase for her toy or presents that I brought back. Then she'd stare at me and turn her back. Even when I walked her, she came but she wouldn't look at me. When we went in the car, she would come but wouldn't look at me.

It would take a couple of days to get back in her favour. She wasn't letting me off the hook easily. Whereas Lexie threw herself at me. She had her toys but she planted herself on top of me, licking, frantic as if she couldn't believe I was there. She didn't make me work to get back in her favour!

Our visits to the vet were the same, the vets couldn't examine Tetley because Lexie would literally crawl into their arms and prevent them from examining her. She would kiss and lick and roll around the floor with the vets. We often thought she was protecting Tetley because Tetley hated being examined but there's also a pretty selfish motive on Lexie's end and that's getting her gut rubbed. They either take her in the back or I bring her back to the vehicle so Tetley can get examined. She loves people and she loves people loving her. She is loyal to that.

Our holistic vet would request Lexie be put outside when Tetley was being examined. She would have to be tethered because she got in the way. We talked about how she does this at home, in general, when you're playing with or petting Tetley. She didn't give anyone else a turn, all turns were hers. She would come over and instigate something with Tetley so Tet would get fed up and leave and she could crawl in and cuddle.

The holistic vet always said it was unhealthy because Lexie needed to understand her place and turn and be respectful but she never did and we honestly didn't do a lot to curb it. We gave them both an enormous amount of attention and love but not a lot of boundaries. In hindsight, we probably could have worked on that more but hindsight is 20/20 and Tetley got so much hiking, fetch, and workout attention, while Lex lay next to me or cuddled me seemed harmless enough. They had different needs and we still were always sure, with both of us, to be as fair as we could in our home. It was the other people who Lex really manipulated to get constant attention.

When my friend, Mary Ann and her husband Mark, took care of the girls for a night when we had an out-of-town wedding, Mary Ann remarked how loyal Tetley was. Tetley didn't like to stay in other people's houses if we weren't there. Lexie just did not care. I believe Lexie is more insecure about her place in the world. Perhaps it's trauma or a chaotic early life, but whatever the reason, Lexie sticks herself to people. That night she left the living room and went to bed with Mark, whom she had never met before this.

Tetley stayed with Mary Ann and stayed by her side the

entire time. Tetley had known Mary Ann for many years and she was friendly to Mark but she was loyal to Mary Ann. Lexie, on the other hand, was belly up in bed with him because he was rubbing her belly.

People often told us that Tetley made them like dogs, even though she was too much with a ball and covered people in slobber from her sticks, she was rather polite. Tetley didn't get in people's spaces or faces unless fetch was involved. She held back and let you invite her to you. She didn't kiss people or lick people. She didn't jump or push herself on people. We always joked Tetley has self-respect but Lex has none. Tetley was more confident and knew her place in the world, but Lex was the dog that licked everyone's tonsils.

When Justin's father, Gord and his wife Helen, took care of Tetley when we went on a holiday once, before we had Lex, she ran home! She had never walked from their house to ours. We live about 5-7 kilometres away from each other. Tetley had been there many times but we never walked that route.

When we came back from our holiday, Helen and Gord were mortified to tell us that Tetley ran away from them and they found her almost back home. Gord had let her out and went back in to get a coat, when we went back out she was gone. He looked around his property because he didn't think she could have gone very far. After a couple of minutes of him and Helen searching they realised she wasn't on their property.

Helen stayed there looking for her and in case she showed up but Gord got in his car and went down their street searching for her. She just couldn't have gotten that far. As he made it from his street to the Main road through town he was more concerned. He didn't think she made it that far so he went back on his street for one more look but there was no sign of her. He wondered if she had made a beeline for home so he went back to the main road and drove to our street. As he made his way up Country Path he saw her furry butt in a full run. He stopped, captured her and brought her back to his house, where she was tethered and leashed the minute she went outside.

She was 2 at the time. She had no intention of not being with her mom and dad. We often had people drop in to take her for a walk, dog walkers or just friends who could help us out when I was working corporate. One couple took her to their house once and she was not happy about it. She refused to go in. She stayed outside, even in the rain. They had to bring her home.

On the occasions she went missing when her dad *wasn't* watching her, people would try to get her in their car to bring her home but she wouldn't get in so they would come up and tell us where she was and we would go get her.

She was and is loyal. While Tetley has deteriorated over the last year she still only offers kisses to us. If she kissed you, it meant she really liked you. I would occasionally see her take a liking to people and she would offer them a lick or even sit or lay next to them, which was rare for her. She stuck close to us but other than her Uncle Chad or Auntie Mary Ann whom she would cuddle up with, she often greeted people but was more standoffish with them.

I feel at times I can relate to Lexie's need to throw herself at people. While I've been challenged with relationships with people I never have with dogs. People are both a desperate need and a weary fear. I've been hurt by people. Many times. And yet the need to be in community, and friendship and to know we are important, cared about and that we matter are intertwined in our relationships.

Lexie was also hurt by people. She was innocent. She was a little baby and humans both harmed her and abandoned her. Like people, animals get imprinted with these fears. I made Lex safe. I was her safety in this world and it was like a balm to her scared little soul, when we met. I feel that bond with her, as someone who also had been innocent and harmed. I feel the need to protect her, to let her be who she is in spite of all she has experienced, and to be safe for her. And I have been that. For that I am proud.

Far too many people get special needs dogs, whether it's emotional or physical and see them as throw away. They are turned over to a shelter or rehomed or in worse cases, euthanised because of the work required. I cannot imagine not going the extra mile for them when they give us so much. How can we expect loyalty from them but not give it to them?

I was Lexie's safe place and she was mine. She taught me to love. Tetley opened my soul to the greatest adventure of my life. She showed me power and purpose and focus and relentlessness in the pursuit of life and what it means to truly live and be alive. But Lexie taught me how to love, how to lean into something that was soft, how to love someone unlike me or maybe help me find those parts of me that were like her but were lost. She taught me how to slow down, and how to embrace love. She taught me how to receive unconditional love and adoration. She taught me that I didn't need to be anything remarkable to have that love.

She gave me pure love, with no strings attached. There wasn't someone or something I had to be to get it. She forgave easily, she loved relentlessly, and loyalty to her wasn't about a person but a way of being. She gave me, and so many who have been blessed to know, the inability to be in a bad mood, hold a grudge or hold back your full self.

Tetley is more of who we were in those early days, worka-holics, relentless in the pursuit of life and success. She was driven with no other agenda than to chase and retrieve that ball or stick. She had a purpose and she was going to live it, at all costs. Her loyalty was to us, her purpose and her breed.

Lexie's loyalty is to her heart. She doesn't need it to be a special person. While she loved certain people, she also just really loves love. She loves comfort and cuddles and softness and that is what she is loyal to.

I love her for that loyalty. That safety and certainty brought it out in her. That her hard past didn't make her saucy but made her more loving. It's like she is always very aware, even though she was so young, that there is a harsher side of life and she is grateful. In her gratitude, she gives what she received. Unconditional love to everyone she meets. She doesn't make anyone work for it. She doesn't wait. She isn't polite. She doesn't care if you want it.

She knows the full presence of her body, pressed to yours, or her belly up in the air with you rubbing it, will make us all better people. Lexie knows that it's not reserved love we need but abundant, adoration of each other, forgiveness and presence that will make us all better.

My loyalty to my girls never wavered. They are always my priority. The way we do things changed but their place or importance never did. I wasn't only loyal to my girls, but to the routines we held, and to the other dogs in my life.

When we went to my parents in Point Verde, my sister-in-law Alyssa and I always took all the dogs on adventures. She had Hunter but the family always brought their dogs. Pepper, Baylee, and Dewy came on adventures with us.

I loaded all the dogs into the vehicles, they were stuffed in everywhere and took off for a swimming hole or in the woods behind mom and dads. I never left any of them behind. We headed into the marsh into the trails behind the house, hiking up to Kern Hill and looking out over the expanse of forest. That was my pop's favourite lookout. He told me once that anyone who didn't believe in God had never seen the forest at sunrise or sunset.

We rigged up on cold winter days, balaclavas, and ice cleats and headed out on adventures. Sometimes it was so cold the dogs would run back to me and I would hold their paws in my hands to heat them up. I tried boots on them many times but they wouldn't walk with them on. Tetley and Lexie always ran back on cold winter days to get their paws warmed up.

One day, in Point Verde, we all headed out for a hike. Alyssa,

Mom, Me, Tetley, Lexie, Hunter, Baylee and Pepper. The sun was shining and the skidoos had beaten a nice path for us. Our faces were red and numb from the cold but we kept going. Tetley found a junk of wood and all the dogs chased it as we played fetch on the frozen marsh.

Me. Hunter. Tetley. Lexie in Point Verde on a frigid walk playing fetch with a junk of wood.

Sometimes the kids would join us. I often found myself surrounded by nieces and nephews, Hailey, Tyler, Eric and Kyle with 4 or 5 dogs, running through mud and bog with the kids making up stories about our adventures. They would tell me stories of the giants and fairies in the woods and make up tall tales about everything as we traipsed through the woods as they yelled "hurry, hide, they're gonna find us" about whatever they were making up, and we would run into the woods, with the dogs following, never know why but always ready for it.

Because of the dogs, I was heading on an adventure, all the time, and I included the kids and dogs that were there. If I was going, whoever wanted to come was invited. Point Verde was where I found myself at the centre of all the dogs.

It took me a while to realise this was reason they loved me. Because I included them. They chased me into the woods and into the vehicles. I never cared if they or the cars were dirty or wet. I packed towels and snacks and we made the day of it. As the dogs started to die or got too old to go, first Dewy, then

Pepper and Lexie and Baylee got too crippled to go, Alyssa and I still took Tetley and Hunter.

We adjusted our outings from longer hikes in the backlands of Argentia and sometimes drove to the lookouts where Lexie could join us for short walks and Tetley and Hunter could play fetch. Or we would head to the ponds and ocean for a swim at the lighthouse in Point Verde or Argentia.

It wasn't optional, we were out. During my brother's wedding, after my hair and makeup were finished, in gale-force winds with Hurricane Larry barrelling toward us, we loaded up the dogs and headed to the water to get them out. I put a garbage bag on my head to save my hair.

Loyalty isn't sometimes, it's all the time.

My girls have an amazing relationship with Justin. He is a great dog dad. But I'm their mom. Sometimes we tested their love and loyalty by seeing whose car they'd get in, they almost always chose mine. Justin said it wasn't fair because they expected adventure with me.

Tetley loved to drive around with Justin but if I was going she was coming with me. She also ran to me if she was hurt. Lexie, too. When Lexie had seizures she came to me, got into my arms, rested her head on my shoulder and waited it out. She then slept next to me after it.

Tetley was always hurting something. Justin's friend, Trevor, threw a ball for her one winter day when they were getting ready for skidooing. Tetley always dropped a ball and most people picked it up.

We had a lot of snow that year and our fire pit was covered in a blanket of snow. He threw the ball, not realising it was there. Tetley hit the corner of the rock wall, slicing open the taut fur and skin on her ankle. I didn't realise it at the time but she came into the house, which was odd when people were outside.

I checked her over and didn't see anything. I asked Justin if anything was wrong and he said she might be tired from fetch. I didn't believe it. She never got tired. As I was cleaning the house she kept following me and staring at me. She went back to her bed, stared at me and her teeth started to chatter.

I knew something was wrong so I had another look over her and that's when I saw it, the skin and fur were rolled up on the inside of her ankle, exposing the flesh and tendons underneath. It was Saturday and that meant *another* emergency room visit. We called the Vet and ended up at Topsail Road Vet Clinic. Lexie and I sat on the floor while Tetley was sedated and stitched up. Lexie lay outside the room looking in.

Tetley's sedation was reversed and she was sent home with a couple of stitches. She might have been outside with her daddy that day but she knew who to come to when she was hurt. Dogs in need always seem to find me. Tetley was always mine but she was also very independent so she wasn't clingy. But as she's gotten older she doesn't like to be away from me much. As she declined, I'm her safety now.

There's a dog that lives nearby, Connor (name changed), he is a beautiful dog and I would have adopted him long ago if the owners would have given him to me. We first met Conner before we had Lexie. He showed up one day and he was just the sweetest dog. He spent the day with us and Justin and I hoped no one was looking for him. We wanted to keep him.

His owners did find us. I had put up some posts online about him and his owner showed up to get him. We sent him home telling them if they ever wanted to rehome him let us know. Connor would come back and forth over the years and the owners always came looking for him.

One day I pulled into the driveway and Conner was on the patio. I hadn't seen him in a long time and often wondered if he had died. As I got out of the vehicle, the girls started to bark but I noticed Connor was covered in blood. My heart sank. He looked like he was hit by a car. My patio was covered in blood and his fur was covered in blood with open cuts everywhere.

I called his owners who came almost immediately to get him and take him to the vet. I followed up with them and they said he was vet-checked, given medication and released. I was surprised because he seemed to be pretty banged up. I was going to visit him a couple of times but it never happened.

A long time passed again when I got up early one morning and Connor was on my patio. He was a mess. He clearly had not been treated since the accident. His wounds had healed, but not healed, and his skin was raw. This time I didn't call his owners. I called my friend who worked in rescue and was also a police officer.

She told me to go to the RCMP detachment and they would be forced to deal with me and the dog. The owner found out I was sitting there and he came down while I waited for the police to come out. He approached my vehicle and I told him I wasn't giving him back the dog, he needed medical care.

He called his wife and I could hear everything she was saying. She called me everything you can imagine, screaming obscenities on the phone. She was en route and said she was going to beat my face in for taking her dog. She called me a high and mighty bitch who treated my dogs too well and not everyone was going to. I was scared, I won't lie. But I wasn't giving up the dog.

The police intervened and I followed them to a vet clinic where the SPCA took care of him. I found out the next day they released him back to his owners. His vet care and SPCA bill cost $900 and they paid it and got him back.

I followed up with the police several times but heard nothing. I've never seen him again and do not know if he died. I was happy they paid for his treatment and hope they continued to provide for him.

I was devastated, once again, in our system, that fails these dogs time and time again. I found 2 beagles once and turned them into the SPCA, they were clearly starving, abused and neglected. They promised me the owner wouldn't see them again. The owners lied and said they just bought them off a hunter and were giving them a better home. I found out through the grapevine they were just put in a cage again.

I found a beagle on Topsail beach one morning, he lived in a cage. He wasn't injured but I had to give him back. The police told me he was cared for and that was that. Our laws are the pits. But I find even the laws we have aren't enforced.

My heart has been broken a thousand times over dogs that aren't even mine and nothing I can do about it or for them. I doubt Connor is still alive now and if he is I hope they gave him the treatment he needed. I told the guy who owned him, I just wanted the best for Connor. I would even pay for his vet care if necessary. I had many conversations with him over the years when I returned Connor.

I didn't hate him. The point people miss is it isn't about them. It's about the dogs. They are so loyal to us, even when we don't deserve it, I try to be loyal to them because I know they deserve it. They deserve so much better.

We live in a divided world, keeping score and holding back and not being loved until we know someone else loves us back. We live safely. But Lexie teaches me every day that playing safe with our love and forgiveness only leads us to live a life of walls and a life less than we could have. Imagine if we all just greeted each other as if we loved each other. Lexie never cares about who you are, what you have, or what you can do for her. If you are a good person and she gets a good vibe she will throw herself at you. That is loyalty to love.

What more can we desire in this world? Than to be loyal to love? Maybe, just maybe, that's the loyalty we all need more of. That we don't care about anything other than the moment? What if we didn't hold grudges and just loved each other in the moment that we are together?

When Lexie sees someone she hasn't seen in a long time she throws herself at them. She doesn't make them work for her love. She is as enthusiastic as the last time she saw them. She doesn't do what humans do, she doesn't hold herself back. She doesn't make people explain where they've been or why they've been absent.

She isn't like Tetley, waiting for you to come to her. She isn't like me, behaving the same way sometimes. We need to be honest about our less-than-ideal traits if we want to be more like dogs. Lexie throws herself at people. She doesn't care if it's the first time she met you or if she hasn't seen you in two years. When she recognises you she excitedly welcomes you to her. She doesn't hold grudges.

I wonder how much better would it be if we did the same. If we left the scorecards behind? If we didn't tick the boxes of who did what, when we last saw them, when they came to us or not, what they were available for or weren't?

As humans, we complicate things with our scorekeeping. Dogs never do. The reason Lexie has so many best friends is less because she's opportunistic but it's because she is being true to who she is. She is love and she makes everyone feel that love.

Wouldn't the world be better if we could all be more loving?

Tetley is loyal to her people. And I respect this. Because I am loyal to my people. Loyalty to me has always been like Tetley's loyalty. You are my people and I will stand by you, with you, and be there for you. I will be loyal to you. I expect the same loyalty in return.

But side by side, I wonder which one is better? Which one serves us more? Let go of what people did, who they are or are not. Is there a right or wrong way to have loyalty? The kind of loyalty most of us want is the kind Tetley has. She reserves herself for those she dearly loves. She is respectful of people's spaces and makes sure of who people are before she gives herself to them.

She's wild. But she's cautious. She is observant. She keeps score. She knows those who like her and do not. She knows who will throw a ball for her and who will not. She notices who will notice her behind Lexie's attention-seeking behaviour and who will not. She remembers. Lexie notices only the opportunity to love and cuddle and she takes it every time.

Perhaps there's not one way to be loyal. But maybe loyalty isn't as simple as I always thought it was. Maybe loyalty isn't just standing guard with a sword, maybe it can also be laying down and loving without any baggage, score cards or fear.

Maybe both ways of loyalty are needed in various situations. Maybe Tetley's version of loyalty will keep us safe from those who would do us harm and Lexie's version of loyalty ensures we never keep ourselves too safe from that which is worth risking ourselves for.

CHAPTER 16
THE ENDING IS THE MOST IMPORTANT

Lexie's 11th birthday party outside at Berg's. Photo by Chrissy Corbett Photography.

Just because we get old doesn't mean we have less to offer or are less valuable. Our golden years, slower seasons, and last days can still be an amazing adventure. It might be different but not less incredible.

Our journey together has been wild and amazing, hard and incredibly joyful at the same time. Tetley and Lexie have been my ride-or-die. They have always been here. I cannot imagine life without them. I always knew we would come here, to the end, but even knowing couldn't prepare me for the heartbreak I feel, constantly, as I walk Tetley to the end, this year.

I had always believed Tetley would outlive Lexie. I told Justin when we brought Lexie home "I don't feel like Lexie will outlive Tetley". It was just a feeling and given her list of medical problems it seemed highly probable she would go first. Tetley is so driven, such a fighter, I know it's most of the reason she's still alive at such an old age.

Tetley has changed substantially over the last couple of months, even during the writing of this book. She's lost weight and has UTIs, yet she still eats with gusto and gets up every morning looking for her workout. I look at her, both with love and incredible sadness as the window on our journey is closing and there's nothing I can do to save her. Old age simply cannot be changed.

And for both of them, I know how lucky I am to have them still, with their ages and their problems, few get to have the length or the depth of the journey we have had. That's why I've adjusted my schedule, reduced work hours, changed my life, stay home more and spend more time with them... this will all just be a memory soon and as much as I've loved every morning run and sunrise, every adventure and hike we've had, I wouldn't trade this time together for anything.

I'd sign up to do it all over again. I wish I could transport myself back to 2008 or 2012 and start over. I want it to be a scene from a movie where God appears and gives me another chance, not because I'd do it differently but because I'd do it all over again for another 20, 30, or 40 years.

The hardest thing to comprehend is the short age of dogs. Maybe when we get to the other side we'll understand. I'm starting to wonder if it's simply because we need different lessons at different stages of our lives. Kelsey asked me once "do you think they are with you just for a certain amount of time for a certain reason?" My answer is yes. Yes, I do. How else can I explain that they both gave me exactly what I needed that I didn't even know I needed at the time I needed it?

So how can I not spend the ending with them in the best way I can? People tell me I'm devoted because I take such good care of them, that I drive 30 minutes to the only place I can get Tetley in a fresh, clean water source. They tell me I'm crazy to hire naturopaths, order special food, and have video calls with a health expert for Lexie... especially so close to the end.

This year people have said "don't put any more money into them now" as if they were an old car that's ready for the scrap yard. They are *my girls*. They gave me everything. They were here for me when no one else was. They are the ones who got me through my hardest days and celebrated with me on my best days. They were with me for everything, no matter what.

People say that we don't know what we have until it's gone. But I don't agree with this. Some of us know exactly what we have. We know exactly what we are losing. We never took a moment for granted.

I won't torture my girls with drawn-out useless medical procedures, won't do anything invasive or drag out suffering but I'll do everything I can to make them comfortable, even change my entire life for them.

For some people, the journey is over when the activity and the ease are over. For me, this has somehow become the sweetest part of our journey together, the chance to say goodbye, the ability to care for Tetley and come full circle in our journey while slowing down and spending more lazy time with Lexie.

To me, the ending is the most important part, the time we get to honour the journey and thank them for all the amazing years we've had together. While there is so much Tetley can no longer do there is still a lot of stuff she can do. There is her drive and determination, which knows no bounds. I'm trusting that I'll know when the time is right. She has been telling me in various ways that it's coming and to get ready. I was prepared after her

CCD diagnosis but she bounced back. Maybe she gave it to me; this last year.

I know we are always coming here, the end, but it also feels surreal. Even though I know we had an epic adventure and did far more in their lifetime than most come close to doing, it's not enough. I want it back. The amazing days. I want Lexie younger again, and healthier, and I want to drive across the Witless Bay Line with Carolyn's Jeep following my Terrain and I want to start over. I want it to live it *again*.

The ending has reinforced even more powerfully the lessons they taught me. This is my chance to give them the loyalty and devotion they gave me. While I've always done my best to adjust my life, schedule and adventures for them based on their needs, this year has been constant big adjustments. I don't leave them alone much. I don't go far and rarely even go for a long hike unless Justin is home with them or we have a sitter.

When I do get out on the trails all I can see is them. There's not a trail they haven't done with me. When I run on my street I see Tetley running ahead and Lexie in the bushes everywhere. I tell them every day that while they taught me so much they never taught me how to live without them.

But that's not true. That's what this year has been about. I have to go places without them because they can't go. I have to leave them behind more. When I started walking without Lexie, it was hard. Then without Tetley, it was hard. But I did what they taught me to do - keep going no matter what - one foot in front of the other.

Charcuterie at Port Rexton Yurt.

This year I've done things we couldn't do in the past, adventures of a different kind. I rented a yurt in Port Rexton where we had a charcuterie party. We drove to all sorts of beaches where Tetley could swim and Lexie could mosey around, smelling new smells.

I took them to the Port Rexton Brew Company, where they had an "Oh My Cheeses" grilled cheese and a lot of attention. We took long drives to the trailheads we once loved to hike. While we couldn't hike them, it was nostalgic to visit them and honour how much adventure we really had. Tetley was standing looking out the window, sometimes even getting on the armrest for old times' sake. She is still who she is, just trapped in an old body. I have yoga and workouts in the garage and on the deck, depending on the weather, so the girls can still be involved.

Lexie firmly plants herself in the console on our drives, with her head snuggled into my neck or behind my shoulder. She wears her new sunglasses and watches intently to see where we might be going. I took the girls to Berg's Famous ice cream in CBS for Lexie's birthday party this year. We always have parties but this year I decided to go for an ice cream one. With Tetley less able to raise hell it's easier to go to these places.

Chrissy came along, Lexie wore my straw sun hat for the drive, while she was in the console. Tetley was in the back looking out the window. Adventure can change but love never does. We spread out the quilt I brought, the girls lay down and I took out their party hats and special hankies. I went into the store while Chrissy stayed with them. I bought chocolate and vanilla ice cream cups with whipped cream. Sometimes I'd let them have a few licks of our ice cream but I never gave them full ones. I never wanted them to get bad bellies. But at their ages now I gave them the full ice creams.

Lexie was beside herself, it was her birthday after all. She had the princess party hat. She got her birthday toys and treats while I sang Happy Birthday to her and her song that I made up to Cotton Eye Joe "Where did you come from, where did you go, where did you come from Lolly Jo?" Her tail didn't stop wagging and her eyes were as big as saucers as she gobbled ice cream.

She was covered in it. It was in her eyebrows and ears as she hurried and tried to get as much as she could. Tetley took little polite bites as Lexie plowed through hers and then gobbled Tetley's.

They attracted the attention of a little girl and her family. She was about 2 and she came over, sitting with Tetley, petting her. With the ice cream gone, and the little girl showering Tetley, Lexie turned her back to us and put her cranky pants on. We had to sing to her to get her back in the party mood.

Chrissy took professional pictures for us and I am so happy to have them. While they are from Lexie's party, the photos of both of them are some of my favourites of Tetley in this season of her life. She's so old now her face is silver and it tells a story of a life well lived. I tell her every day that she is about 2 millimetres from a unibrow.

In the months leading up to Tetley's diagnosis, she could no longer walk much so I bought myself a pair of rubber boots that went to my knees and we drove to all the places we could drive to access water for her to swim. I had so much fun and joy watching her swim and how much she loved it. I did the same with our daily adventures when Lexie couldn't do our walks anymore. I changed what we could when we could, for them. People say they are lucky to have me but I am lucky to have them.

The choices I made in my life were to make them a priority. Sometimes it's been hard and there were days I didn't know how much more I could take. With no sleep and Justin away for months at a time, I was exhausted, but instead of saying goodbye to her before we were ready, I adjusted my life and my schedule.

I invite friends for meals and drinks on the patio instead of going to a beach or a restaurant. Justin hung lights and we bought a propane firepit, I hung out on the deck, with the girls at my feet. I invited business connections for meetings on the patio. They got to meet the girls and relax in a nature setting instead of being in an office or on a zoom call.

We played games and watched movies. I bought a TV for my bedroom, one thing I swore I'd never do, but Tetley is content while she is in the bedroom. I moved my spin bike upstairs so I could still work out. Yoga is now completed in the living room instead of the rec room.

For Tetley, mornings are slow and sluggish, which Lexie absolutely loves. My writing and quiet time have become mornings instead of evenings, with a nice coffee and Lexie at my side while we wait for Tetley to get moving.

Once she's up and her paws hit the ground she's ready to roll. We make our way to ponds for adventures. Once she's settled then I focus on work and school. Less really is more, sometimes.

The lessons I had learned in life with the girls have now become even more pronounced as I give back to them what they gave me. The community, friendship and loyalty that I found in my people have reminded me that the way we live our lives in the good days comes back tenfold in our bad days. My friends and family are the only reason I've been able to continue to care for them the way I have.

My mother took care of them for me when Chrissy and Carolyn and I went on a hiking and adventure trip to Red Island. My father took us in his boat in a gale of wind and rain. We were the only people on the island and we explored, hiked, visited other islands, cooked food and had songs in the cabin. We had an incredible adventure, only possible because of the support I had to go.

Family, friends and community have made it possible for me to take care of my girls this year. I couldn't do it alone. Caring for our loved ones can take so much but it's easier to carry when we have people who help us and lean in for us when we need them.

That's what happens when we cultivate healthy relationships in our lives. It's great when it's good but it's amazing when it's bad. Knowing we're not alone and have support is what makes it possible.

Lexie is playing nursemaid, pinning Tetley down, washing her face, stealing her snacks, and taking advantage of her condition to get even more snuggles and keep us all happy and grounded on these hardest days.

It's the bravest thing I've ever faced, walking them to the end, knowing that the journey is going to be over and I'll have to live without them longer than I got to live with them but I realise the life I'll get to live is *because* of them, not without them.

They will become the foundation of everything that I am and have and do and create because they are part of who I am. They are in the very fabric of my being. I am who I am because of them. They made me into who I am so I can never really live without them. They're as much a part of me as I am them.

I ask myself if I'm clinging to life, to her life, but I've promised her I would let her go when she tells me she's ready. She's declining and we're preparing but for now, she's showing all indications that she's still enjoying her life. I don't want to cling to her for me.

Tetley and I are spirit connections, soul mates almost, twin flames. If she could be a person, she would be me and if I was a dog I would be her. She came to me in this lifetime and she and I have a different relationship than I have with Lexie. Tetley taught me to shirk off the conditions of this life, to be myself, and to embrace the wildness and instincts within.

Lexie is my heart dog. She taught me to love. She looks at me like I am the best thing she's ever seen. Adoration is the only word to describe it. Justin says Lexie's addiction to me isn't healthy but I laugh and tell him he's just jealous she doesn't love him as much and he agrees he is. And we laugh together about it.

Lexie taught me to love. Deep, unconditional, soul-filled,

love. I don't have to be anything for her. She just loves me. Tetley is demanding and Lexie is loving. There are gifts in both of those medicines. I know they came to me together to give me those two very different gifts at the time in my life when I really needed them. Maybe some people get that in one dog but for whatever reason, I got it in two different ones. Maybe what I needed at the time was too big for one and I needed the totality of different things to get through to me.

Or maybe it was because of who I was when they came to me. Tetley got me outside, into life, into the woods, and into adventure. Which I desperately needed, more than I could ever know. But Lexie, four years later, came to me right before I started my trauma recovery. She came to me in the depths of pain and darkness and changing life priorities. She was there while I was becoming who I was meant to be instead of who I thought I needed to be.

I have no doubt that wasn't available in one dog because of who I was at the time. But they came to me, yin and yang, love and power, softness and strength, relentless in their own different ways. I think a dog like Lexie was not something I could handle before I worked on myself. She softened me.

Tetley and I have a different bond. She reads me, reads my mind, and knows by the clothes I'm wearing what is happening that day.

Glenn told me once, while he was helping train Lexie, that he's never seen anything like it, how she would watch me and how we communicated without words. I mean he did teach me nonverbal communication with her but it was deeper than that. It was like she was reading my mind and I'm sure she was because of all those times I thought to myself "last one" then she would go lie in the pond and refuse to come out as if she knew it was the last one without being told.

There are some dogs that change us and she changed me. So did Lexie. I don't believe they came to me at the same time as a coincidence. People say you get only one great dog, one life-changing dog, in your life but I don't believe that either. All of my dogs changed me. And certainly, Tetley and Lexie are both heart and soul dogs. I believe we get the dogs we need at different times in our lives.

The girls balanced each other, and me. They gave me unconditional love and taught me more than I could ever fill in one book. They gave me everything that I hold dear and what I value most in the world. None of it is success or money or any of the other things I've spent my life chasing. I'm just grateful that even while I was chasing that I was also chasing life with them. They never came second. They were a priority, always.

The things I value most are my beautiful girls, the friendships of the women in my life, the amazing opportunities that I've been given, the people I have met on the journey, and Justin, who gave me the support to raise the girls the way I did. Not many men would stand back and put up with the chaos we created, not to mention the money I spent on them! And that they came into my life at all, that they chose me feels like fate, somehow.

I'm grateful for that. I hang onto that when the fear of losing them washes over me. It's fate that I had them at all.

From the moment I picked Tetley up in Ottawa, I was so happy that I was denied another dog by another breeder. It was meant to be. I am always grateful for the people who didn't want Lexie and the snow day that we had so Justin was with me when the woman kept calling that day. The only thing I can imagine worse than losing them is if I never had them at all.

The sequence of events that brought us together, in each case, was too wild to be a coincidence. Even the fact that I got turned down by a breeder *and* that I left Lexie behind at first.

They have given me more than I could ever give them in return and while I'm still lucky enough at this moment to have them, the reality is that time is winding down. This book was both a book I've wanted to write for a long but also a reflective and honouring journey as I walked back through the life we have lived together, and the amazing adventures we have had, and my hope is that sharing our lives with people that it will open these simple but powerful reminders of what's truly important in life.

None of us are going to live forever and in the end, what we have is less important than who we become. I think it's silly to believe we won't ever have regrets. We're human. But I do believe that my healthy fear of knowing this is all temporary as well as my fear of living with regret has helped me live a life I can be proud of, for me. It might not be a life that someone else would choose or that others think has value but it's valuable to me and that's what matters.

When the journey with the girls is over I want to be able to look back on the experiences with love, and affection and I want to be of clear mind and heart to make the decisions I may need to make for them.

I also want the same for myself. At the end of my life, I want to be able to look back at it and say I chose my life and lived it in a way that I could be proud of. I don't want to be walking through that tunnel at the end and see the version of me I could have been if I had been braver.

Instead, I want that wild spirit to run through me as it runs through Tetley. I want to be relentless in the pursuit of the things that bring me joy like Lexie is. I desire to be fearless and leave the past where it belongs, firmly in the past.

I want to embrace the present moment and find joy in the here and now. I want to have focus when it's time to focus and play when it's time to play. I want this to be a bouncing-off moment where everything we have experienced wasn't for nothing but it was for love.

Because love really does cure everything, even the never-ending living grief that is a constant companion with senior dogs. *What would love do?* is the question I ask myself to bring myself back to the awareness of the only thing that matters. Am I acting in love? Love wouldn't cling or keep alive for the wrong reasons. Love wouldn't let go too long. Love wouldn't be frustrated or rushed or get upset with caring for those we love in their final years.

Love wouldn't be put out for changing our lives, staying home more, or spending more money to keep them comfortable. Love wouldn't find it an inconvenience. Love would stay, until the very end, because it's the ending that matters more than anything else.

How we start is important and how we live is critical but how well we walk to the ending is divine. I believe the greatest testament of our lives is how we handle those later years when the adventures slow down when the bones hurt when the bills mount when we stay home more, and when coffee happens on the dog bed instead of the hiking trails.

The ending is when we are asked to change, to be even more selfless than they have been. I figure if they gave me everything, I can do the same for them.

In a throwaway society, how well we love them at the end, is really the sweetest time with them. It's easy when they're young and healthy, it's heartbreaking and yet the greatest act of love I've ever given to another, this time in the end. I give them everything they gave me and more because really I could never ever come close to giving them what they gave me.

Wherever this story finds you, however long it is, whether we are still here, knee-deep in ponds or not, or whether we are still cuddling and watching the clouds or not, whether we're all here or we're all gone, I hope these words and this story inspires you to find the beauty in the mess and the mud, to find the joy in the journey, not just the destination. I hope you slow down when you need to and speed up when you need to.

And most of all, I hope you find your heart open to the purest, deepest, and most profound love that exists...and I hope you face every adventure with the same 360 spins through the hallway, out the door and in the car that Tetley did and that when it's time to love, you love with your whole being like Lexie did, that you never hold back on love. I hope you find the courage to fling yourself into whatever life you find worth living. We have just one life and if we do it right, that's all we need.

My girls and I have lived. And we have loved. And I think that's more important than how many years we get but what we do with those years that matter most, not how long we live but how well we live. No regrets. That's what I remind myself every single day as the twilight closes in on us. We have lived without regrets and what more could we ask for? In the midst of it all, there was love, deep, unconditional love. And in the end, isn't that what it's all about? Love.

Some day the sun will set on our adventures for the last time. But today is not that day. We're heading to the pond now, Lexie in the console wearing her new sunglasses and Tetley ready for her daily swim. We'll blast the radio with our favourite songs, belting them out for our drives like we do every day. For all that changes, some things remain the same, for now anyway.

Stay Wild & Loving,
   Tonya, Tetley & Lexie

Me. Justin. Tetley & Lexie.

Nora Roberts
"Everything I know, I learned from dogs."

ALSO BY TONYA WHITTLE

Unchained: A Journey To The Soul From Head To Heart

Unchained is a soul-awakening account of life after childhood trauma, of one woman choosing to let go of who she thought she was so she could become who she was meant to be.

Tonya Whittle's story reflects what happens to so many women when they pretend trauma didn't happen: who they become, what they do, and how they create a vision of themselves for protection. But what happens when the life someone is running from collides with the life they've created? *Unchained* shares Tonya's own journey through the collapse of a life falsely created, exposing her wounds and forcing the truth. Tonya encourages other women to take off their own masks, face their truths, and do the inner work necessary to live life fully, ultimately leading to healing and rebuilding.

Unchained takes women on a journey to the soul, from head to heart, from fear to faith, from girls gone wild to wild soul women. For anyone who feels disconnected from life, who is just getting by, simply existing, Tonya reaches out to encourage them to let go of the things that have happened to them and thrive despite those traumas. In the face of #metoo and #timesup, her story serves as an instruction manual for how ancient wisdom, and the process of facing the past, lead to an amazing future—no matter what happened.

www.ingramcontent.com/pod-product-compliance
Lightning Source LLC
Chambersburg PA
CBHW021137090426
42740CB00008B/823